Radical Earnestness

Radical Earnestness

English Social Theory 1880 — 1980

FRED INGLIS

Martin Robertson · Oxford

© Fred Inglis, 1982

First published in 1982 by Martin Robertson & Company Ltd.,
108 Cowley Road, Oxford OX4 1JF.

British Library Cataloguing in Publication Data

Inglis, Fred
   Radical earnestness: English social theory
   1880 – 1980.
   1. Sociology — History
   I. Title
   301'.09'034 (expanded)   HM24
   ISBN 0-85520-328-5
   ISBN 0-85520-401-X Pbk

Typeset in 10 on 12pt Atlantic by Pioneer, East Sussex
Printed and bound in Great Britain
by T.J. Press (Padstow) Ltd.

For Eileen

Despite appearances, political thought is of the same order. It is always the elucidation of a historical perception in which all our understandings, all our experiences, and all our values simultaneously come into play — and of which our theses are only the schematic formulation. All action and knowledge which do not go through this elaboration, but seek to impose ex nihilo values that have not been drawn from our individual and collective history, which would make the calculations of means a completely technical thought process, reduce knowledge and practice below the level of the problems they are trying to resolve. Personal life, knowledge, and history advance only obliquely. They do not go straight, without hesitation, toward goals or concepts. That which one too deliberately seeks, one does not achieve. On the contrary, ideas and values are a bounty to one who has learned to tap their source — in other words, to understand what he lives. At first they yield to our signifying and speaking life only like points of resistance in a diffused milieu, are circumscribed, the way perceived things are, only through the complicity of a background, presupposing as much shadow as light. We should not even say in this case that the ends prescribe the means. Ends are nothing but their common style, the total meaning of everyday means, the momentary shape of everyday meaning. And even the purest of truths presuppose marginal views. Not being entirely in the center of clear vision, they owe their meaning to the horizon which sedimentation and language preserve around them.

Here the reader may complain that we leave him empty and that we confine ourselves to 'how things are', explaining nothing. But the fact is that explication consists in making clear what was obscure, juxtaposing what was implied. The proper place of explication is therefore at the beginning of our knowledge of nature — which is precisely when this knowledge believes it is dealing with a pure pure Nature. However when it is a matter of speech or of the body or of history, where there is a risk of destroying what one is trying to understand, for example, of reducing language to thought or thought to language, one can only make visible the paradox of expression. Philosophy is the inventory of this dimension, which really speaking is universal, and a sphere where principles and consequences, ends and means, turn full circle. With respect to language, philosophy can only point out how, by the 'coherent deformation' of gestures and sounds, man manages to speak an anonymous language and, through the 'coherent deformation' of this language, to express what existed only for him.

(Maurice Merleau-Ponty The Prose of the World, *1974.)*

Contents

Acknowledgements

The whole emphasis of this book falls upon the rich and varied implications of 'membership', 'community', and 'tradition', as the meanings of these words are lived in intellectual lives. The book itself has been written at a time when, in Britain, intellectual life is itself once more openly menaced by the interest groups of the time-servers and gangsters who live inside and outside the gates of the academies. Against these, the idea of a university is powerless without the material realities of membership and friendship, as well as the rather harder and more wintry virtues of solitary independence, resistance, doggedness, and the absolute resolution to get on with the task in hand and not to be bought out by the cosy privileges and soft snobberies which are still amply available to bright young-to-middle-aged academics.

Accordingly, I thank and honour the men and women who set such an example at the present time, and especially those of my friends who, knowingly or not, have been influential in shaping the version of an intellectual life worth living as offered in these pages. David Satterly, more than he would recognise, has pointed out to me the straight way of thought on many occasions; I am grateful to Dan Jacobson, John Burrow, David McLellan, Krishan Kumar, Roger Poole, Nicholas Garnham, and Charles Taylor for their eloquent and original contributions to my graduate seminars 'Knowledge, Inquiry and Values' and 'Interpretation and the Human Sciences' and for all they have taught me during those sessions and at many other times. Bernard Williams, Patricia Williams and Basil Bernstein all gave characteristically quick and unselfish help when it was pressingly needed; John Williams, as before, gave lavish hospitality in the United States; Joe Grixti was invaluable in the preparation of the index; Roy Parker helped with the pages dealing with the work of Richard Titmuss; Cressida, of course, has been a good-tempered and discreet guardian of my desk throughout the rapid writing of the book.

No doubt it is invidious to pick out someone formally treated in the pages that follow but — like all his friends — I owe more than I can say of my intellectual (to say nothing of my personal) formation to Quentin Skinner, to his generosity with his own ideas, to his patient exposition of them to slower-witted listeners such as me, to his heart-lifting sense of the comic. Above all, I pay tribute to Eileen McAndrew, for all that she has taught me about the necessary connections between compassion and understanding, detachment and ardour, and how much any of the human sciences simply are theories about how to lead a life you can be proud of.

Lastly and indispensably, Maureen Harvey typed, as she always does, equably, accurately and by the hour. Michael Hay and his colleagues have proved the best and promptest of publishers.

Formal acknowledgements are also due to the following individuals, publishers, and executors for permission to quote from copyright materials in their charge: the Royal Economic Society and Macmillan, London and Basingstoke, for extracts from the work of John Maynard Keynes; Basil Blackwell for a paragraph by Alisdair MacIntyre taken from *Philosophy, Politics and Society,* 2nd series; Jonathan Cape Ltd., and the Estate of C. A. R. Crosland for extracts from *The Future of Socialism;* Victor Gollancz Ltd., for the extract from *The Making of the English Working Class;* A. P. Watts Ltd., for the lines by W. B. Yeats; Faber and Faber Ltd., for the extracts from the *Selected Essays* and the poem *Little Gidding* by T. S. Eliot, and also for the lines from *Credences of Summer* by Wallace Stevens; George Allen and Unwin, for the extracts from the work of Richard Titmuss; the estate of Sonia Brownell Orwell and Secker and Warburg Ltd., for the extracts from the work of George Orwell; Oxford University Press, for the extracts from the works of R. G. Collingwood, and for the lines from *The Way of the World* by Charles Tomlinson; Chatto and Windus Ltd., for the extracts from the works of Edwin Muir, F. R. Leavis, Richard Hoggart, and Raymond Williams, as well as paragraphs from *Concepts and Categories* by Isaiah Berlin, for which acknowledgement is also due to Hogarth Press Ltd; Beverly Hiro, for lines from *A Seventh Man* and *The Look of Things* by John Berger, and Messrs. Weidenfeld and Nicolson, for extracts from *The Moment of Cubism, Art and Revolution* and *G*, by the same author; Merlin Press, for extracts from *Writing by Candlelight* and *The Poverty of Theory*, by E. P. Thompson; Thames and Hudson Ltd., and the estate of Adrian Stokes for extracts from the author's *Critical Writings*.

PART I

The Intellectual Origins of the Present Crisis

Prologue
Text and Method

This is an academic textbook; it is a fragment of an autobiography. Saying so is not intended to advertise the author as its interesting subject matter; it is merely to acknowledge that what is spoken of in these pages as a tradition began life, at any rate in the schematic form implied by the contents page, as a particular reading list. But to glance at the list of names which prefigure the historical peaks along which I try to draw the line of an intellectual contour makes it clear that the reading list has many more celebrated predecessors, of which one famous one is Raymond Williams's *Culture and Society: 1780–1950* which stars in chapter 8.

That obviously formative book lives in its turn in a tradition. Tradition is a term to return to in some detail. Say instead, Raymond Williams spoke to a particular audience and, in the pointed cliché, at a critical moment. *Culture and Society* came out in 1959; Williams speaks movingly elsewhere of the years in which he was writing it, *to* which he was addressing it; he must have been somewhere towards the end of his work during 1956. His great associate, Edward Thompson, here cast as the hero of the succeeding chapter, frequently names 1956 as the most important date of a socialist's postwar calendar — the year in which the Russian tanks cruelly put down the people's rebellion in Budapest, and Janos Kadar's high-principled trimming installed him in power in Hungary for a generation. In the same extraordinary few weeks, Gomulka[1] pulled Poland away from the grimmer, drearier domination of the USSR and Anthony Eden joined with Guy Mollet to drop parachutists on the Suez Canal.

Williams and Thompson had an audience in mind, and they spoke to it, not from the platform but from the body of the hall. Time and, no doubt history itself, has since given them seats on the platform. They cannot now avoid being made to sit up there. Even more is that true of other authors this book treats of who are dead. To write in brackets after T. H. Green's name the dates (1836 – 1882) places him in a specific position in the book — first, with William Morris. The reader adjusts to the signal, whether or not he knows Green's name and work. 'Victorian' 'Idealist' 'Hegelian' 'Evangelical' 'Oxonian': these might be the first, placing moves on the part of the sympathetic reader starting to orient himself to the argument, to join the audience. Then to encounter F. R. Leavis (1895 – 1978) jolts the same reader, irrespective of his knowledge of Leavis's work. It places the argument much more sharply up against the present day. And of course the same is even more true of the entries Raymond Williams (1921 –   ), Edward Thompson (1924 –   ) and John Berger (1926 –   ); they signal the harder, always presumptuous effort to give a novel account of work which is very much unfinished, whose internal meaning cannot (of course) be understood and judged until the author is dead, even if he never writes another word. Each of those men, if they ever look into these pages, might pull back and demur vigorously, at the company they are forced to keep, at the misrepresentations of what they have written, at the uses to which they are put. Of the dead authors it is certain that, for example, Leavis would have been vehement in his rejection of the seat allotted to him on the platform, and Adrian Stokes, more manageably, just puzzled.

This book was finished in 1982. Its historical moment is less readily marked on the clock by headlines and by tank tracks than 1956, although the names, the 1982 names, Iran, Afghanistan, Zimbabwe, Kampuchea, Poland, Gold, Oil, announce a looser, more turbulent, less institutional power system than in 1956. The difficulty of responding to 1982, let alone grasping it, is indicated by the other distinctly *English* names, in this book. But that makes the point. The reading list is called to justify itself to a particular audience at a particular time. That audience may be, certainly is, vastly dispersed over the world, and most of it will never hear this small voice. But it is composed of those who, in the teeth of a long record of British bullying, self-congratulation, hypocrisy and murderous cruelty, have also found something to honour in British intellectual life as it has *resisted* the awfulness of its own, dominant culture. In among imperial rule, child labour, poisonous snobbery, the depredations of class, horrible chauvinism, the routine stupidities of the deadly sins as lived in the British style, in among all these a view of the world has been kept alive capable still of speaking seriously of matters of life and death, and of giving both some point and scale by insisting on such traditional measures as freedom, justice, generosity, tolerance, laughter, disobligingness, love. Most of all, the best versions of that intellectual life have insisted, against much of the toughest eggs in other schools of thought, that after all men do their often very poor best to make their own history although not in circumstances of their own choosing, and that even without the substantial evidence of such examples as Lenin or Hitler, it is still true that individuals can do something to will events.

So the Englishness of the school of thought I am picking out is addressed to those in the thinking world who may have found usable that particular temper. But I pick it for present experience. Political science, as practised sometimes in the books of numbers and sometimes in the more world-weary versions of the history of ideas, has been apt for a season to claim that it had and has no credible interest in teaching the world for the world's good. Well, this small book can influence very little indeed, but I intend it for the world's minor improvement. Along with the nastier features of the national polity, English intellectual life has made it possible to turn some utopian symbols into reality, has passed on ways of valuing and imagining human virtues which have helped to prevent their being lied out of existence, has shown how to criticize and fight off the blatant ideologizing of their advantages by the rich, the powerful, the greedy, and the cruel. This book honours a line of men who have kept up such a language. Its method therefore is not only to understand its chosen texts by placing them in a given culture and politics; it is also to recommend what they say as having point and truthfulness and eloquence in a world whose political languages are largely incredible to reasonable men and women.

And so the mode of thought into which I recast my singular version of the English dissenting thinkers is a customary and embattled one. If I am right, the congeries of academic disciplines under such names as social and political theory, history of ideas, sociology, even hermeneutics and cultural studies, are reluctantly and variously turning back to the view that the proper study of political man not only seeks scientific understanding but also answers to the questions of how to live well and to strive for the good and just society.

There is a clear revival of interest in an active, valuing and interpretative version of the human sciences. There are distinct moves towards an armistice between the idealists and the materialists. These signs of the times taken with the concentration on language as the central, problematic subject-matter for any one preoccupied by the question (Leavis's great question, which may be taken to stand as epigraph to this prologue), 'What for — what ultimately for? What do men and women live by?' suggest a cue for rewriting the syllabus of social and political theory, and redrawing the line of a long, honourable, and sometimes neglected community in English thought. That same line has like-minded contributors from both Europe and the United States, and indeed in the case of such advocates of Romantic subjectivism or a more political dissent from established realism as Kierkegaard or Emerson on the one hand and Saint-Simon or John Dewey on the other, the mainland Europeans or the Americans are every bit as vehement and substantial as the Englishmen. In the case, obviously, of such towering figures of the century as Marx or Nietzsche, then we have to turn obliquely to such thinkers as Darwin and Dickens to find a mind at work in England capable of pulling together and theorizing a comparable hugeness of experience and evidence.

Nonetheless, I stress a tradition in *English* thought, and am concerned to do these four things, as plainly and straightforwardly as may be.

(i) To place a specifically English tradition within the movements of the intellectual climate towards a more polemical and morally wideawake political theory. To do this is to insist on the need for a more local, historical, and concrete mode of analysis than generalist and holistic theories often favour.

(ii) To trace the membership of that tradition in terms of its stubborn idealism, and durably liberal and critical temper, and to connect these characteristics to the line of radical dissent in English politics.

(iii) To connect a line of well-known names in a new and necessary configuration, and to vindicate, by way of a detailed scrutiny of their work, the ringing claim that you cannot separate scientific understanding from moral experience.

(iv) To insist on the richly contextual nature of the history of ideas as properly conceived, and therefore to identify this 'configuration' as settled on the larger map of English thought processes, and that map as a projection on the part of a reforming and (again) liberal segment of the bourgeoisie intent upon repairing the worst ravages of capitalism, keeping up the low-key Romanticism of their inheritance, and maintaining in a more or less equable spirit the great class-compromise of their history.

The names of the writers imply two strands in this line of thought, the first made up of those writers who deal more or less directly with politics and policy — politics so to speak, with a capital P — the second made up of those whose subject-matter is cultural, and for whom the spiritual health of polis and people is the ground of theory. T. H. Green, as uniting both strands and as reminding us of the return of Hegel to contemporary thought, and William Morris as Romantic artist and active socialist, stand at the head of the line. Collingwood, Keynes, and Leavis follow as the three points of an essential hermeneutic, and as giants of twentieth-century liberal theory in England. The subsequent chapters indicate ways in which that theory has developed, and end with an optimistic review of the work presently in progress.

At every point the study of development implies the certainty of breaks and discontinuities. No sufficient mode of thought could survive the drastic ruptures and cruelties of the past century with its form and content unchanged. The literally inconceivable extension of communication systems which make information so much vaster and news unmanageably more abrupt and tumultuous, these compel social theorists to stretch, rebuild, and on the pain of necessity, to break with the conceptual framework they have learned to use, in order to be able to think and act rationally in the world at all. And yet the imperative to maintain connection with existing modes of thought is deep and irresistible. To think at all, but certainly to think politically, is to make honest sense, to connect idea and reality, through both space and time. To do this, as everybody knows in their everyday lives, is to make the past contiguous with the present, to find an idiom and a way of thinking both radical and conservative, traditional and new.

The tradition commended in these pages carries such an idiom and mode of thought. What is admirable about it is, precisely, its commitment both to the idea of a good and just society and to the actual, concrete details of the real world its practitioners inhabit. Across deep differences of temperament, discipline, categories of inquiry and the nature of the concepts with which they think, these men embody an intellectual tradition and a *practice* which never fails to match up honourably to the wide variety of their historical circumstances.

1

Tradition and Englishness:
Politics and Belief

What is an intellectual tradition, and what good may it do us if we have one? Tradition is a word which comes big upon the page, and yet in the present chaos and uncertainty of the world it may sound like nothing so much as a name with which to console others for the inexpressible dignity of your advantages over them. As we watch the land masses of the turning globe, and the nation-states of its chance, tattered, divisions, what do we see? Here, Latin America, largely under the despotism of uniform and holster, of quite arbitrary and dreadful torture and casual execution; there the Soviet Republics and the long, grim line of grey and wasted prisoners, stiffened in the cold of the labour camps; over here, the baffled and bottled rage of wageless American blacks, over there, the blank-faced starvation of a million or two South-East Asian children. The dim responsibility for the steady toll of slaughter and slow death we give to a squadron of fearful names — Bokassa, Duvalier, Pol Pot, Campora, Amin, Mobutu, Vorster; otherwise, the mere list of countries stands for the assorted versions of a universal political condition in which the great names of human rights, of freedom, dignity, justice, equality, known and called for by more people than ever before, are more clearly put down by avoidable cruelty and want than ever before. The names of the countries, rehearsed, let us say, in a parliament or a university seminar in a western democracy, prefigure the helpless response: Chile, South Africa, Iran, Argentina, Czechoslovakia, Ulster, Angola, Biafra, Eritrea.

But condemnation of world brutality and hypocrisy cannot easily stop with those straight-forward offences against the master-symbols of modern politics. Marx's famous truism that, with the revolutions of 1848, all history became world history, is vastly more inescapable a recognition of the present terms of international political economy. All the *official* institutions of world trade and finance — the World Bank,[1] the IMF, the central currency trading stations — now agree with the long-standing reports from academic sources that the poor nations of the world have no chance at all within the present system of coming within sight of the standards of living of the rich, and that the said standards of the rich depend in turn on keeping things that way. And so, if you are looking for targets for international humbug, hypocrisy, and calculated exploitation, what their own newspapers may still be counted upon to refer to as the free nations or, less contentiously, the Western democracies, provide as ready examples for prosecution as anywhere else. The comfort and comparative independence in which, say, between two-thirds and three-quarters of their electorates live, is built visibly enough upon an insane rate of pillage of the world's natural resources and the steady immiseration of a good half of the world's population. Only the sociology of ignorance combined with the unfailingly reliable inclination of human nations, often adventitiously constituted and riven by internal wounds and struggle, to go extravagantly to war against their most plausible allies and own best interests, could possibly begin to explain why that wretched half of the earth should allow matters to stay as they are, in a state of clear, callous, and improvable inequality. Any serious and reasonably well-informed citizen of West or East, or any other point of the geo-political compass, can only feel himself to be torn down the middle, on the one hand by the unalterableness of world economics, or rather by the fact that those giant structures drive headlong under their own colossal momentum, and that little rational let alone altruistic control may be exerted on them; on the other hand, the conscientious *moyen*-liberal can see and hear more clearly than ever before the piercing justice and rightness of those exceptionally exacting images of human fulfilment and freedom and self-critical awareness which circulate under the best banners of democratic and socialist theory.

In this hapless position, to ask for an intellectual and moral tradition within which to live well and reasonably, is, if the inquiry is pursued with anything like vigour and courage, likely to make you either a cynic or a fideist. In the contemporary West it is all too clearly the cynics who are running the show. The fideists come in two sorts: the last and by now exhausted details of Christian soldiers, who at least are in the position of being able in the face of convincing evidence to talk sensibly of wickedness and evil as being inevitable, and grace and redemption as being individual in origin and very hard to come by; the other fideist is now certain to be some sort of Marxist, and his surely irrefutable condemnations both of the murderous drive of capitalist production and the moral evasiveness of its liberal ideologies can only take the pilgrim as far as being able to name those wrongs for what they are. For Marxism has too dreadfully disgraced itself when purporting to set up its utopias, and given itself so wholeheartedly when in defeat or among the guerrilla to teaching hatred, spite, and vengefulness that it can no longer stand as a name for all that may be admirable in the imagined future of socialism.[2]

Christianity and Marxism by no means exhaust the possibilities for those who want to choose an intellectual and moral tradition within which to think about the world. But choosing, in the ingenuous, naked existentialism which the word means in ordinary moral discourse, is hardly the form or structure of our finding our modes of thought. 'Choosing a tradition' as a phrase and as an action has about it all the fine flourish of the boulevardier of the cultural supermarkets. It suggests that you may hitch your way to the campuses of California, or even of Oxford and Cambridge, and pick out an intellectual style from the libraries, much as you may a uniform from the motley boutiques, surplus stores, Blow-your-mind shops and Digger emporiums in the youth markets of university cities. But modes of thought like, one would guess, modes of dress, are more atavistically rooted in a culture than merely garments can show; it is a banal enough observation that the barmy antics of Fifth Avenue Hare Krishna are more American than Hindu. And so, to speak of choice in relation to tradition is not to say something perfectly vacant, but it *is* to make thought, feeling, judgement rather narrowly voluntarist affairs.

TRADITION AND NOVELTY

The idea of tradition is itself powerful and, though substantial, elusive. As an explanatory concept it has perhaps had, among the human sciences, the longest run for its money among literary critics and their great-uncles, the theorists and hermeneuticians of biblical scriptures. It is quite often invoked by anthropologists, but in a surprisingly general way, as merely marking the basket in which they may pile up custom, ritual, symbol, totem, and so forth for future analysis as to either meaning or function. In among the ethnographies, tradition is as ready a term as innovation, each tidily balanced against the other to distinguish little more than what has always been practised from what is being done apparently for the first time.

This simple distinction has however the merit of connecting the sometimes precious usage of academic discourse to the homelier, clumsier, intermittently crass speech of everyday life. When people speak in the real language of men and refer to tradition, the word may be used approvingly or not, but it carries a strong and binding element whose meaning and power of adhesion cannot be traced precisely back to social structure or system of ideas or to the relations of production, but which penetrates all these with its unmistakable endurance and presence. Conservative thought has by definition written of this continuous presence with a sort of grim relief; in poetry T. S. Eliot, in philosophy, Michael Oakeshott, in history, Lewis Namier, in aesthetics, Ernest Gombrich, in politics, Karl Popper, in music, Benjamin Britten, this uneven but impressively mixed bag of expatriate and home-brewed intellectuals and artists have all at different times and in different cadences during the past forty years touched the resonant chords of traditionalism, in both thought and feeling, in order to justify them. In perhaps the most famous and moving lines from *Four Quartets,* T. S. Eliot may stand as first and best — or at least most conveniently compressed — spokesman for tradition.

> This is the use of memory:
> For liberation — not less of love but expanding
> Of love beyond desire, and so liberation
> From the future as well as the past. Thus, love of a country
> Begins as attachment to our own field of action
> And comes to find that action of little importance
> Though never indifferent. History may be servitude,
> History may be freedom. See, now they vanish,
> The faces and places, with the self which, as it could, loved them,
> To become renewed, transfigured, in another pattern.[3]

The lines, in all their subtlety and qualification, speak also however for the line of Western thought which most sets itself *against* tradition and its necessary assumption that merely to quote the facts of continuity suffices to justify it. The deep conservative resists change because he values whatever structures have been won from the intense inanity of things, and are capable of turning accident into experience. Such structures will do, however cruel and foreshortened, absolutely because they provide meaning, and once their hard-won, provisional security has been broken open, the wilderness is come again, and there is no knowing when its desert places may be given a recognizable shape and location.

Since, let us say, the French Revolution and the advent of Romanticism, the deep conservative cannot be found speaking any of the European languages with any degree of plausibility or intelligence. He is not Edmund Burke, nor de Tocqueville, nor is he any of the four names I listed as standing for a present day conservative intelligensia. It may be that the deep conservative may still be found in the churches of Islam or Buddha, although his immortality there would require him to adopt precisely the exclusiveness and inflexibility which characterize Iran and Saudi-Arabia today. I do not know. But our business here is with a very much more domestic mode of thought, and the degree of moral and political reflection which it permits counts as its tradition.

The quotation from *Four Quartets* might stand as epigraph to any present day history of European ideas which aspires, as this one does, to stretch reconciling hands either to those who join Nietzsche in rejoicing at the final rupture with past morality or to those who with Marx look forward to the key of all mythologies as being turned by a victorious proletariat in the future. For Eliot speaks eloquently of the profound patriotic attachment in which political action must begin, and measures it against a larger comprehension whose powerfully historical reach attempts the necessary impossibility of an understanding both quick to present experience at the same time as outside and superior to it.

> Why should we celebrate
> These dead men more than the dying?
> It is not to ring the bell backward
> Nor is it an incantation
> To summon the spectre of a Rose.
> We cannot revive old factions
> We cannot restore old policies
> Or follow an antique drum.
> These men, and those who opposed them
> And those whom they opposed
> Accept the constitution of silence
> And are folded in a single party.
> Whatever we inherit from the fortunate
> We have taken from the defeated
> What they had to leave us — a symbol:
> A symbol perfected in death.[4]

With his characteristic dignity and calm, Eliot brings together the inheritance of liberal and conservative, of the Enlightenment and the church, of — in his terms — Bach and Beethoven. The intensely *personal* struggle of Beethoven with the form of the quartet is matched to the grandly impersonal resonance of the traditional liturgy borrowed and transfigured by Bach. And although he is left rather lamely with 'a symbol', the poem itself is intended to bring that symbol to perfection; for the artist in post-Romantic thought is an iconographer, that, is a maker of images which *are* their own religious meaning. In the first days of the Enlightenment its greatest theoreticians sought to break absolutely with tradition: Kant gave every individual a way of moralizing his own unprecedented and historyless individuality; Hegel insisted that all historical eventuality signified a *progress* into a future certain to realise itself as rational improvement.

By the time we come to the smaller, more rightly cautious, of our latter-day spokesmen we find them, with Eliot, balancing a picturesque but feudal past against a banal but comfortable present. The liberalism inaugurated by the *Encyclopaedia* or by the Terror (whichever you prefer) crossed the channel with several generations of refugees. Its indestructibility is the subject of this book, but no one could claim that pure liberalism, in its first, gleaming essence, has survived into the present, any more than the conservatism of, say, Richard Hooker, survived the Commonwealth. In that essence, the liberal acid attacked all traditionalism, all presences of the past in so far as they denied the clean, well-lighted premises of the new, rational present. Tradition and authority were the swearwords of liberalism.

It is the most familiar platitude of political history since the French Revolution that the bright young radicals turn into something much more stolid and unmoving, as the ideas for which they fought against the past move into the seats of power and themselves become the new past. In a brilliantly compressed summary of Hegel's main scheme and of the imperative to live and think morally within it, whatever else about Hegel is hopelessly dated, Isaiah Berlin wrote:[5]

The history of thought and culture is, as Hegel showed with great brilliance, a changing pattern of great liberating ideas which inevitably turn into suffocating straitjackets, and so stimulate their own destruction by new, emancipating, and at the same time, enslaving conceptions. The first step to the understanding of men is the bringing to consciousness of the model or models that dominate and penetrate their thought and action. Like all attempts to make men aware of the categories in which they think, it is a difficult and sometimes painful activity, likely to produce deeply disquieting results. The second task is to analyse the model itself, and this commits the analyst to accepting or modifying or rejecting it, and, in the last case, to providing a more adequate one in its stead.

It is seldom, moreover, that there is only one model that determines our thought; men (or cultures) obsessed by single models are rare, and while they may be more coherent at their strongest, they tend to collapse more violently when, in the end, their concepts are blown up by reality — experienced events, 'inner' or 'outer', that get in the way. Most men wander hither and thither, guided and, at times, hypnotized by more than one model, which they seldom trouble to make consistent, or even fragments of models which themselves form a part of some none too coherent or firm pattern or patterns. To drag them into the light makes it possible to explain them and sometimes to explain them away. The purpose of such analysis is to clarify; but clarification may expose shortcomings and subvert what it described. That has often and quite justly been charged against political thought, which, at its best, does not disclaim this dangerous power. The ultimate test of the adequacy of the basic patterns by which we think and act is the only test the common sense or the sciences afford, namely, whether it fits in with the general lines on which we think and communicate; and if some among these in turn are called into question, then the final measure is, as it always must be, direct confrontation with the concrete data of observation and introspection which these concepts and categories and habits order and render intelligible.

Berlin's point is not that of the *bien-penseur* who tells the hot-eyed young radical how he too used to stride the streets with Shelley in one hand and a revolver in the other, looking for priests and royalists to shoot, but who now in mature, time-serving, property-owning middle-age, takes his holidays on the Greek islands and his opinions from the *Financial Times.* Berlin redescribes the inevitable life and death of great systems of ideas, and their inevitable passage into other systems, until the original has undergone such rich and rare sea-changes that it can barely be recognized. He acknowledges that we all live within a variety of sometimes incongruous frames of mind, and move in and out of these as suits our circumstances.

Berlin, with his large tolerance of the vanity of human wishes, would be unlikely to make strictures upon what the English in their peculiarity do with their ideas. He has remarked as a commonplace[6] that of course particular cultures *do* colour systems of ideas in virtue of their language and the concepts familiar to it as well as in virtue of its special history, and the selection and distortion that history causes men to make from a system. There have been those who have praised the English tendency to adulterate the heavy spirit of Continental philosophy with honest English water, and those who in exactly the same metaphor have derided the inherent wateriness of English metaphysics.[7] There have been others, of a robustly insular tendency, who have stood firmly upon what they take to be the English tradition of political thought and have warded off the metaphysics and the politics in the name of that nationally sceptical temper which is seen to powerful advantage in David Hume, who after all wrote little by way of political theory, and in James Mill, who is an unlikely runner in any classic race. Thereafter the allegedly anti-theoretic and sceptical temper of the Englishman as he does his thinking in public upon the nature of public life can find only such decidedly modest and motley representatives of the genre as Sidney Webb, Lord Macauley, Walter Bagehot, G. H. Lewes, the anthropologist E. B. Tylor, Thomas Huxley perhaps, or the stridently philistine rhetoric of Carlyle. Of course the exceeding modesty of their intellectual gifts — a modesty variously appraised by their holders but not at all overestimated by at least one of their number, Lewes, whose wife presumably served as a constant reminder of what it was to be a genius in those days — was obscured by the cultural haze in which they worked and which served, when seen in the right light, to give an aura to small but congenial features.

The climate which exudes such haze is part of our subject. English intellectual culture in the second half of the nineteenth century was marked by the parent society's tendency to inordinate self-satisfaction, the exultant philistinism Matthew Arnold chronicled and named, by the arrogance of power and chauvinism which its geographical and misleading economic successes encouraged. It picked out the ideologies which spoke to the dominant drives of its temper.

So did, so does any political culture. But the difficulty for the historian of ideas who is concerned, as I am, both to be faithful to the historicality of those ideas and to find answers, with Collingwood, to the question of what ideals to live by and what (if anything) past ideas may tell us about how to live well in the present, is to identify those thinkers of Victorian England who, living as they were bound to do, in their own context, nonetheless live on in ours. After all the tense, difficult arguments about text and context as I have briefly rehearsed them it is true that forms of thought are longer lived than those who thought them first. We do not have to fall into the chic notation of the Parisian deconstructionists[8] in order to see that there is a figurative use to be made of the trope that 'the discourse speaks itself' and that the man we think of as, shall we say,

Herbert Spencer, is only and complexly the function of those texts with
that name on their spine as well as the many footnotes and exegetics
which incorporate and extend them. Modes of discourse arise from a
form of life. To think at all in that form of life — and a form of life is
necessarily a social matter, inevitably a national because linguistic one,
and in our situation strongly a class one — is to find an available mode of
discourse and to bend it to your purposes.

THOUGHT, ACTION AND BELIEF

The definition of discourse returns us to the definitions and significance
of tradition and Englishness. Assorted emphases in the human sciences
and in real life have made it unlikely that anyone any longer supposes
that voluntarism, which is to say the doctrine that the individual will is
the paramount cause of political and historical motion, is credible in its
pure form. Sociology at large, and structuralism, functionalism, and
Marxism, have all in different ways reduced the place left in the theory
of social action for the individual and his will to a very small corner. And
yet it is its strength and its paradox that what began as the drastic
uprooting of pre-Revolutionary thought[9] settled into the many forms of
English reformist and revolutionary ideology. Imported from across the
Channel the new criticism of the Romantic and Enlightenment thinkers
and creative artists found a ready intellectual horticulture for their
grafting and transplanting. Kant, Herder, Condorcet and Hegel found
Coleridge, Godwin, Bentham, Byron, Mary Wollstonecraft, Wordsworth.
The twin, mighty lines of English utilitarianism and romanticism surged
into their mutually tense, polar duality.

Such an account might do as a preliminary cartoon for the directory of
ideas. These ideas arrived from *there* and met indigenous ideas, and
were synthesized into *this* novel theory within the tradition. Well, it
happens that way, as any scholar of ideas knows. Supremely, it happens
that way when the originator or the receiver of a system of ideas is a
genius, and makes of what he reads something novel and momentous.
The list of names on the contents page of this book is witness to the fact
that voluntarism *has* something to it: these thinkers made a distinctive
intellectual moment out of their opportunity; to read them and not other
writers is to be open to change of a certain kind. Someone who not only
understands them but learns to use them to interpret his own world,
learns to enter their discourse, to inhabit their frame of mind, but to live
in it with purposes and inclinations they could hardly have foreseen.

At first sight, this claim amounts to no more than that new ideas are capable of changing the whole way a person sees the world. It is not a trivial claim, but it is a familiar one. But to change the way you see the world is necessarily to act and to be a different person in the world.

Any theory about the role of theory in society is bound, if it is to be convincing, to contain an account both of its rivals and of itself. Moreover, social theories have another characteristic, as yet unnoticed in the present argument, which must now be brought out. It is a characteristic which sharply differentiates the role of theory in the human sciences from that of theory in the natural sciences.

The way people think about things (that is, natural science — 'things' includes human bodies) is appropriate or not depending upon the nature of the things in question: the way people think about people, themselves, is part of the reality about which they are trying to think in appropriate ways. The concepts which we employ to grasp what we are become part of what we are; or rather that we use them in this way becomes part of what we are. Thus in social theory we are using concepts to understand beings who define themselves by means of their use of concepts, in some cases the concepts that we are using in trying to understand them. So to construct a theory and to propagate it is to afford people a new means of self-comprehension; to give the theory currency may well change the very behaviour which the theory attempts to describe. Hence the much noted fact that social theories, unlike theories in physics, can play a role in their own verification and falsification . . . If the methodological part of this essay is correct, then actions are uninterpretable and unidentifiable apart from beliefs.[10]

To tie a knot between ideas and beliefs, and between both these and action is to identify what Marxists usefully call 'praxis'. The notion is useful because as Macintyre has shown us, and as the theorists of speech-acts have gone on to demonstrate very fully,[11] there is no way of understanding social action as rational and autonomous unless it is ideally paraphrasable in a language which identifies beliefs, motives and intentions. 'Praxis' is as immediately theoretic *and* practical as any significant action performed even by the most unreflective of plain, blunt men or women.

These few remarks may serve to hold together a more complex field of force than is usual in the conventional models of social action. We typically speak of action as simply consequent upon belief and both as succeeding thought in a causal, linear way. Our real behaviour is more instantaneous, even after long pondering: rather, we may say that action *embodies* and *realizes* thought, belief, and purpose, and that the action only has its meaning in so far as it is successful or not. The field of force which we are considering in order to understand action at all is defined (although not contained) by thought, certainly, but also by language, theory, rationality, and practice; above all, but ungraspably, by *culture*. These concepts take on a structure, and according to the concepts we emphasize, so we shall see the structure from a given perspective. Yet, to make Macintyre's point again, that perspective takes in and is part of the action we consider, redescribe, interpret, evaluate. Satisfactory understanding entails an effort of moral sympathy; after the sympathetic understanding the spiral of thought and experience curves away to a point at which distance permits detachment and criticism, and curves back inwards towards the subject again in order to check the validity of the criticism; then on, out once more.

This spiral is the movement of mind in history. The metaphor of spiral reminds us of the by now classical difficulty of historical relativism. We claim understanding of past actions from a larger or at least a posterior position; how can we ever know that we know better?

Briefly, we can't. But at least we know that we know *subsequently*. We are obliged to live in history; our only means of thinking about the present is to consider how we got to be in our present circumstances.[12] That rueful necessity is as commonplace to the human scientist as it is to the overspent householder. And that reflection back on how we come to be where we are is a reflection whose images are provided by the past. We can only think about the present in the materials made available by the past.

'Materials' is the right word. For the break with the past is when we create new patterns out of old materials, and where 'materials' denote the facts of social life — the human systems, their relations and means of production, men's and women's ideas about these. To be human at all entails the imaginative capacity to take the old materials and to think new thoughts with them. The thoughts, as we have seen, are carried into action, and history proceeds.

To write like this is to seek to tread the fine line between idealism (roughly, the doctrine that reality is socially constructed[13] out of the ideas you may have about it) and materialism (the epistemology which claims that social life is constructed from its material conditions as identifiable in the systems of economic and technical production). But however probable it is that the enterprise the book represents tilts it strongly towards idealism, the offered definition of action as the practical embodiment of theory stands squarely whether you declare for idealism or not. In this showing, any such embodiment is traditional. It means what it means within the form of life which realizes it.

This detour through a condensed account of recent theories of social action is important not only because it prefigures a main theme of this book but also because it proposes an account of tradition, both intellectual and cultural, which makes it platitudinously the context of all action, as well as the continuing identity of a culture. Tradition is to a culture what personality is to an individual. Your personality may change considerably even in maturity (though less often than is supposed) but you remain the same person. Even in the splintering discoveries of the twentieth century — accidental, evil, benign — about the fluidity of the self, the contingency of its composition, the inaccessible but determinate forces which give it essential shape both outside and underneath consciousness, its inadequacy before even its own best moral standards, yet we continue to act and believe in ourselves as *our selves,* and within the tradition of English thought reconstructed here, to think of ourselves and the selves most precious to us and most recognizable to us as the realm and fount of value.

This is the first premise of the English tradition; if Alan Macfarlane is right[14] it is also the oldest. Now in spite of the dreadful damage done by Marx, Freud, and the larger destructiveness of world war and world prosperity, to liberalism's cherished master-symbol, the individual, it remains true that for better and worse the celebrated absolutes of English society still turn around the values of liberal individualism: fulfilment, freedom, sincerity, honesty, personal dignity, choice, creativity, happiness, individual rights. And where these terms are capable of more collective versions, the English tradition revises them in an individual direction — happiness, creativity, rights, even (perhaps most of all) freedom — are all defended and upheld at almost every level of political discourse as the absolute embodiments of the freely choosing, self-determining individual. The same language is more aggressively spoken across the Atlantic, and there sounds in the accents of a different popular-political language — not only the greater aggressiveness, but, even now, the contextless nature of the individualistic claims, and their paradoxical connection with patriotism. And again, the low-key, decent suburbanity of individualism has been exported along with O levels and the erratic forms of post-colonial independence in Africa and the Caribbean and there set in a drastic atonality to accompany the unheeded demands of the black nations for an economy and a polity they can call their own.[15]

THE ENGLISH MIND

We can plausibly trace the main outlines of demotic liberalism back to their origins, or at least the point of historical intersection at which it makes sense to begin. And if we do, it may then be possible to see the essential terms of what became the preoccupation of this book, and the tradition of thought, the mode of feeling, it calls, 'radical earnestness'.

The point at which two powerful new currents of thought intersected was most percipiently marked in by John Stuart Mill, greatest of English intellectual systematizers. His work lies just beyond the reach of this study, but he serves as its first marker because he beautifully typifies the English intellectual's strong capacity both to absorb what he wants, and only what he wants, from the predominate climate, and then with his own strong photosynthesis, to transmute what he selects into his own system. At the same time Mill captures the essence of certain main tendencies and gives them a clear name, so that his audience may use the names as handholds with which to stay upright in the headlong, deep, and muddy torrents of political argument.

Our typical intellectual is English in all this: that, above all, he seeks to keep his ideas and those he borrows from headier spirits paraphrasable into the real language of some men — not of any men, but of his circle of decent herbivores. English liberal idealism is not a man-eating rhetoric, and it is none the worse for that. This strong, vegetable impulse in the tradition fertilizes itself with a heavy mixture of traditional literature.

It is only an assertion, not here documented or argued for, but it seems likely that the English intelligentsia maintains a special, close, and friendly relation with literature of a kind not experienced by other Europeans. In 'England, your England', George Orwell refers rather blithely to the English 'lack of artistic ability'.

This is perhaps another way of saying that the English are outside the European culture. For there is one art in which they have shown plenty of talent, namely literature. But this is also the only art that cannot cross frontiers. Literature, especially poetry, and lyric poetry most of all, is a kind of family joke, with little or no value outside its own language-group. Except for Shakespeare, the best English poets are barely known in Europe, even as names.[16]

For French intellectuals, the two names which command their national allegiance are Descartes, supremely, and Voltaire, more ironically; neither their incomparable painters nor Flaubert and Baudelaire are *there* for them as Descartes is, and after Descartes, Marx. For Germans, the dominant names are no doubt Kant and Hegel, and only thereafter, Marx and Nietzsche. In Italy the tremendous bulk of the church shadows everything which is written. In Eastern Europe, above all in Russia, the long inheritance[17] of the surveillance and imprisonment of ideas has given literature extraordinary significance simply because political talk is either sycophantic or *samizdat*. But then the novels and the poems go a little mad, because they are outlaws and in perpetual disguise; they have to live a Robin Hood kind of life, disguised as itinerant friars and with a price on their heads.

Generalizing quite so sententiously about other countries and their life of letters is a risk. Perhaps that short comic strip about the foreignness of Europe will nonetheless serve to throw into relief what Orwell calls the family joke of literature. For English literature, Europe's greatest and most varied, has been present to its national intelligentsia in a taken-for-granted way peculiar to them. Not Church nor Party but a liberal-to-whiggish view of Shakespeare, Milton, Boswell's Johnson, *Tom Jones*, the Romantic poets especially Wordsworth, Jane Austen, the Brontes, Dickens and the early George Eliot, has provided the metahistory of the intellectual class and a few, at least, of their pupils who have practised official politics.

Time and again the English intellectual tries to explain his ideas or to interpret those of others by resituating them in his literature. The whole action of works such as Trollope's parliamentary novels (or his Church of England ones as well), of Henry James's *The Tragic Muse*, Thackeray's *The Newcomer*, Meredith's *Sandra Belloni*, to say nothing of Disraeli or a novel like Mrs. Humphry Ward's *Robert Elsmere*, endorses the closeness of the connections of family, property, marriage, world-picture, between intellectual life as lived at Oxford and Cambridge, and political decisions and policies.[18] The world D. H. Lawrence portrayed picnicking early in *Women in Love* vividly dramatizes the juxtaposition of Cambridge, Bloomsbury, and Westminster, the seats of intellectual, political and drawing-room power about which Lawrence was, at the personal level, unanswerably right ('it isn't that life has been too much for them, but too little') is a world in which political ideas are clearly and readily handled in a domestic language. You may say, if you like, that (for instance) it is the confinement of philosophy to the tea-table which has made Oxford linguistic analysis at its most parodiable so stifling and trivial an activity. But there is also a strength in both the structure and culture of a polity where political ideas may be readily discussed whatever the everyday circumstances.

Strength or weakness, I offer it as a feature of the way in which the English intellectuals treat political ideas that they keep them close to the necessarily domestic idiom in which fictions are told. This has meant that ideas imported from Europe or from the States have been assimilated into this domestic idiom, partly in order to tame them, in any case to place them within the organizing field-of-force of the English ideology. For as well as the reference to literature as a means of insisting that general ideas transform themselves into intentional action by discovering a narrative, the programme of individual experience as drawn through the eighteenth century by the empirical philosophers from Locke to Hume, and sharing with a jurisprudentialist like Edward Blackstone or the first and greatest utilitarian Bentham a developed scepticism and a cultivated distaste for grand theory, taught four lessons. It taught a habit of recourse to concrete examples in argument, a calm refusal of formal metaphysics, an unexamined criticism of 'over-abstraction' (which meant other people's abstractions), and a general preference for non-systematized or pluralist theories of political life.

Now there has grown up of late a reflex dismissal[19] of the English ideology as summarized in these familiar lineaments: empiricism, concrete detail, evidence collection, scepticism, hatred of theory or jargon, and so on. The dismissal claims that, according to Marx's originating use of the term, this structure of concepts is, strictly, ideological in the sense that it conceals much more than it reveals; it works to prevent any more roundly totalizing theories which would show how intellectual practices interlock and how empiricism and the rest repress any interrogation of the present scheme of things in the name of a different social order; it breaks the connections between political and economic practice and the comfortable academic life led by those who dream up and profit by the ideology.

Well, there is much truth there, as we have seen. It is very easy, as the briefest consultation of the middle pages of *The Times* will show, for the complacent and the well-off and the philistine to dress up their prejudices as the English ideology. But an insistence on an empirical base to thought and a systematic scepticism is a minimum condition of sanity. A rational belief in and striving towards a better life and world is only possible if that life and world are not only imaginable but *feasible*.[20] An impossible Utopia, as long as it is situated this side of Paradise, may be used in many ways — as pain-killer, daydream or as justifying murder

— but all of them deadly. The strength of English thought and its irresistible powers of assimilation and exclusion and honest popularizing lies in its triple tensions: between dissent and practicality, between individuals and institutions, between experience and hope.

John Stuart Mill algebraicized these tensions as the pull between Bentham and Coleridge: Bentham as standing for the public calculus of rational interests in a mass society: Coleridge, as the emblem of his own dictum, 'men ought to be weighed, not counted', standing for the solid, experiencing and historical individual, most himself in his feeling life. Public versus private, later vulgarizers might even more crudely say, and indeed it is in those terms that the Englishman has often portioned out his life — here, private life as feeling, personal, warm, sincere; over there, public life as vast, rational, impersonal, productive, uncontrollable, lethal.

ROMANTICISM AND DISSENT

The best thinkers in the tradition have accepted the descriptions, but not their necessity nor that of division. Poised, as I put it, between dissent and practicality, we certainly can think of the last hundred years' work as rewriting the deep contradictions of Romantic feeling and Enlightenment rationalism. But the thinkers bring to that task the language of dissent as first spoken[21] and shaped by the Puritan divines of the Civil War and the Commonwealth — and indeed responded to by centre constitutionalists like Clarendon, Marvell, Fairfax. The Christians of the Revolution, dominated by Milton and figuring great pamphleteer supporters such as Stephen Marshall, Thomas Cartwright, Richard Baxter, as well as Ireton, Lilburne, Cromwell and company among the soldiers, and, at the limits of zeal, Bunyan and Gerard Winstanley,[22] are the prime speakers of the dissenting rhetoric.

It is possible to ring their bell backward even further past the Elizabethan debates on political freedom to Wycliff and the Lollards. It is the Whig interpretation of history that these names indeed constitute progress itself, and there is something if unhistorical to say for this view once more. But the seventeenth century casts a sufficiently long historical shadow on the English mind, and the qualities of the prose of the Puritan divines serve as recipe book for the eminent Victorians T. H. Green and William Morris with whom we begin in earnest.

The divines brought to political immediacy a moral earnestness whose intensity sought to fill any empty metaphysical space by sheer force of personality. This was the earnestness of the Anglicized Calvinism with which they had learned to see all and everyday life as charged with heavenly significance. They brought their evangelicalism, that complex frame of mind as much a habit of command and address to an audience, a consciousness of patriarchy, as it was a commitment to belief. With these qualities, they also brought a self-righteous suspicion of power itself, cultivated against the monarchy, and allied this to an almost instinctual intransigeance and bloody-mindedness when faced with the symbolism and fact of coercion.

Such qualities cut both ways; in many versions, Milton's among them, they include bigotry, arrogance, sanctimoniousness, bullying. As a checklist however they serve to identify the structure of style as well as method and modality in our more recent subjects. T. H. Green and Morris lived from the moral earnestness and intense evangelicalism of their forebears; they too sought to fill an even larger metaphysical void than Milton created by the force of their will and their passionate commitment to an ideal way of life.

These two men are by no means the only ones to choose as heroes of the tradition, and foremost dissenters of the Victorian age. They live and stand, as it is the point of this chapter to expound, in the dense field-of-force which held Victorian ideas and ideology. They enter here on two cues. First, because they engaged head-on the two contradictory motions of post-1789 Europe and sought to hold them together. That is, they saw that the Enlightenment, the new forces of capital and class which the Fourth Estate and their much more prosperous fellows in England released, was a source of *progressive* new life. They saw, that is, that a new kind of society was upon them, with a new system of institutions and collectivities, and that this needed new versions of rational organization for its control and development. They saw the paramountcy of science and scientific forms of calculation. At the same time, however, they responded with all their beings to the Romantic resistance to the new world. They identified with the celebration of subjectivity, the dangerous and exhilarating recognition of the joy of spontaneous feeling. Above all, they spoke out against the expressive death of bourgeois society, its stifling conformity, its meanness and acquisitiveness, its wizened provincialism, all rooted in a poisoned set of social relations. Green and Morris signify all they do because in such different but complementary ways they struggled to unify what has been called[23] the dialectic of the Enlightenment: private Romanticism and the rationalism of public bureaucracies.

The form and content of that struggle for unity is the second reason for starting with these two men. Both were products of the new public schools; both started from the cultural power base of Oxford; both won wide public acclaim and influence; both were individuals of extraordinary personal force and presence. Both may be taken to typify the best versions of the tradition we are taking: strong in conviction, in sense of public duty, in feeling, *manly* in some very deep, pure sense. They signify that social formation without whose energy, temper, and genuine influence, English life would be a great deal less free, decent, open, and upright than it is. In the teeth of normal human unpleasantness, they embodied ideals essential to the best life of their culture; their lives were part of that best life. They remain living examples of how to dissolve the antipathy of public and private, theory and experience.

2

The Long Summer: Idealist Radicals and the Oxford and Cambridge Intelligentsia — T. H. Green and William Morris

At first sight T. H. Green is not the most obvious choice as an intellect of the streets. He was born in 1836, fourth child of a West Riding vicar, and very soon motherless. His father, a genial, intelligent and notably unauthoritarian but authoritative man gave his son the freedom and the education to provide the origins of his strenuously evangelical temper and his determined insistence on an ethics of self-determination. Like later heroes in this book, R. G. Collingwood and R. H. Tawney, Green was a pupil at Rugby school some short time after Thomas Arnold had made it the symbolic citadel of the moral uprightness and zeal, of the intellectual stamina and vigorously debated scholarship, for which subsequently the public schools have so unbashfully celebrated themselves. Like Collingwood, Green spoke harshly of the anarchy and pointlessness of much of his public school education; but when all is said and done about the stifling conformism and the hatred of things of the mind encouraged by public school gentlemanliness, it seems still to be true of Rugby School, as of Winchester and certain other of the English public schools, that something in their traditions and structure made and, even now, makes, possible for a few a certain cast of radical and interrogative intelligence. Some odd alchemical conjuncture on the margins of these schools brought together for the better part of a century the schools' professed liberalism and commitment to intellectual inquiry, their allegiance to reform and their official distaste for gross acquisitiveness, their nursery discipline and saturnalian freedoms for young men of eighteen, their celibacy, and high, objectless yearning for the noble and self-sacrificing. This peculiar social formation held men at each limit of this study: Green and Morris; Crosland and Thompson.

In Green's case, as no doubt in the other cases too, the strongest formative structure he encountered — and lived within all his life — was the university, and for the social formation of which we speak the university in question could only be either Oxford or Cambridge. Green went to Balliol in 1855 and became a Fellow of the college after mixed but considerable academic success in 1860. He remained at Balliol for the rest of his life, becoming, notably, as well as Whyte's Professor of moral philosophy, one of the first Fellows to marry (in 1871) and retain his fellowship, the first university teacher to be elected a City Councillor, naturally as a Liberal, a member in 1864—6 of the Royal Commission inquiring into 'the schools attended by the children of such of the gentry, clergy, professional and commercial men as are of limited means, and of farmers and tradesmen'.[1] In this and similar connections, Green was in the vanguard of the Radical movement which sought and expected so much from the extension of national education, whose first big victory was Forster's compromising Act of 1870.[2] Yet his most substantial and perhaps admired contribution to education was to be found, first, in his collaboration as college tutor with Jowett, the Master, over the establishment of a special hall of residence to accommodate able students too poor to afford the usual college bills; second, in the activity and busy, relevant sense of duty and application which he brought to his membership of the Taunton Commission; third, in the governorship of King Edward's School, Birmingham, which his report led to; fourth, in his vigorous championship, with that of his wife, of the education of women and their admission to Oxford. Mrs Green, a woman of great independence and intelligence, kept all the years of her widowhood in Oxford, and remained for many of them on the council of Somerville College, and the Association for the Higher Education of Women. Lastly, Green's commitment to education generalized itself in his life. The central place in liberal thought of education as the rational process of self-realization is clouded in as famous an expositor as Matthew Arnold by that something not only in his manner but in the substance of his argument which Robert Bridges (surprisingly) caught in a phrase when he called Arnold 'Mr. Kidglove Cocksure'. Arnold's life experience, not unlike Green's (Rugby, of course) though obviously Higher Church, led him to over-value the redemptive power of culture[3] and to leave himself helpless without either an ethics or a politics. His moral recommendations rest on a perfectly unexamined gentility — good manners being all that his class had left after the removal of Christianity — which provided him with a useful critical terminology for an assault on the grossnesses and omissions of cultural life but quite unable to provide a political account of how to repair them. Politics only transpire in his writings as a source of either nervousness or nastiness.

Arnold has featured so largely in English social theory of a belle-lettriste kind because he was a man of letters, and spoke so sympathetically against the industrial depredations which were too much for the sensibilities of those who wished neither to give up a comfortable life nor to seek more power and wealth than was seemly in north Oxford or north London. But his strengths were drastically limited. They rested largely on his combination of a fine tact in poetic analysis and a winning line in cultural oratory.

The other major contender as chief spokesman for radicalism among the intelligentsia to rank with Green is, as we have noted, John Stuart Mill. Mill however may be set aside for our direct purposes on three grounds: that, strictly, he antedates the past century of social theorists; that his social thought, though vast and architectonic in magnitude, engages only unsystematically with such main radical issues and topics as education, poverty, social structure (in relation to justice and equality); lastly, that for all its generosity, the form of utilitarianism which he spent his intellectual life trying to justify is now argued to be critically weak in areas in which industrial society most needs an adequate social ethic. What is missing in Mill's life and its praxis is just that visible and day-to-day reciprocation between practical matters and the effort to locate these within an intellectual totality which won Green his enormous following.

A life's work as enormous as Mill's cannot be dismissed by anyone; the dismissal would be clearly insupportable as well as insolent. Mention of his name here serves perhaps to identify the utilitarian dominance which it was Green's self-appointed task to resist and, by the example of his life and thought, to hold back in at least the academic capital of Oxford for twenty years. Furthermore, it is a characteristic and, no doubt, elective affinity of the thinkers in this book that, unable to dispense with the organizing power and convenience of utilitarianism[4] they wrestle with it as an omnipresent point of reference and resistance. Utilitarianism is largely unignorable, and most of all in its reformism. Thus Mill, like Green, would have counted himself a political reformer, and responded warmly to Green's typical insistence that 'the nature of the genuine political reformer is perhaps always the same . . . The passion for improving mankind, in its ultimate object, does not vary'.

There is a noticeable difference between the present position of political reformers and that in which they stood a generation ago. Then they fought the fight of reform in the name of individual freedom against class privilege. Their opponents could not with any plausibility invoke the same name against them. Now, in appearance — though, as I shall try to show, not in reality — the case is changed. The nature of the genuine political reformer is perhaps always the same. The passion for improving mankind, in its ultimate object, does not vary. But the immediate object of reformers, and the forms of persuasion by which they seek to advance them, vary much in different generations. To a hasty observer they might even seem contradictory, and to justify the notion that nothing better than a desire for change, selfish or perverse, is at the bottom of all reforming movements. Only those who will think a little longer about it can discern the same old cause of social good against class interests, for which, under altered names, liberals are fighting now as they were fifty years ago.[5]

Such accents link Green firmly to Mill as liberal intellectual; in any simple collision with state oppression, they would have stood in the same opposition. As Green's later revisionist disciple D. G. Ritchie was to say, 'There is no reason why the Idealist, after making clear his objections to Hedonism, should not join hands with the Utilitarian.'[6]

But the objections to hedonism, which for Mill was in any case a deeply contested and ambiguous notion, are not the heart of the matter. The good utilitarian and the good idealist may equally assent to the importance of being earnest; they may be joined by the good Marxist. The importance of Green's kind of earnestness, however, is exemplary, and the significance of his biography is that it betokened the effort to live, in thought and deed, a unified version of his particular world-view. Hence his readiness as our example. His creative effort was to build together metaphysics, morality and practical politics; it was to insert the giant achievements of Kant and Hegel in a class society and according to decent, liberal principles of welfare, social concern, reason and justice. The question now at issue is whether the not very strange death of liberal England which took place between 1914 and 1918 made Green's creation obsolete or not.

T. H. GREEN: THE IDEALIST IN POLITICS

Green's most thorough expositor in recent years, Melvin Richter, is in no doubt that Green is done for. The admiration he clearly feels[7] for the man (and who could not share it?), he no less firmly separates from the status of the man's work. This is a stance shared by many contemporary historians of ideas about the subject-matter they study; the stance, in the disagreeably amused mode not altogether avoided even by so intelligent a commentator as Collini, implies that the ideas of old — in these cases, the ideas of social reform in the late nineteenth century — may have had some sociological (though little logical) validity then, but to understand their context is to discard their present relevance. Most deeply of all, the stance connotes the historical relativism which is one of the knottiest problems at the centre of social theory. Collini, for example, very much an advocate of the kind of history of ideas discussed in the final chapter below, comes roundly out against his own subject-matter as no longer usable in any form; indeed, his intention is to show that this is now the case:

It should be clear by now that it is no part of my intention to attempt to restore Hobhouse's reputation or to advocate a return to his methods. On the contrary, my aim has been to emphasize that his thinking was embedded in a set of assumptions which no longer demands our allegiance, and addressed to a range of problems which no longer commands our attention. Above all, his theories sustained and were sustained by a pattern of moral attitudes which enjoyed a special prominence during this period.[8]

By the same token, in a last eddy of confidence inspired by the success of Oxford analytic philosophy, Richter ends his book on Green by murmuring: 'Technical developments within philosophy had discredited the intellectual case for Idealism. And its decline coincided with the downfall of the Liberal Party and stemmed from many of the same causes.'[9] He goes on to note that 'the disappearance of Nonconformity as a political force' was one such cause, although there are plenty of stalwart Labour Party chairmen left in east Derbyshire and west Glamorgan who would be puzzled even now by this unannounced superannuation, and concludes gracefully, as so many historians of ideas have, that, by the 1920s, 'the Liberal epoch had come to an end, and with it the tenure of Green's influence'.

Well, Green's influence in the sense of an intense and irresistible presence which filled the minds of his many followers was no doubt over. The force which seemed to one pupil as like to conversion as may be imagined outside formal religion — 'his existence was one of the things that gave reality to the distinction between good and evil'[10] — was bound to be forgotten after his death. But 'the Liberal epoch' ended partly because of the drastic historical ruptures of the 1914—1918 war, and partly because so much of what it had once only imagined was now proved, much of what its reformers had envisaged as within real social capacity had begun to be filled, and much of the complex and difficult relations between moral possibility and social structure had been charted and incorporated into political practice, and were themselves changed, as Hegel and more sketchily Green, had always insisted that they were bound to be. However quick modern historians of ideas[11] are to guard themselves against charges of meliorism and however much they are determined to sound realistically world-weary about the impossibility of progress, the fact remains that liberal arguments about state intervention and its justifications, about positive and negative freedoms in relation to this secularization, and about the self-realizing individual whose manifold existences in a rational society were the unenvisageable purposes of this advance, had won and held real victories since Green's early death in 1882, and were ready to go on to new ones under the same banner.

This is not to claim that Green, and Hobhouse and the company of Fabians after him, brought about these victories by themselves. Green was only forty-six when he died; most of his books were published under Nettleship's editing after his death; he was only a local councillor, a fine man, and a university teacher. We may however claim that even if Idealism did not lead to the Delectable Mountains, inasmuch as there is truth in historicism when it professes that we can only understand and value the present by reconstructing it in terms of its past constituents, so Green's life and thought and his creative struggle to make them indivisible, provide a handhold for our present understanding of the good and the real.

Green began from his assertion that these two, the good and the real, are coterminous. That is to say, he insisted that ethics (the study and the precepts of moral behaviour) grounds itself in metaphysics (the investigation of what really exists according to Kant's principles of critical reason, which necessarily presuppose the prior existence of minds and concepts and seek to define their reliability). So when he asks:

The question, What is our moral nature or capability? — in other words, What do we mean by calling ourselves moral agents? — is one to which a final answer cannot be given without an answer to the question, What is moral good? For the moral good is the realisation of the moral capability, and we cannot fully know what any capability is till we know its ultimate realisation. It may be argued therefore that we either know what the moral good in this sense is, and accordingly have no need to infer what it is from our moral nature, or else we do not know what it is, in which case neither can we know what the moral nature is from which we profess to infer what the moral good is.

The answer is that from a moral capability which had not realised itself at all nothing could indeed be inferred as to the moral good which can only consist in its full realisation; but that the moral capability of man is not in this wholly undeveloped state. To a certain extent it has shown by actual achievement what it has in it to become, and by reflection on the so far developed activity we can form at least some negative conclusion in regard to its complete realisation.[12]

At once we engage with an English-based and, we may say, post-Wordsworthian version of Hegel's teleology. (*The Prelude*, finished in its first version in 1805, twenty-six years before Hegel's death, may be proposed as the Romantic individual's version of Hegel's metaphysics. Green, like Mill, admired Wordsworth above all poets.) History is constantly realizing its own best possibilities, but can only do so in logic in the terms made available by present, specific opportunity. The specific nature of this realization of your opportunity is all you can work with; your judgement, however, of what it is worth measures itself against whatever your temperament and education make it possible for you to guess of the nature of the absolute.

The absolute, or the finished realization of the irregular, ineluctable progress of society towards reason-in-spirit, has a far less fearsomely abstract look about it in Green than in Hegel. His treatment of moral advance and the measures necessary to encourage it implies less staring through high windows than Hegel's version of the achieved spirit.

Green does not attempt to mitigate the ambitiousness of Hegel's historicism and Kant's deontology, or theory of duty-for-duty's sake; but he earths it in an intelligible picture of *what to do*. He does not inhabit an empyrean view of faceless individuals all equally to be treated as ends and not means as Kant requires, but in a series of more detailed recommendations about disadvantage, stupidity, and class.

Green's strength is that he was far more wideawake in the world of everyday dealings than is usual for metaphysicians. But this is not to say that all his more abstruse dealings must therefore be cashable in the currency of health and social security. At every point, Green drives his argument home to the stage at which he may identify experience and community. For he is caught, and knows that he is caught, in a tense irreconciliation. He wants to make compatible the splits between individual and membership, spontaneity and obligation, between — most painful of all — virtue and happiness which Romanticism in its many guises tore open in the web of social life. Whether or not that web was ever as snugly woven as some of the sentimentalists supposed is not something Green, to his credit, speculated upon even in his lectures on the Commonwealth; there too, true to his historicism, he said 'English puritanism originated in the consciousness of a spiritual life which no outward ordinances could adequately express'.[13] But his business was always to place human response in a recognizable model of shared mentality, a mentality which represented the only vehicle of knowledge. So, a fact 'is not a feeling, but an explanation of a feeling, which connects it by relations, that are not feelings, with an unfelt universe'; hence knowledge 'compels an inference to the unknown', and — the telling selection of the formulation is Nettleship's — 'while it is true in a sense that in inference we do not go beyond experience, it is so because in experience we already go beyond sense'.[14]

The strain is apparent in the conceptualization; but this way of putting the idealist case is a long way from Hegel's, and far more congenial to the English habit of rooting argument in the commonsense though commonly unidentified category of 'experience' than German idealism makes possible. Of course, congeniality is no criterion of rationality, but idealism in this architecture not only gives plenty of room to the hoped-for armistice between idealists and materialists, or at least those this side of the absolutely dedicated physicalists of Quine's school; this idealism also offers accommodation to social scientists in our tradition who recoil from the simpler head-counting of empirical sociology and the more bellicose trenches dug between facts and values by social theorists and political scientists of many colours.

Green is a considerable help (in a way in which Mill is not) in qualifying, long before it was enforced by the uncertainties of modern physics, the distinction between fact and value, and in placing his decidedly partial versions of the facts in the selective cognitions of very particular social structures. Thus, again, in his treatment of subjectivity and objectivity, notions which even today are thought of as routinely counterposed in perception and validity (and the validity of what is subjective is the more fiercely defended just because it *belongs to* the actor and is mistakenly thought to be indisputable as a consequence), he provides a theory of consciousness as active and creative in making worlds which do not belong to the actor alone. On this view the whole is ultimately knowable in its objective reality, and our subjective apprehension of it is as great as our consciousness will allow, staked out as it is along the empirical and transitional events which are our mental states but itself the nontemporal ground of observation and ordering.

The strength of this account is that it mediates action and structures; it is not easy to recollect for the historian of ideas how vigorously Green had to work against the grain of Humean empiricism in order to theorize his picture of the actor in society. Green was not in a position to test his theory against the demands of the linguistic coherence which would now be asked of him, and continued to write of metaphysics in a style which, so to say, guarantees its truth to reality by assuming (and never questioning) a perfect transparency of meaning. These are developments rather than criticisms which we shall follow up later. For the moment it is the vigour and completeness of Green's whole scheme which is so attractive.

For at the heart of that scheme is a radical thesis about freedom. Green would have claimed it to be true. A hundred years later, after the new military technology from the tank to the neutron bomb has made it clear that the limits for social optimism are very narrow indeed, and when it has come to seem only rational to speak up for pleasure as an end in life, Green's thesis is not so much true as *potential*. That is to say, without it, it would be hard to keep alive the idea of a common good, of recognizable progress, of social hope, at all.

It is this. Human nature is inherently self-reflexive; this reflection is not passive but dynamic, and impels the individual towards self-awareness and self-fulfilment. This realization of self cannot be confined to the individual, because self-awareness reveals our membership of a society of self-aware others.[15] The more developed our personal self-awareness, the more we acknowledge how partially we know what a realized fulfilment would be like, and the more we strive to transcend the existing moral life and create a new, superior one. Green endorses Kant's 'good will' as the transcendent good, and redefines it as the *social* impulse 'to know what is true, to make what is beautiful, to endure pain and fear, to resist the allurements of pleasure, *in the interest of some form of human society*'[16] (italics added).

In this enterprise, the centre of freedom is not choice, as it would have been for Mill ('negative' freedom as Berlin calls it[17]), but thought itself, and thought as the motive for action. The energetic motion of thought inevitably discovers the uniformity of nature, and this uniformity dissolves the 'false individuality of self'[18] by the repetition of encounter with mind and minds, and affirms true individuality not as momentary, impassioned, exclusive, and self-absorbed feeling, but as the energy of communication.

It is easy enough for a gun-slinging analyst of language to shoot holes in some of the more exposed parts of Green's case. There is no call here to defend the asserted monism or world-uniformity which the absolute idealist is committed to find. Green's importance for us as historians of ideas is that he created an English idiom for the bringing together of metaphysics, ethics, and action, and for us as social theorists in the present, that he imagined a language for the description of consciousness and the self which remoralizes their action while making it relatively clear that his moral vocabulary only works within a given form of social life.

So far, so good. Green specifies no sheer disjuncture between the actual and the desired ideal. The ideal is immanent, as Hegel said before him,[19] in the actual. But when Green comes to deal with the actual, his treatment depends veeringly on his prior intellectual equipment. (It is a point whose general accuracy his very system requires; *of course,* he would say, my social theory is partial. The point then becomes, how do we insert its partiality into a more satisfactory, later version of the totality?) His ideas commit him excellently to the equality of citizens. The capacity for self-realization *is* the defining human quality. What constrains it are social limits. Change those limits, and you enable changed men. Nettleship quotes an attractive passage which makes this point about suffrage:

The winner is no party, whig, conservative, or radical. The whole nation wins by a measure which makes us for the first time one people. We who were reformers from the beginning, always said that the enfranchisement of the people was an end in itself. We said, and we were much derided for saying so, that citizenship only makes the moral man; that citizenship only gives that self-respect, which is the true basis of respect for others, and without which there is no lasting social order or real morality. If we were asked what result we looked for from the enfranchisement of the people, we said, that is not the present question; untie the man's legs, and then it will be time to speculate how he will walk.

Our present system of great estates, as I believe, gives a false set to society from top to bottom. It causes exaggerated luxury at the top, flunkeyism in the middle, poverty and recklessness at the bottom. There is no remedy for this poverty and recklessness as long as those who live on the land have no real and permanent interest in it . . .

It is this debased population that gluts the labour-market, and constantly threatens to infect the class of superior workmen, who can only secure themselves, as I believe, by such a system of protection as is implied in the better sort of trades-union. This is an evil which no individual benevolence can cure. Ten thousand soup-kitchens are unavailing against it. It can only be cured by such legislation as will give the agricultural labourer some real interest in the soil.[20]

This way of speaking sorts happily with Green's extensive writing on education, and all he says on education partakes of the special aura he gave in life and thought to his own brand of 'citizenship'.

That citizenship was no doubt special to the highmindedness and objectless yearning of a class of undergraduates which had absorbed evangelical feeling but lost its religious belief. Green provided a framework of meaning, and even when the twentieth century sensibility pulls back in both irony and more or less amused revulsion from his more solemn comminations on the allurements of sensuous pleasure, and the ruin caused by drink, no radical bosom can fail to return an echo to his strictures on the class divisions in Victorian education, and to his singular insistence that liberal-democratic commitment to universal education is not simply an adjunct of benevolent class-feeling, but followed from and was entailed by the metaphysics of an ethics of universal self-realization. No self *could* realize itself without education and knowledge. It is the force of this argument which makes his backing of Oxford High School for boys — a backing which included his own not easily afforded £200 plus an annual scholarship in his own account, as well as the support of his profound convictions — so satisfactory an endorsement of a vision of the good man as the good citizen, and the good citizen as prefiguring the good life not only of 1882 but of a generation or two to come.

In every nation, perhaps, there must be a certain separation between those who live solely by the labour of their hands and those who live rather by the labour of their heads or by the profits of capital, between members of the learned professions and those engaged constantly in buying and selling, between those who are earning their money and those who are living on the income of large accumulated capital; but in England these separations have been fixed and deepened by the fact that there has been no fusion of class with class in school or at the universities.

Within the last thirty years there has arisen a new order of proprietary schools, Clifton, Cheltenham, and the like, very useful in their way, but equally maintaining in practice a strict class exclusion. They are schools for the sons of members of the learned professions and for those commercial men who never appear behind a counter. These schools, however, are quite of recent creation. Till they arose, the class of parents who now use them, together with the great body of shopkeepers, unless by a happy accident they had access to a well-managed grammar school, sent their sons to different sorts of private schools. But between the different sorts of private schools there were and are the strictest social demarcations. Farmers and ordinary shopkeepers will send their sons to one kind, at one rate of payment; richer men of business and professional men to another kind, at a higher rate of payment. The boys sent to the one kind of school will look down with contempt on those sent to the other, and though they may be necessarily thrown together in after life, there will never be that freedom of social intercourse between them that we notice between men who have the same memories of school and college.[21]

Green goes on to sketch out for the first time in the United Kingdom a diagram of tripartite and quadripartite education in which intelligence would be the sole criterion of merit. We have no call to be condescending about a progressive vision which would have looked daring and contemporary to the honest Beveridgeans who drafted Butler's 1944 Education Act. And we would have even less such occasion when we reach the peroration of this lecture:

So the knowledge among the artisans of Oxford that at any rate no barrier of social exclusion stood between their sons and the highest university education would, I believe, give them a new feeling of reverence for knowledge and of respect for those who can impart it. Perhaps this may be thought a student's flight of fancy, but at least there can be no doubt of the definite and much needed stimulus that will be given to the elementary schools of the city by the opportunity of distinguishing themselves in the scholarship examination of the high school; and of the improvement that will thus result the working classes will have the immediate benefit. Our high school then may fairly claim to be helping forward the time when every Oxford citizen will have open to him at least the precious companionship of the best books in his own language, and the knowledge necessary to make him really independent; when all who have a special taste for learning will have open to them what has hitherto been unpleasantly called the 'education of gentlemen.' I confess to hoping for a time when that phrase will have lost its meaning, because the sort of education which alone makes the gentleman in any true sense will be within the reach of all.[22]

Liberalism cannot easily appear in a more appealing light; we have seen how rightly, in the great class—compromise Green was no small instrument in negotiating, education must figure centrally as the medium for transforming the equality of human capacity (in Green's phrase; we would now say potential) into commensurability of achievement and respect.[23] In this he shared with reformers and revolutionaries alike, with Marx and Mill, ambitious hopes for the redemptive aspects of the aesthetics of consciousness. Our latter-day educationalists would drastically alter the content but not the form of his hopes.

The deep lack in his metaphysic of ethics was a credible theory of capital's contracts and obligations, and this failure shifts us to the second hero of our Victorian origins, William Morris. Green, in advocating the aesthetics of consciousness, had little access to and less interest in the works of Marx appearing during the 1870s, and although with Mill he repudiated the market morality, he ignored his own inadequacy in trying to negotiate this absence.[24] Indeed, for all his forceful advocacy of a justifiably increased state legislature and statist politics, he was so unable to account for the victories of Josiah Bounderby or the Onedin line that he continued to regard capital accumulation as a necessary freedom in individual self-realization.

For all the greatness of heart and personal heroism of mind which Green brought to his task, he lacked the intellectual apparatus of economics, and the experiential luck to spot his own major deficiency. William Morris broke with reformism on the basis of his wider experience. It is this which makes him the structural complement to Green in the 1880s.

WILLIAM MORRIS: ROMANTIC TO REVOLUTIONARY

It will be noticed that this subheading transcribes the title of Edward Thompson's fine biography of William Morris.[25] Thompson's book written, as at times this book intentionally is, as a work of hagiography, acts as a reminder of the continuities between the late nineteenth and the late twentieth centuries: a number of our spokesmen did some of their speaking and thinking on that primitive instrument of mass communication, the platform of a large public hall. Morris joins Green as hero of the tradition before the first, colossal disruption brought about by the 1914—1918 war, because he too worked out many of his best ideas on and for the public platform.

In this, he commends himself to the historian of radical earnestness and of English social theory. Of his heroism, as that of Green, there can be no doubt, and the status of heroism — of what it is to live in such a way as evokes admiration and perhaps emulation — is close to the centre of these studies. But to begin, so to speak, with a theory of heroism is not so much to take the risk of sounding simplemindedly Victorian — we may be none the worse for that — as to push out of focus the most immediate problem of method. The essential interest of Green's and Morris's lives is that in their lives, and in this rather strict sense, they were methodical. That is, the method of their thought can hardly be considered aside from the practice of their public lives.

In both a necessary and a banal way, this must always be so for any thinker. But our business is rather less with the thought of thinkers, and more with the practice of intellectuals. The animated cartoon of the thinkers is caught by the storybook image of Descartes staring at the stove and Kant staring at the steeple, just thinking.

> The great mind
> Sat with his back to the unreasoning wind
> And doubted, doubted at his ear
> The patter of ash and beyond the snow-bound farms,
> Flora of flame and iron contingency
> And the moist reciprocation of his palms.[26]

Well, if it is the matter of influence in dispute, there can be no dispute that Descartes and Kant have affected the way of the world vastly more than any of the men in this book. But what is at issue is not stature and its magnitude but a way of thought in the world. Green and Morris shaped a way of thinking about the world by making their way in it; how they realized their experience *was* their practice as intellectuals.

True, no doubt, of all of us, though we may escape triteness by recollecting what has been already mentioned, that experience is itself a less intelligible concept than everyday usage suggests. Even to speak of 'having had an experience' implies its difference in status from a mere event. To have had an experience is more than just having had something happen to you; it is to have acknowledged it as an encounter between you (in all your peculiarity) and it (in all its accidental nature). Somewhere at that meeting point is what the experience means, and that that can be made to mean something (even if you can never say what) is the essence which confirms it as experience.

But there is no pressing need to do more than note that every man and woman intuitively theorizes experience immediately and continuously. Assorted thinkers, Descartes supreme among them, sought to make mind and matter absolutely distinct; the Hegel who dominated Green sought to make mind all-encompassing. Our more socially and politically tendentious line of theorists makes shift with a rougher and readier philosophy of experience than the professionals may be happy with. Even though T. H. Green himself was deeply committed to sustaining a fully professional philosophy of practice, the lessons we have taken from him leave him open to many changes of strictly philosophical mistakings and misguidance. His importance to us is less the convincingness of the system, than the way he undertook it and the components he insisted on including.

The same is true, and very much more so, of William Morris. He does not offer any complete theory of political and cultural workings. But that is true, is indeed a typifying feature, of the other human scientists in this book. The greatest, perhaps the only total theorizer in English social theory of the nineteenth century is, as we have seen, John Stuart Mill: the ambitions for an English totality thereafter dried up in the petrified monuments of Herbert Spencer and the evolutionists,[27] or ran out into the sandy, porous revisions of liberalism as written by J. R. Hobson, L. T. Hobhouse and Graham Wallas.

Like some of the most ambitious and greatest-minded of his contemporaries, like Weber and Durkheim, like, indeed, Marx himself, Morris left no last will and testament, organizing his intellectual property and naming his proper heirs. Now sorting a system of ideas out of what was not systematically intended is a notoriously tricky practice. Indeed, intention itself is the most contested difficulty at the heart of the matter. Let us say, for the present, that to understand what Morris could have meant — as to understand what Green could have meant — it is necessary, so far as possible, to recover from his writings a sufficient account of his intentions interpreted in terms of the conventions which made them even thinkable in the first place.[28] To essay these always difficult and delicate acts of reconstruction is to practise history (a drastically different matter, as Collini says, from 'talking-up antiques').[29] But, as the chapter on Collingwood emphasizes, history does not even start there, least of all the history and practice of ideas. It begins in the set of mind and interests which brought the historian to the subject matter in the first place, and these may be small or large, trivial or important, independent or sycophantic, but all and inevitably of the present. So, to interrogate Morris for his systematic thought is certainly to try to understand him as he would have wished to be understood; it is also to hunt through his writings for what he can tell us. It is to bring all the help we can find to the conduct of our own practices. It is in this way that historical language is a magic language, and the historian, like the poet, becomes a magus. For to redescribe the past successfully is to see it differently; it is to reorder the action of memory, either personally or collectively and therefore and quite literally to change the way one understands things and acts upon them. T. S. Eliot, as we have noted, is not remarkable for his contribution to radical thought but he is remarkable for his contribution to radical poetry, and his account of the constant reordering of tradition effected by the advent of an insistently different poetic style fixes in an agreeably Hegelian way why it will indeed make a difference to resituate a William Morris in a different company to the one he usually keeps in the literature. In a famous passage, Eliot wrote:

No poet, no artist of any art, has his complete meaning alone. His significance, his appreciation is the appreciation of his relation to the dead poets and artists. You cannot value him alone; you must set him, for contrast and comparison, among the dead. I mean this as a principle of aesthetic, not merely historical, criticism. The necessity that he shall conform, that he shall cohere, is not one-sided; what happens when a new work of art is created is something that happens simultaneously to all the works of art which preceded it. The existing monuments form an ideal order among themselves, which is modified by the introduction of the new (the really new) work of art among them. The existing order is complete before the new work arrives; for order to persist after the supervention of novelty, the whole existing order must be, if ever so slightly, altered; and so the relations, proportions, values of each work of art toward the whole are readjusted; and this is conformity between the old and the new. Whoever has approved this idea of order, of the form of European, of English literature will not find it preposterous that the past should be altered by the present as much as the present is directed by the past. And the poet who is aware of this will be aware of great difficulties and responsibilities.[30]

By this token, I may try to change the tradition of theory and practice of which I write not merely by putting Morris's books in it, but also by putting his life's experience in it. Men and women battle to make sense of their, and other people's lives; as we have noted, they make theories in order to turn events into intelligible experience. But events themselves only vary according to the extent that an individual may turn event into opportunity. Morris's enormous gifts were such as to make many such transformations possible.

His life, therefore, is like Green's exemplary. He was born as the son of a wealthy speculator in 1834, was brought up in circumstances nominally similar to Green's as the child of the genteelly evangelical bourgeoisie and pupil of its schoolmaster in one of the new public schools, in this case Marlborough, and went to Oxford in 1853, a little while after Green. But the intellectual style of Exeter College was enormously different from that of Balliol. Morris was caught by that old, potent social formation of Oxford, the high, heady mixture of Pusey's Anglicanism and Romantic medieval imagery. He dropped the substance of the first pretty quickly, but kept its intense, bodiless yearning in his poetry; the second he incorporated into his admiration for the work of John Ruskin. These broad, strong components he wove into the thick-textured, powerful unity of his life. Such weaving is comfortably metaphoric: Morris found many means of expression with which to think through the difficult, searched-for variety of his life.

First, he wrote his many long poems. Although Edward Thompson in *William Morris* makes the best case for them that he can, they remain poetry of a kind made possible by the great Romantic poets, Keats, Wordsworth, Byron, Shelley, but with their implicit, unacknowledged deathliness and irresponsibility now sounding the dominant in its music. *The Defence of Guenevere* and *The Earthly Paradise* have their interest for a literary antiquarian, but they matter for my purposes as the responses of incomprehension − or the thought of a man who is refusing thought. One now familiar and useful way to place the poems is to say, as E. P. Thompson and F. R. Leavis before him have said, that Victorian poetry went fay and weak before the noisy, vulgar onslaught of the historical reality of the time. The real creative energy went into the novel, whose prose and structure were strong enough to encompass the new facts of life: the giant forces of production and capital whose combination had released all this amazing industry. Thompson's criticism is joined by that of the Frankfurt cultural critics Theodor Adorno and Herbert Marcuse[31] who voiced a more general commination over the ideological uses to which the successful bourgeoisie put their art under the energy of industrialization. They blamed the bourgeois poet and his readers for making art a sacred refuge detached from the awful ugliness of cash and production but endorsing that awfulness by recommending ecstacy in front of its own allegedly higher and more personal reality.

Both explanations are necessary and neither seems quite sufficient.

Morris, like other cultivated and less creative young men of the time, came to poetry as the readiest medium of reflection. The poets to hand, his great predecessors, had responded to the original power of Romantic ideas by turning them into statements of passionate and spontaneous individuality — 'the growth of a poet's mind'. They had devised a mysterious and beautiful landscape for this drama — the Lake District, the shrine of Melancholy, the Dark Tower, the West Wind. But as the paramount social creation of the century began to emerge — the industrial city — the Romantic agony and its unpeopled landscape turned out to be no place to live. The Arthurian legend, even for Tennyson, could support only domestic love affairs and the pastel picturesquerie of the water colour.

Morris took from medievalism what Marx took in his first formulations of the economic laws of history: the firm recognition of mutual interdependence in social relations, the systems of production which offered skilled workers the experience of absorption and meaning, the framework of belief which transcended class formation, the unexploitative relations of country and city.[32] But Morris's engagement with the experience of production was much closer than Marx's, and he brought to that experience the Romantic commitment to the humanly redemptive power of art. The strong surge of ideas for which the conventional starting points are the French and American revolutions not only detonated strong charges below any received scheme of social ethics, and handed over to the individual the extremely high tension power-line between passionate spontaneity and moral integrity, but it also gave to art its function as unique regulator of that alternating voltage.

Morris started from art. It is his strength and his originality, that he brought to his social and political theory his practical experience in the production of art. The poetry he wrote I fairly pass by as no more than fantasy in a weak sense of the word. The doctrine of self-expression made possible by Romanticism cannot find poetic experience upon which to grip; the self in Morris which finds poetic expression is part wistful, part yearning, and part gently hopeless. It is worth noting that when this tremendous polymath and genius turned from his full length translation of Homer and, in later life, learned Icelandic in order to translate the great sagas, the harshness and cruel courage those stories celebrate gave to his verse a steeliness and ruggedness which King Arthur never prompted.

The important questions Morris put to his creative energies were not, at the second stage of his development, verbal and literary. When he left

Oxford in 1856 he was already friend and member of the Pre-Raphaelite Brotherhood, was recruited by them and their infectious enthusiasm to start a career as a New Renaissance painter by decorating the Oxford Union with murals and went on to set himself up with his sizeable family wealth in studio life in Red Lion Square as full-blown painter-poet. He and his friends in the Brotherhood were caught up by the then magically attractive leadership of Dante Gabriel Rossetti, and the fervent faith he planted in them to learn from painters before Raphael how to recover brightness of colour and freshness of looking. We cannot pause for long over Morris's painting; what he was able to begin to bring to bear on it were some of the characteristics for which so many of his contemporaries at different times of his life praised him: his forcefulness, energy and strong convictions, his utter truthfulness and manliness, his irascibility and lively sense of humour.[33]

But his centrally important work in art and craft was not in his statuesque Arthurian tableaux (he must have known this; he painted very few full-blown paintings). After his marriage to the amazingly beautiful Jane Burden in 1859 he turned his wealth into the beauty of the Red House at Bexleyheath, which he designed with his friend Philip Webb, and subsequently into the setting up of his famous Firm, offering wallpaper and tapestry design, stained glass, carved wood and furniture — the main items in the recipe book of the arts and crafts movement,[34] still irresistibly influential all the way from Liberty's to Selfridge's and back to Habitat. It is not a trivial point to make. Morris contributed vastly to 'the English ideology', and never more so than when he was designing. Quite against his intentions, English sentimentality, the sweet, remembering prettiness to which the scale of its landscape, its wild flowers, its suburban gardens lend themselves, joined forces with the cynical voracity of the productive systems to domesticate, and to turn into high chic Morris's utter integrity of workmanship, its fineness and clarity, its honest shapeliness and decency.

Yet, at the same time, Morris was in as practical a way as possible committing himself against all that production, capital, and consumerism made of his work at the time and in Sanderson's extravagant showrooms since. For he was working at exactly the intersection between art and craft, expression and workmanship, guild workshop and studio, popular and fine culture. His celebrated chintz designs — blackthorn, honeysuckle, marigold — deny the aesthetician's distinction between art and craft,[35] at least in so far as it confines itself to a view of art as an unenvisageable end and craft as a matter of the precise application of technique to means. There is far more to say to the argument than that, of course; here it is enough to emphasize that Morris's answers to the questions posed in his design dissolve the distinction between art and craft, and that the solution is a political one.

How shall we say that the sturdy, graceful, and eloquent honeysuckle design is political? I shall say it in the special sense to suit this case, and yet it is the sense implied by the acknowledgement Nikolaus Pevsner pays Morris as first pioneer — with Ruskin as theoretician — of modern design.[36] Pevsner recognizes that 'what raises Morris as a reformer of design high above the Cole circle and Pugin is not only that he had the true designer's genius and they had not, but also that he recognized the indissoluble unity of an age and its social system, which they had not done . . .' and he goes on to praise the manliness and sturdiness I have named as Morris's signature on his designs, and his ensuing breadth and stateliness, all of them qualities plainly and firmly inscribed in the work, chastening and above all criticizing by their robust accuracy, their fidelity both to natural forms and the requirements of pattern, the ostentatious goods of the Great Exhibition with their implicit assertion of art as the property of the powerful and rich.

It is hard not to digress into a grand encomium upon Morris's skills: his daughter's fine memoir[37] and her extensive quotation from his letters brings out his brilliance, his diversity, and the modesty with which he displayed both. But the relevance for my view of Morris's practice as a social theorist is that his designs, for chintz, for chairs ('built for Barbarossa'), for stained glass illustrations, embody a fiercely critical — and because critical by positive, superior example, creative — account of contemporary market products. At the same time, the conditions of production at 'the Firm' of Morris and Company (the nominal partners Marshall and Faulkner soon dropping out after 1862) were intended to learn from the human productive possibilities inherent in medieval craft guilds.

As his political commitments grew, he sought always to theorize these relations between art and craft, production and the human producer, in a series of remarkable lectures given between 1883 and his death in 1896 to early socialist organizations in Britain. To begin with, however, he extended his work in the Firm in a national direction by founding the Society for the Protection of Ancient Buildings, nicknamed 'The Antiscrape'. Crude restoration, even cruder Gothic imitation, the distaste of bourgeois landowner and clergymen for any architecture since the Reformation, had meant — still means in 1982 — that fortunes had been made out of the demolition and entirely insensitive alteration of ancient buildings. Morris's sense of history and his civic passion was outraged. In two papers to the Society, he wrote:

> it is living art and living history that I love. If we have no hope for the future, I do not see how we can look back on the past with pleasure. If we are to be less than men in time to come, let us forget that we have ever been men. It is in the interest of living art and living history that I oppose so-called restoration. What history can there be in a building bedaubed with ornament, which cannot at the best be anything but a hopeless and lifeless imitation of the hope and vigour of the earlier world? . . . Let us leave the dead alone, and, ourselves living, build for the living and those that shall live. Our ancient architecture [he went on] bears witness to the development of man's ideas, to the continuity of history, and, so doing, affords never-ceasing instruction, nay education, to the passing generations, not only telling us what were the aspirations of men passed away, but also what he may hope for in the time to come.[38]

From 1877, when the society was founded, to his death, he remained an active campaigner under the standard struck by these declarations.

They place, as Morris's running of the Firm also places, a particular view of history at the centre of social experience. Too often liberal theorists speak of history as simply the aggregate of every individual's actions; too often, Marxists speak of history as the lawful necessity of economic process. Morris, secure in a view of history as the material social practices visible among other things as architecture, is able to resist the goofy liberal's view of progress as waiting on the certainty of personal decency, and the lockjawed Marxist's view of history as always to be superseded by a shiny new world. From the designs of the past — the tapestries, the buildings, the organization, the *visions* — Morris sought patterns of possibility which could be recovered (so to speak) and redesigned for the present, and the present in the future. Hence his absorption in prehistoric and medieval models of product and production, hence also his natural turning to forms of utopian fiction in *A Dream of John Ball* (1887) and the magnificent *News from Nowhere* (1890). More generally, his vivid sense of the tragic difficulty of making historical ends meet and maintaining a tolerable continuity in social life pulled him between a strong faith in the institutions of the past in which men and women had put their trust, and just as strong an ardour to destroy the institutions which maintained a hateful and killing oppression and system of injustices. He catches himself time and again in the bitter, painful tension between reform and revolution, slippery terms both. His years of political activism from 1883 with the Social Democratic Federation at first, with the Socialist League after it broke away a year later, and from 1890 with what amounted to his ward Labour party, the Hammersmith Socialist Society, this broken and difficult experience and its inner logic, led him gradually and uncertainly to be convinced of the need for armed revolution.

At times the pull was unmistakeable, as in his satisfying outburst against the Jubilee in 1887, 'now the monstrous stupidity is on us . . . we must not after all forget what the hideous, revolting, and vulgar tomfoolery in question really means nowadays'.[39] But Morris didn't very often allow himself the indulgence of broadsheet polemics, for all that he not only paid for the League's monthly magazine *Commonweal* from its inception in 1885, he also wrote substantial amounts of it for ten years. What most characterizes his political thought is its lived engagement with the facts of everyday political practice.

This is nowhere plainer than in his grappling with two exceedingly practical institutions, the nature of parliament and the nature of work. His contribution to the first always disputed question in political literature may be contrasted on one hand with T. H. Green and on the other with Friedrich Engels, Marx's great equal and collaborator, Morris's own acquaintance, and after Marx's death in 1883 doyen of the International Communist movement, correspondent to a dozen European parties and rarely in touch with English activities. Engels had an off hand, even a disdainful view of the future of socialism in Britain; after Marx's death, we may rather summarily say, Engels inclined more and more to the strong determinist view of the advent of socialism: revolution and terror, the necessity of totalitarianism, the dominance of the natural sciences as models of thought and of the development of society, the unimportance of the individual in history.[40] Against this General Staff view of politics, Morris counterposed not only a vision of the fine ends of life capable of inspiring delight and happiness, but also a keen sense of actuality — of what these qualities are really like when work is both useful and beautiful.

Morris is one of the very few social theorists of any colour to write in believable detail of a happiness whose conditions were structurally inseparable from a picture of freedom and justice.

Being determined to be free, and therefore contented with a life not only simpler but even rougher than the life of slave-owners, division of labour would be habitually limited: men (and women too, of course) would do their work and take their pleasure in their own persons, and not vicariously: the social bond would be habitually and instinctively felt, so that there would be no need to be always asserting it by set forms: the family of blood-relationship would melt into that of the community and of humanity. The pleasures of such a society would be founded on the free exercise of the senses and passions of a healthy human animal, so far as this did not injure the other individuals of the community and so offend against social unity: no one would be ashamed of humanity or ask for anything better than its due development.

But from this healthy freedom would spring up the pleasures of intellectual development, which the men of civilisation so foolishly try to separate from sensuous life, and to glorify at its expense. Men would follow knowledge and the creation of beauty for their own sakes, and not for the enslavement of their fellows, and they would be rewarded by finding their most necessary work grow interesting and beautiful under their hands without their being conscious of it.[41]

This simple passage is taken from an address given in Hammersmith the very day a peaceful demonstration in Trafalgar Square was most bloodily broken up by the police, and three demonstrators killed. Some of the best of Morris as in the passage: the bluffness and geniality of temper, and the care to make his prose and tone plain and wholesome and 'good as bread'; throughout the lecture, he is careful to go gradually, to explain what may be too hard for his audience, to be homely and vivid in his examples (how many intellectuals today are careful to work out how they may be well understood by a ward party meeting?). And when in a *Commonweal* essay 'On some 'Practical' Socialists'[42] he rises to a more stirring and generalizing exhortation to action, he does so in a rhetoric whose radical earnestness of address has about it the ring of the open-air pulpit for which in Morris's hagiology, John Ball, leader of the free peasants in Kent in 1381, was the greatest occupant.

Will the body of the woman we love be but an appendage to her property? Shall we try to cram our lightest whim as a holy dogma into our children, and be bitterly unhappy when we find that they are growing up to be men and women like ourselves? Will education be a system of cram begun on us when we are four years old, and left off sharply when we are eighteen? Shall we be ashamed of our love and our hunger and our mirth, and believe that it is wicked of us not to try to dispense with the joys that accompany procreation of our species, and the keeping of ourselves alive, those joys of desire which make us understand that the beasts too may be happy? Shall we all, in short, as the 'refined' middle classes now do, wear ourselves away in the anxiety to stave off all trouble, and emotion, and responsibility, in order that we may at last merge all our troubles into one, the trouble that we have been born nothing but to be afraid to die?[43]

Anger is the embodiment of generosity in a great-hearted man; he is angry because changeable circumstances debar men and women from the plenty he would give them.

This is Morris's difference from a noble-spirited theorist of liberalism such as T. H. Green. He says:

I have thought the matter up and down and in and out, and I cannot for the life of me see how the great change which we long for can come otherwise than by disturbance and suffering of some kind . . . Can we escape that? I fear not. We are living . . . in an epoch when there is combat between commercialism, or the system of reckless waste, and communism, or the system of neighbourly common sense. Can that combat be fought out . . . without loss and suffering? Plainly speaking I know that it cannot.[44]

The certainty of 'loss and suffering', of tragedy in the largest sense, is inscribed for Morris in historical processes. He understood, as liberal theory did not, that there is not only a conceptual, but a military distinction between reform and revolution. This gave him a much sharper and less friendly eye for the comings and goings of Parliament than those of the liberals and social democrats[45] who produced the genesis of the Fabian Society. Morris saw with extraordinary prescience the assimilating and anaesthetic properties of the Houses of Parliament, and the need there would always be for a vigilante body of members to chasten and call to order parliamentarians who succumbed to the assorted indulgences of the West End.

He brought all this wide range of theory and insight to its most complete statement in his last three creative-political writings, *The Dream of John Ball,* which is what it sounds like − the encounter of Morris, returned in time to 1381, with the Kentish revolutionary, *The Pilgrims of Hope,* an often clumsy but still striking verse account of the Paris commune of 1871, and most impressive and best known of the three, *News from Nowhere,* published in 1890, and an account of Morris's journey forward to the communist Britain of the twenty-first century.[46]

News From Nowhere underlines what I said earlier about the ready use made of literature by the English intelligentsia. No doubt it requires slightly different handling to straight political theory, but it sits perfectly at ease with Morris's lectures and *Commonweal* editorials; it represents his most complete efforts to realize the communist society and in doing so takes as much from his profound admiration of Dickens as from his reading of Marx. Morris doesn't have Dickens's intense vitality of visualization of course, and this lack comes out not so much in a uniformity of characterization, which might be encouraged quite properly in a communist utopia, as in the remorselessly pious tone of the narrator's incomprehension before the absence of money, poverty, ill-health and human nastiness in this paradise regained, and the similarly savourless benignity of his informants. The power and range of his imagining, however, comes out in the comprehensiveness of the social vision – the deeply plausible detailing of dress and demeanour, and the connecting of these to the disappearance of capital, the restoration of work to the status of craft, the deployment of technology to dispel toil, drudgery and mean labour, the full stop of the advance of production. Instead of simply uttering with Engels a curse over 'the holy family' as the master property-symbol of the bourgeoisie, Morris presents a new image for the reconciliation of desire, love, and the relations of men and women.

The most telling and capacious metaphor Morris catches and holds in his novel is that of the Garden City – the idea he bequeathed to the actualities of the Garden City movement, and the many Town and Country Planning Acts since the Attlee Government's first in 1947.[47] The ambiguity of this metaphor and those realities fixes Morris in our tradition. In Chapter 17 of *News from Nowhere,* Morris describes 'How the Change Came' by general strike and armed revolution between 1952 and 1954. It represents the solidest political thinking in the book, moving from deep recession caused at least in part by trade union militancy, and proceeding to the crisis of confidence and legitimacy, vacillation by a liberal government between concession and military repression, general and successful strike, counter-revolution and the defection of the soldiery, and the ultimate triumph of the forces of socialism.

It is, as Anderson says, 'an extraordinary theoretical feat'[48] within which Morris provides an entirely credible programme for a new English Revolution. And yet, both before and after this chapter, Morris provides his always haunting, sometimes lovely evocations of the successful union of garden and city in the Thames valley. Morris gives us architecture not only as the highest art, but also as the mode of thought within which to imagine productive relations and the good society.[49] As we know it was largely the Fabian reformers who took the vision and made it, in their gradual way, actual.

T. H. Green, in my simple algebra, stands for one power line in the English intelligentsia: the classic citizen-intellectual from Oxford, reforming friend to Governments, practical reasoner, zealous and upright, eloquent and effectual; his is the grand, discreet style of English radical life and thought. Morris powers a very different line: hugely gifted, boundless in variety, energy, and expression, fragmentary and diffuse in the results of his actions; but the prodigality of his work, the wealth of imagery he makes available, the precision and concreteness of his thought, mark him as the greatest visionary of modern British industrialism, and a momentous standard against which to check my subsequent luminaries.

PART II

Englishness and Liberalism

3

Power and Policy: The Fabians and John Maynard Keynes

With a now famous title, George Dangerfield signals the advent of war and the decisive political rupture of twentieth-century England. In chapter 4 of *The Strange Death of Liberal England*,[1] he catches in a silhouette the converging and crushing forces which were to destroy liberalism:

That Albert Hall meeting on the night of 1 November 1913, presents us with a very convenient phenomenon, for on the speakers' platform sat, in serried ranks, the united grievances of England. For the first and the last time Irish Nationalism, Militant Suffrage, and the Labour Unrest were met together . . . for what? Simply to demand the release from prison of a messianic strike-leader whose mind — to say the least — was a trifle unbalanced, and whose methods were definitely not sanctioned by Trade Union leadership? Or was Trade Union leadership itself under fire? One thing, at least, is certain; the vigorous and passionate oratory, rising in increasing volume and a variety of accents beneath the roof of the Albert Hall, was not — as some people rather ingenuously imagined — merely the irritable expulsion of reformist steam. It resembled rather the gathering of a heavy cloud, caught up out of some teeming sea; for its strength was drawn from every factory, every workshop, mine, wharf and slum throughout the length and breadth of England.

Since Dangerfield's strictly political analysis in 1935, various people have pointed out that the death of liberalism was not strange at all, and the historians of ideas, particularly those of the Oxford and Cambridge New Wave whom we shall meet on their own terms in the last chapter,[2] have unpicked the strands of some very rough tow-ropes indeed in order to show how variously mixed and woven the different threads were. T. H. Green has so far embodied for us the reformist line of idealist social theory and practice; William Morris has been the hero of an English revolutionary praxis, and one which transpired from an astonishingly wide engagement with the facts of culture and productive life. According to the definition of tradition which I proposed earlier, it would be gratuitous to say which way the influence of these men went, as though influence were less a field of magnetic force and more a simple current of a certain voltage running down one wire, and available as energy to anyone who plugged it into his head. Morris's influence was and remains enormous and incalculable, though like anybody else's, it varies according to historical circumstances, may dwindle and quite die out, and then flare up again quite unexpectedly and boldly as it has done today in the English Marxists Edward Thompson and Perry Anderson. His influence as a designer, draughtsman, and visionary of the environment, has been consistently exerted since his death. Ebenezer Howard and the Garden cities of Letchworth and Welwyn directly followed Morris (we can speak quite uncomplicatedly of influence there) and initiated the line of social planning and construction whose excellent results via the industrial estates of Saltaire and Port Sunlight are the best corners of the New Towns in Basildon, Harlow, Telford, Peterlee, Cumbernauld, Milton Keynes. These are indeed the powerful expressions of social practices, and carry theory into the heart of experience with an obviousness which few theorists have the luck or the materials to make possible.

Well, the best New Town building adumbrates a reform or a revolution, depending on where you think the shadow of history falls. The lines of less tangible progress are harder to see. For the Fabian society, formed in 1884, progress was to be visible in decent housing and the 'gas-and-water socialism' which was the careful, practical self-definition of the quietist Labour party when it first formed a (minority) government in 1924.

The Fabian society named itself in a clumsily donnish joke after the Roman emperor, Fabius Cunctator, 'the gradual' — or that at least was the paraphrase which Sidney Webb and his future wife Beatrice Potter fixed as the society's political style in the phrase 'the inevitability of gradualism'. The society began[3] as an odd mixture of intellectual proletarians and parvenus meeting in shabby rooms in Clement's Inn, London, and quickly dominated by the formidable quartet, Bernard Shaw, Sidney Webb, Sydney Olivier, and — for twelve years — Graham

Wallas. They announced their commitment in the first of the now famous Fabian series, the *Tracts,* under the bracing, simple title, *Why Are the Many Poor?* They were at once joined by Annie Besant, first feminist, atheist, woman trade unionist, and gallant sexual freedom fighter of the day, and by the beautiful Beatrice Potter who became Mrs. Webb and shared a partnership of fifty years with Sidney in the patient, detailed advocacy of forms of welfare socialism.

The Fabian society came and went through a dozen alliances, quarrelsome, factious, fraternal, with other new socialist and radical organizations. H. G. Wells, a member for twenty-five years, criticized it in accents readily recognizable to any present day Fabian for its dribble of political activism, conducted in echoing basements to thin cups of tea and unshaded light bulbs. Bernard Shaw, for all the selfless and self-deriding conceit with which he worked for the society, was a weirdly feckless paradox in the style of its ideas, though a genial and bracing one; more precisely, he was a glittering advertiser of Fabianism's exceedingly characteristic rationalism, its typically liberal indifference to tradition, its complacent conviction that it certainly knew better than they did themselves what was good for the working classes. These attitudes and methods were turned into the careful, necessary and invaluable methods of Fabian social research — single issue policy agendas for future Labour ministers. The social formation of the Fabians was clerkly, auto-didactic, London-suburban. They were the henchpersons of a so far unrealized political power, and they had no idea what to do about it. What they did do, however, was to insist that the dry upper air of the one-time idealists should be thickened with a few facts of life as learned not so much in the systems of production themselves, as on the streets outside.

We may take the Fabians as a benchmark of late nineteenth-century criticism of liberalism; they signify, from a position very different to that of William Morris, the extent to which liberalism was under direct intellectual strain and challenge. Morris himself criticized the Fabians for muddling 'the co-operative machinery towards which modern life is tending with the essence of socialism itself'.[4] Their members came and went: Graham Wallas (1858–1932), one of the most sensitive, dogged, and upright, gradually and painfully drifted away from the Society and what he saw as its mechanical policy studies, its lack of sufficient moral idealism, its offhand disdain for liberal ideas he still found admirable; ultimately he broke with the Society's anti-intellectualism.[5] In his long worked-at and, in a quite unsolemn way, steadfastly earnest book, *The*

Great Society[6] Wallas proposes as 'the master-task of civilised mankind' the strenuous business of discovering the conditions of the good society, and this endless search as impelled by the life-driving belief that enormous social progress is possible and that, in a term he shared with Hobhouse, 'a harmony' between men and women and their whole environment 'far deeper and wider than anything we can see today' may be rationally and purposefully striven for.

The high moral tone characterizes Wallas (led him to biographize Francis Place) and is sensibly contained by the venture which found expression in his *Human Nature in Politics*.[7] In a way which broke both with day-to-day Fabianizing about the necessity of an elite intelligentsia writing the ideas down for the honest worthies of the Labour Party, and also with the heartfelt fatheadedness with which the old liberals believed in the improvability of the hearts of all men, Wallas sought to theorize realistically the nature of human nature, what in it was contingent and what was necessary.

We may say, summarily, that Wallas drastically lacked an adequate psychological vocabulary; the structure of his concepts is too airy and too temporarily tacked together to offer very much more than the doubtless correct view that the political consciousness created by capitalism is meanminded, irrational and moblike, feckless and suspicious. Such a moral social psychology is a fair place to start from, but it is hardly more than a litany of commination. For the first time in social theory, however, Wallas wrote into the terms of reference a direct experience of and respect for the texture of *social* life as lived by the politically unassertive, tolerant, easygoing, and gregarious segments of the working class.

For our purposes Wallas does little more than identify an intellectual blank. He criticizes the liberal idealist's over-confidence about progress, but he has no theory of either class or power with which to chasten liberalism. He sees that it cannot contain the strains of Dangerfield's three rough beasts slouching to the Albert Hall — Labour, Women, and (as we may generalize it) Imperialism — but can only counterpose his faith in democracy as composed by a rational electorate and a responsible intelligentsia.

His associates in the Fabian society, and his intermittently close friends, L. T. Hobhouse (1863—1929) and J. A. Hobson (1858—1940), were in varying degrees energetic to name, resolve or dispatch the contradictions of liberalism before it was overtaken first by the new insurgency of the working class movement after 1911, and subsequently and so hugely revised and attenuated by the 1914—18 war.

Both Hobhouse and Hobson were colossally productive. They both wrote too readily — with a fluency and freedom undamaged in Hobhouse's case by very much recognition that after the war he had only old banalities from which he vainly tried to remove the tarnish (the most lowering example of which is his gamely titled and listlessly performed *Elements of Social Justice* (1922)), and in Hobson's case by an always insufficient awareness of the deep intractability of his subject matter. The most famous of his thirty-two titles is no doubt *Imperialism: A Study*,[8] and it is useful here as a tract which identifies the inadequacy of liberalism's self-image, especially in its model of capital expansion. *Imperialism* gave the social theory of the time a name rather than a concept. His economics, for all his considerable satisfaction with their range and purchase, were of far too pat a push-me-pull-you form. Imperialism in his view was the complementary result of domestic under-consumption displaced into imperial over-investment. His insight that imperialism provided no visible profit to the community at large is true but drastically incomplete: it lacks what Marx could have provided and Lenin at the time *was* providing, a theory of capitalism's inherently exploitative and power-asserting momentum, and it lacks any theory of sectional interests as directing investment. In spite of his necessarily pre-Fascist and non-psycho-analytic effort to chart the phenomenon in *The Psychology of Jingoism* (1901), he came up with neither a psychological nor a satisfactory political explanation of imperialism. In the very different contexts of England he sensed the forces which in Weimar Germany burst open the connections between crowds and rational power, between capital and economic understanding. But he and his fellows lacked the social experience, the opportunity and, we may say, the genius, to force a system of interpretation out of these shadowy perceptions.

It would be the height of complacent anachronism to blame Hobson for not understanding the economic and political dynamism of the empire until he had seen what the war did for productivity and consumption, to say nothing of its less creative and deadlier consequences. And indeed Hobson went on writing, revised *Imperialism* in the light of Lenin's criticism in his famous work on the same subject,[9] and followed John Maynard Keynes as a very much lesser but usefully asperient critic. But he stayed within the lightweight apparatus of a neo-Fabian political economist. He wasn't a pupil of the great Alfred Marshall, professor of political economy at Cambridge, and he was a working London journalist and man of letters; he had neither the intellectual strength nor the cultural circumstances to break with his frame of mind.

The Fabian society and those they argued with may be very briefly compressed, as an example of all that Keynes was not, in the career of Leonard Trelawney Hobhouse. He went, like Morris, to Marlborough, nephew of a famous radical peer, was an undergraduate at Corpus Christi, Oxford from 1883, caught by the residue of Green's powerful, heady influence, took a first in Greats, the Oxford Literae Humaniores degree in 1887, left university teaching in 1896, lived also as journalist, occasional civil servant, political activist of a genteel kind, public intellectual and returned famously to academic life as first English professor of sociology, at the London School of Economics in 1910. Thereafter he remained an active journalist, writing for *Tribune,* whose full-time columnist he had been, for *The Nation* and for the *Manchester Guardian*, of which he was a director, a leader writer, and an emblem for many years.

His emblematic force comes out with congenial warmth in his pre-1914 journalism of the kind revised and rewritten in *Democracy and Reaction.*[10] As with Wallas so with Hobhouse, we find a mind and a man strongly committed to the admirable possibilities of modern democracy, and battling manfully with his confident sense that the old liberalism simply wasn't up to sustaining it. The battle was lost and won by the set of sun in about 1916. There is so much to admire in Hobhouse: the tirelessness, the ready pen, the steady work, the intellectual taking not to the streets, not even to Fleet St, but to the solid, radical, free-trade-and-thought offices of the *Manchester Guardian*, New Cross Street, and there carrying on the great English business of keeping the old bus on the road, of finding new ways to think old thoughts. He wrote a decent agenda best and first in his journalism: old age pensions, national insurance, wage boards, wealth redistribution[11] — not a bad list by the early 1900s. But he dithered endlessly over how to bring about change, over the attractiveness of market freedoms, over the justification of inequality. Stuck by Green with the notion of a conflictness common good, he broke his back trying to resolve what he saw of political life with a more and more improbable metaphysics. With greater experience and less intellectual stature than Green, he saw his dominant idea of Progress as the inevitable victor in the class struggle destroyed by the war, and fell gradually backwards down the slope of old Reaction itself. Hobhouse embodies the forms of reform and idealism which could only survive 1918 by turning away from the real sources of social energy.

A risky phrase, and John Maynard Keynes (1883–1946) is a risky man to take out of the bounds of theoretic economics these days. But what he always and abundantly demonstrated was an absolutely confident and, one might say, in practice infallible sense of where the sources of social energy in terms of production and capital really lay.[12] That 'really' is not an idealist's invocation of *Geist*. Keynes was astonishingly quick to decide what reshaping of existing institutions was possible in order to release economic energies otherwise locked up and unusable. We may say against Marxism that in at least this corner of the sciences of man Keynes proved the truth of Kantianism: once you change the concepts by which you see the world, you can change the world. Once Keynes led the policy-makers to see investment, and neither savings nor prices, as the dominant economic category, they could be persuaded to understand the new role he proposed for governments in free markets. To unpack investment into its multiple, ambiguous constituents as a texture of expectations and choices about available (or even hoped for) resources[13] was to move economics very drastically beyond Alfred Marshall's powerfully static equilibrium model and to retrieve it from the clean, well-lighted market place Hobhouse and Wallas were constantly trying to open up to the noisy, smelly bazaar outside. Keynes put the new economics squarely (for example) down in the economic consequences of the 1919 peace treaties or the (to Marshallians) unrecognizable disorder of the 1929–31 series of economic crashes.

This is to move too fast. Keynes contrasts so extremely with the Fabians first of all because of his direct access to the power centres of the country and of the world. In this he also contrasts with every other figure in this book. Not only that: in addition his moral, political, and philosophical style sorts ill, at first sight of him and his biography, with our title 'radical earnestness'. Pick up his over-anthologized and therefore over-emphasized essay 'My Early Beliefs',[14] and recognize the tone and manner of the Kingsman, leader of King's hyper-exclusive club the Apostles, son of a Cambridge economist and his bluestocking wife, old Etonian, intimate of the Bloomsbury set and of G. E. Moore, their admired and mocked honorary Pope of the passions and their morality. All the pressure of the Edwardian English *haute-bourgeoisie* came to bear upon Keynes's absolutely astonishing intelligence, and gave it its unforgettably idiosyncratic and deeply class-typical timbre and posture: great warmth and charm, sheer cold bloody-mindedness, assumed world-weariness and flippancy, electric quickness in the judgement of others, and a suddenness of self-criticism and of great generosity as unexpected as a blow. Above all, his life and his life's work is characterized by his unfailing belief that intelligence and reason can always be made to win the political and economic day, if resolution and good luck sufficiently combine.

The breadth and *chiaroscuro* of character, its lambency and reticence, its frank zest for power, its Bohemianism, the backing of its wealth — Keynes was a celebrated collector of both modern paintings and rare editions, and married to Lydia Lopokova formerly a brilliant dancer within Diaghilev's ballet — fit uncomfortably, as I have said, with the plodding worthiness of Hobhouse and Hobson. But Keynes's Cambridge was the Cambridge of Leslie Stephen (father of Virginia Woolf and great Utilitarian) Henry Sidgwick, Maitland, and G. E. Moore. Keynes breathed in every bit as moralizing and idealistic a surrounding air as Green's successors breathed in at Oxford. Keynes, however, also learned a novel lightness, brilliance, and attractive insouciance which, as he later acknowledged in response to D. H. Lawrence's vehement rejection, turned at times in some of the Bloomsbury set to the shallow, feckless narcissism of Harold Skimpole.

Keynes himself wore this insouciant air and delighted in a sort of Hampstead village encountergrouphood, looking back on it in later years with a rueful self-patronizing which he should really have never let himself get away with.[15] The personal posture he struck implied in its identification with his intermittently appalling associates an endorsement of the empty gentilities of ruling-class culture which was to lead F. R. Leavis to typify Keynes and Cambridge as exemplifying all that was worst in postwar culture.[16] But Keynes's view of private life in relation to politics, his freedom from an over-worthy and leaden insistence on knowing what was best for others, together with what insistently comes through from quite the most powerful, the most historically significant, and probably the cleverest figure discussed in this book, as his egotism, a certain wilful lack of feeling, a nonchalance towards what Tolstoy called 'the mightily important . . . men's relation to God, to the universe, to all that is infinite and unending', all this strength of adjustment enabled him constantly to start again quite cleanly.

In particular, it was just this insouciance which carried Keynes over the violent cultural and political break torn open by the first World War. He remained deeply within the Cambridge and Alfred Marshall[17] tradition of a moralizing economics in one strong current of his being, and in the other, quick, political, pragmatic, absorbed in the fascination and delights of *technique* without worrying too much about either metaphysics or the scientific status of his preferred arguments. This is not to say that he was no scientist, but that, as Moggridge puts it,[18] his intuitions worked rapidly ahead of his theories, and were brought to bear, in virtue of his position, very quickly upon matters of international finance in a way that disregarded their status as economic science or the risk that they might be damagingly unsuited to the future Keynes couldn't plan for. Harry Johnson, from a position neither in Keynes's line nor among the Beaker Folk midget monetarists who now suppose themselves to have displaced his theories, comes out with these strictures.

All in all, it is difficult to avoid the conclusion that Britain has paid a heavy long-run price for the transient glory of the Keynesian revolution, in terms both of the corruption of standards of scientific work in economics and encouragement to the indulgence of the belief of the political process that economic policy can transcend the laws of economics with the aid of sufficient economic cleverness, in the sense of being able to satisfy all demands for security of economic tenure without inflation or balance-of-payments problems, or less obvious sacrifice of efficiency and economic growth potentialities. A good case could even be made to the effect that Keynes was too expensive a luxury for a country inexorably declining in world economic and political importance and obliged to scramble for dignified survival to be able to afford.[19]

But Johnson himself, in a hardly consistent way, having spoken airily about immovable unemployment of a regional kind as simply reflecting a blithe choice on the part, no doubt, of Clydesiders or Appalachian hillbillies, to live off social security for the sake of the leisure, agrees a little later that 'the Keynesians are right in their view that inflation is a far less serious social problem than mass unemployment' (p. 104). This admission returns us to the Keynes whose determined advocacy of economic policies (as opposed to theories) necessarily embodied a political worldview, which, while not being merely his, realizes the whole subsequent tradition of welfare socialism and what is vaguely called neo-liberalism.

Keynes, himself ultimately to be killed by overwork, saw that work remained the paramount value of the western labour cultures, and that therefore to be out of work or to be unjustly rewarded for work was to put in danger the fragile fabric of mutual trust and assent which maintained a decent society. In the famous last chapter of his greatest work, *The General Theory of Employment, Interest, and Money,*[20] he briskly and correctly (still correctly) wrote, 'the outstanding faults of the economic society in which we live are its failure to provide for full employment and its arbitrary and inequitable distribution of wealth and incomes'. Indeed, he goes on to congratulate human moneymaking proclivities as a useful way to contain greed and piracy in 'comparatively harmless channels . . .' For 'it is better that a man should tyrannise over his bank balance than over his fellow citizens' (p. 374), so long, that is, as the State sets limits to such tyranny, legitimizes only modest levels of income inequality, and so long, indeed, as inheriting inequality is made much more difficult. And a little later, Keynes spoke up in the *New Statesman* for these (until 1979) unimpeachable banalities:

The question is whether we are prepared to move out of the nineteenth century laissez faire state into an era of liberal socialism, by which I mean a system where we can act as an organised community for common purposes and to promote social and economic justice, whilst respecting and protecting the individual — his freedom of choice, his faith, his mind and its expression, his enterprise and his property.[21]

The bosom of no comfortably employed public servant could fail to return an echo to these sentiments. But not only were they a lot less obvious in 1939, they depend upon a system of values capable of cutting right across the interests of his class. Keynes was perfectly guiltless of 'false consciousness'; he knew exactly what he spoke for, and he spoke for it in the name of a rational and above all feasible social order. 'False consciousness' may apply to anyone, proletarian or intellectual, radical or conservative. Keynes was quite clear about the system he rescued, and clear, moreover, with a distaste for cant and a contempt for stupidity which comes out ringingly at the right moment, and in a way to remind us of his best provenance and its traditions.

He was, for instance, a stirring pamphleteer. His class origins, his early experience as a civil servant in the India office and his membership of a Royal Commission when only thirty followed by his conscription into the Wartime treasury in 1915, all gave him a self-confidence in the discussion of immediate questions of economic and power policy which is quite unrivalled. When, therefore, Winston Churchill returned sterling to the gold standard in 1925 at the impossibly high rate of $4.86 to the £1 and in the name of the pre-1914 laissez-faire world picture, Keynes launched quite independently a pamphlet, in an edition of a few hundred copies, which instantly became the accepted doctrine of all the Baldwin Government's opponents.

I should pick out coal as being above all others a victim of our monetary policy . . .

The colliery owners propose that the gap should be bridged by a reduction of wages, irrespective of a reduction in the cost of living — that is to say, by a lowering in the standard of life of the miners. They are to make this sacrifice to meet circumstances for which they are in no way responsible and over which they have no control . . .

Why should coal miners suffer a lower standard of life than other classes of labour? They may be lazy, good-for-nothing fellows who do not work so hard or so long as they should. But is there any evidence that they are more lazy or more good-for-nothing than other people?

On grounds of social justice, no case can be made out for reducing the wages of the miners. They are the victims of the economic Juggernaut. They represent in the flesh the 'fundamental adjustments' engineered by the Treasury and the Bank of England to satisfy the impatience of the City fathers to bridge the 'moderate gap' between \$4.40 and \$4.86. They (and others to follow) are the 'moderate sacrifice' still necessary to ensure the stability of the gold standard. The plight of the coal miners is the first, but not — unless we are very lucky — the last, of the Economic Consequences of Mr. Churchill.

The truth is that we stand mid-way between two theories of economic society. The one theory maintains that wages should be fixed by reference to what is 'fair' and 'reasonable' as between classes. The other theory — the theory of the economic Juggernaut — is that wages should be settled by economic pressure, otherwise called 'hard facts', and that our vast machine should crash along, with regard only to its equilibrium as a whole, and without attention to the chance consequences of the journey to individual groups.[22]

The authority and disdain of the piece go along with the necessary anger not merely of a very intelligent man convinced that people are acting with great stupidity (Keynes was always of the view that stupidity was the worst political crime), but also anger as the natural expression of his sense of fairness and of a generosity which cannot at all be contained by the notion of enlightened self-interest. We may say that Keynes wrote generosity into the structures of modern political economy and its expressive institutions. The judgement first arises on reading his no less famous 1919 pamphlet, *The Economic Consequences of the Peace* (it is a measure of their celebrity, that Keynes, not without a trifling, casual immodesty, repeated the title of his first pamphlet in the second). He wrote the first pamphlet immediately after his resignation in June 1919 as senior Treasury official at the Paris Peace conference; it came out in December, and, at once made him a national name in every daily paper.

It remains a marvellous read: scornful, magnanimous, bold in vision and sweep, and unanswerably right. Keynes's prose is passionate and vivid; he sketches in the contours of great historical movements, and puts the small, familiar contingent world of domestic Britain beside them; he dots the narrative with memorable cameos of the powerful and pitiful men who were willing the peace programme which gave Hitler his chance, and made war in another twenty years so likely; he rides a high rhetorical horse, and stays mounted in the saddle.

Paris was a nightmare, and every one there was morbid. A sense of impending catastrophe overhung the frivolous scene; the futility and smallness of man before the great events confronting him; the mingled significance and unreality of the decisions; levity, blindness, insolence, confused cries from without, — all the elements of ancient tragedy were there. Seated indeed amid the theatrical trappings of the French Saloons of State, one could wonder if the extraordinary visages of Wilson and of Clemenceau, with their fixed hue and unchanging characterisation, were really faces at all and not the tragic-comic masks of some strange drama or puppet-show.

The proceedings of Paris all had this air of extraordinary importance and unimportance at the same time. The decisions seemed charged with consequences to the future of human society; yet the air whispered that the word was not flesh, that it was futile, insignificant, of no effect, dissociated from events; and one felt most strongly the impression, described by Tolstoy in *War and Peace* or by Hardy in *The Dynasts,* of events marching on to their fated conclusion uninfluenced and unaffected by the cerebrations of Statesmen in Council . . .[23]

These phrases set the key for a majestic symphony. Keynes goes on to show not only the mean-minded spite inherent in the proposals that Germany should pay the Allies killing reparations, but also that Germany would simply find it impossible, that these vengeful reparations were only likely to exact revenge in return, and appealed for largeness of imagination, forgiveness and munificence on the part of the Allies as the only basis for a lasting peace and a stable European order. Keynes understood in a way his dull managerial successors of today never do that institutions and their bureaucracies *sustain* particular meanings, and that without these meanings the bureaucracy has no point beyond self-preservation (an infinite regress). The terms of the 1919 Peace treaty identified the political power structure and its momentum; different terms, of Keynes's kind, would have balanced the huge, delicate, and topheavy machine differently, and launched it in a different direction.

Why has the world been so credulous of the unveracities of politicians? If an explanation is needed, I attribute this particular credulity to the following influences in part.

In the first place, the vast expenditures of the war, the inflation of prices, and the depreciation of currency, leading up to a complete instability of the unit of value, have made us lose all sense of number and magnitude in matters of finance. What we believed to be the limits of possibility have been so enormously exceeded, and those who founded their expectations on the past have been so often wrong, that the man in the street is now prepared to believe anything which is told him with some show of authority, and the larger the figure the more readily he swallows it . . .

I cannot leave this subject as though its just treatment wholly depended either on our own pledges or on economic facts. The policy of reducing Germany to servitude for a generation, of degrading the lives of millions of human beings, and of depriving a whole nation of happiness should be abhorrent and detestable, — abhorrent and detestable, even if it were possible, even if it enriched ourselves, even if it did not sow the decay of the whole civilised life of Europe. Some preach it in the name of Justice. In the great events of man's history, in the unwinding of the complex fates of nations Justice is not so simple. And if it were, nations are not authorised, by religion or by natural morals, to visit on the children of their enemies the misdoings of parents or of rulers.[24]

Keynes saw, perhaps saw most clearly at the peace conference, just how enormous historical, political, and economic a gap there was between 1914 and 1919. *The Economic Consequences of the Peace* provide us with the loose, flexible liberalism to which *The Treatise on Probability* (1921)[25] was the metaphysics, and for which, via the two volumes of *A Treatise on Money*[26] his greatest and most ambitious work, *The General Theory of Employment, Interest, and Money* was to provide the moral and political economy, and its new republic.

His progress was, no doubt, less schematic than that. But what comes strongly through all these writings is Keynes's fundamental commitment to the notion of personal liberty and the conditions of individual freedom and fulfilment, without this classical liberalism being required either to postulate an idealist's common good or even to suppose that education would enlighten every dark and stubborn working-class heart. He took from the Bloomsbury group what his intellectual segment of the ruling class had defended in some of its formations for a century, its genuine libertarianism, its tolerance of human variety and deplorability; he left out the Bloomsbury narcissism and the over-analysis of personal life, not least perhaps because his own life was so happy and successful. He also left out the grislier aspects of his class's lineaments — its jingoism, its greed, its selfishness. Hence, the public virtues Keynes stood for were the liberty and fulfilment I have spoken of, and their structural complements, the moral and social institutions of work and justice (conceived as 'fairness-of-play').[27] What lubricated the friction of these values in their social interplay was Keynes's great and truthful tolerance. He was, for instance, an energetic supporter with his wife of the arts in society: he was the effectual founder of the Arts Council (as it became) in 1942 during the most unpromising hours of the second world war, and a patron in many other ways. But he had no wish to press artistic interests on those who did not share them. He expected a society to come to value these things, but only after a long time. He intuited first of all that the 1914—18 war (and in a vaster, more uncontrollable and ambiguous way, the 1939—45 war also) had released new, unthought-of and potentially progressive and productive forces. He saw that these forces would create an intoxicating new abundance which it would take twenty years for people to adjust to, become satisfied with, and take for granted; and therefore it would take even longer to grow through to deeper questions and more important matters.

Keynes's grasp of this historical and developmental truth gives the whole frame of his thought its human strength and its larger metaphysicality. In some attractive remarks to Roy Harrod Keynes said that it seemed to him that economics was 'a branch of logic, a way of thinking' and that it was up to economists to repel efforts to pretend that the subject was 'a pseudo-natural science'. He went on

Economics is a science of thinking in terms of models joined to the art of choosing models which are relevant to the contemporary world. It is compelled to be this, because, unlike the typical natural science, the material to which it is applied is, in too many respects, not homogeneous through time. The object of a model is to segregate the semi-permanent or relatively constant factors from those which are transitory or fluctuating so as to develop a logical way of thinking about the latter . . .[28]

With these remarks in mind, Keynes stands intelligibly at the apex of my hermeneutic triangle of forces marked by his name, R. G. Collingwood's, and F. R. Leavis's. In the deep crisis forced by the first world war, by the strong insurgency of the new social movements in Britain, by revolution, Marxism and Fascism abroad, Keynes revised one of the central subjects in the human sciences in order to keep its Marshallian moral centre and to create a novel frame of concepts expressible in plain English with which to control and redirect to more human, just, and equitable ends the irrational depredations of blind and headlong market forces.

To do this, he pondered upon Tolstoy's 'the infinite and unending' long enough to sketch a theory of expectations in relation to time which blithely acknowledged a godless universe and looked to the satisfactions of holding or spending money for yourself as the by no means final device of consumers for warding off the dangerous inanity of event and experience. In *The General Theory* he italicizes his own formulation 'the importance of money essentially flows from its being a link between the present and the future' (p. 293), and goes on to describe it as 'a theory of value and distribution' (themselves essentially social concepts) 'and not a separate theory of money' (p. 294). He replaces money, therefore, in the meanings of experience, and it is in this rather exiguous sense that I speak of his metaphysics. For experience in Keynes's political economy is on the move: money, being placed in time, is the locus of expectations, doubts, fears, happiness, anxieties, and — paramount value in the vocabulary of liberalism — choices. His subtle, responsive sense of the texture of human psychology rescues Keynes's ideological premises from an unsatisfactorily simple utilitarianism of the kind he read in 1902 just as he came up to Cambridge, in Henry Sidgwick's *Principles of Political Economy.* He does not equate happiness with mere material welfare (though he does not underrate the latter either) nor does he crank the handle of his economic model in order to print out any crude calculus of 'the greatest good of the greatest number'. Rather, by placing money in time, and taking it right out of the timeless balancing of the books present in equilibrium theory, he delightedly acknowledges the force and terror of the uncertainty he analysed in *A Treatise on Probability,* and tries with all the daring at his command to catch in a net of concepts what he knows is uncatchable.

Thus, his quadrangular model in *The General Theory* starts from the satisfying demolition of the petit-bourgeois virtues of thrift and saving,[29] in order to present 'the propensity to consume' as structurally essential to the new expectations released by the war, its triumphs of production, its monolithic reminders of the uncertainty and shortness of life. He goes on to register the operation of consumption in both its subjective and its structural dimensions in what he called 'the multiplier' (chapter 10) which must be capable of statistical representation and may be thought of as the series of waves in a tide of historical progress. Its deployment begins by measuring elasticity of output, and uses this to predict the accelerations in waves of the tide which may be caused by investment increases, in turn expanding income, in turn expanding consumption. The multiplier was therefore both measure and control; the politician could for instance calculate the outward ripple of income in terms of the smaller, inner wave of investment increase.

The third term of a four-cornered model which, it must be repeated, is dynamic not sequential, and progressing through time rather than seeking equilibrium, was 'the inducement to invest' and the motivation for investment provided in 'the state of long-term expectation' by 'the marginal efficiency of capital' (chapters 11 and 12). This was simply a ratio for appraising the costs of plant in relation to the costs of borrowing. Lastly and logically Keynes provided a theory of the rates and structures of interest, understood as a consequence of individual and social decisions of 'liquidity-preference' or choices about how readily someone wants access to money.

We do not need to go further into technicality to see how momentously Keynes provided a way of totalizing economic behaviour, and making it both the expression of a society's life and, for a season, amenable to a society's will. It is worth repeating just how refreshing and emboldening an experience it is to reread what he actually wrote when, in 1982, there are so many misrepresenting him. He could not foresee the dreadful distortions which would be wrought on economies by an arms race which does not generate economic life but ruins it,[30] and he would only have despised the more hedonistic excesses of consumerism and its symbol-system, advertising, for wantonly denying the continuing facts of poverty, starvation, illness, cruelty. He expected the social order always but irregularly to move forward to a greater rationality, welfare and cultivation — the 'liberal socialism' he gestured towards. To this extent, he kept the ideal of progress aloft and did much to move it into actuality. In his subsequent work after *The General Theory* and after, too, the first of the heart attacks which began in 1937 and were to kill him through overwork as he did so much to launch the recovery of Europe in 1946, he struggled in the names of reason and generosity to give sane politicians a greater and greater grip upon national and global economy. He invented the budgetary forms we are used to; essentially, he devised the liquidity institutions, especially the International Monetary Fund, under whose shadow we live.

In all this, he kept capitalism, the old bitch gone in the teeth by 1931, on the road. This is to speak of one man with a drastic voluntarism. Let us say he had the genius, and his position at Cambridge, his patrician connections, his social authority and freedom from social structure, gave him the chance to do what he did and to be what he was. That is his heroism. He lived at the intersection of theory, policy and power. His Englishness was to hold quite unsanctimoniously to what was good and what was potential in the society about him, and to shape theories not just for its preservation but for its betterment out of the stuff of life which lay to hand. He improvised institutions right up to his death during the negotiations at Bretton Woods in Surrey around American lend-lease aid, the IMF and the new World Bank. Always, in his vision, those institutions were intended to permit the greater freedom and fulfilment of individuals, and while there is much to be said against the bronzed and beautiful people of consumer advertising in the aesthetics of capitalism, only the very stupid and very selfish could fail to support Keynes's day-to-day efforts on behalf of justice and welfare. His social theory successfully reconciled the claims of determinism and freedom, of individuals and institutions. It did so on the familiar, particular ground of English society, and in the name of a rational and admirable 'science of human affairs'.

4

Resituating Idealism:
R. G. Collingwood

Robin George Collingwood (1889 – 1943) stands at the next corner of our trigonometry; his is the project to write the textbooks for 'a science of human affairs'. His first significance is that, sharing (for my ends at least) very many of Keynes's assumptions and values, emerging from a much less wealthy but nonetheless similar social formation, he too addresses himself to the restoration of a credible moral and intellectual order within which to build a land fit for heroes to live in. Like Keynes he recognized the urgency of a need for a science of human affairs, but where Keynes's was a glancing intuition of the structural necessity for a historical dimension in any version of such a science, whatever the field of its interest, Collingwood, whose interests were foremost theoretic and not political, set himself to understand and explain the central energy provided by historical study in the sciences of man, and then to give a detailed account of how to practise such study in the names of reason, truth, and freedom.

Collingwood turned to the interrogation of history in 1919 much as Keynes went to his book on probability in order to rewrite the theory of uncertainty. As Collingwood writes in his autobiography,[1]

In the last thirty or forty years historical thought had been achieving an acceleration in the velocity of its progress and an enlargement in its outlook comparable to those which natural science had achieved about the beginning of the seventeenth century. It seemed to me as nearly certain as anything in the future could be, that historical thought, whose constantly increasing importance had been one of the most striking features of the nineteenth century, would increase in importance far more rapidly during the twentieth; and that we might very well be standing on the threshold of an age in which history would be as important for the world as natural science had been between 1600 and 1900. If that was the case (and the more I thought about it the likelier it seemed) the wise philosopher would concentrate with all his might on the problems of history, at whatever cost, and so do his share in laying the foundations of the future.

The faith in progress, the belief that the pre-war disputes over liberalism would lead into an enlightened future had come to the Somme and been shot to pieces. The natural thing to do was to ask, how did it happen? Collingwood, turning to ask this question of the human sciences to hand, could find no answer nor any way of even thinking about one. Just as Keynes followed Alfred Marshall in insisting on his subject as one of the moral sciences (as Mill first named them and the Cambridge syllabus still calls philosophy), so Collingwood, looking back on the years at Oxford just before and after the war, described the helpless scepticism that the typical realist philosopher would be likely to recommend to his pupils.

'If it interests you to study this, do so; but don't think it will be of any use to you. Remember the great principle of realism, that nothing is affected by being known. That is as true of human action as of anything else. Moral philosophy is only the theory of moral action: it can't therefore make any difference to the practice of moral action. People can act just as morally without it as with it. I stand here as a moral philosopher; I will try to tell you what acting morally is, but don't expect me to tell you how to do it.'

At the moment, I am not concerned with the sophisms underlying this programme, but with its consequences. The pupils, whether or not they expected a philosophy that should give them, as that of Green's school had given their fathers, ideals to live for and principles to live by, did not get it; and were told that no philosopher (except of course a bogus philosopher) would even try to give it. The inference which any pupil could draw for himself was that for guidance in the problems of life, since one must not seek it from thinkers or from thinking, from ideals or from principles, one must look to people who were not thinkers (but fools), to processes that were not thinking (but passion), to aims that were not ideals (but caprices), and to rules that were not principles (but rules of expediency). If the realists had wanted to train up a generation of Englishmen and Englishwomen expressly as the potential dupes of every adventurer in morals or politics, commerce or religion, who should appeal to their emotions and promise them private gains which he neither could procure them nor even meant to procure them, no better way of doing it could have been discovered.[2]

Both Keynes and Collingwood responded to the realist in the ways that confirm them with F. R. Leavis as spokesman for the moral sciences. They deny the tight grip upon our lives of the technocrat, his panel of experts, and his managerial *semblable*, the planner of social utilitarianism. Collingwood, certainly, spoke for intelligence and the intelligentsia, but he spoke always as 'a man speaking to men' — in Wordsworth's moving formulation[3] — and 'selecting from the real language of men' in order to capture its object, 'truth, not individual and local, but general and operative'.

Wordsworth is a good name to mention in an introduction to R. G. Collingwood. Not only was Collingwood as committed as Wordsworth (and Keynes) to speaking in plain, fine and eloquent English of the ends of life and to recreating the best values of his society, he was also direct heir to much of the strong current of Romanticism which Wordsworth codified for English poetry readers and which so strongly fertilizes the traditions of thought of radical earnestness. Indeed, Collingwood was born a few miles from Coniston Water in the Lake District. His father was, first, a pupil of Ruskin's when he was Slade Professor and, later, his friend and subsequently his editor and expositor of his greatness and ideas after his death. William Collingwood was a respectable painter, though living in great frugality and occasional discomfort as a poor but passionate artist and scholar in the north-west. He had, as his son reports, a large library, he was intensely active, and his dedication to intellectual matters, his cultivation, his zest and energy in painting, archaeology, travel and sailing were all characteristics transferred to his son. The first chapter of Collingwood's *An Autobiography,* a classic of its genre, is the most vivid, piercing and exemplary chapter I know for anyone who attempts to understand the essential mystery and magnetism of the intellectual life. Collingwood's decisive origins start in that round, liberal, and cultivated air.

He writes with perfect unselfconsciousness of his own astonishing precocity, partly under his father's guidance: 'I began Latin at four and Greek at six; but on my own doing I began, about the same time, to read everything I could find about the natural sciences, especially geology, astronomy, and physics; to recognize rocks, to know the stars, and to understand the working of pumps and locks and other mechanical appliances up and down the house. It was my father who gave me lessons in ancient and modern history, illustrated with relief maps in papier mâché made by boiling down newspapers in a saucepan . . .' A page or two later there follows a passage whose endearing power to move one's recognition is only matched by one's incredulous admiration at the premature understanding:

> My father had plenty of books, and allowed me to read in them as I pleased. Among others, he had kept the books of classical scholarship, ancient history, and philosophy which he had used at Oxford. As a rule I left these alone; but one day when I was eight years old curiosity moved me to take down a little black book lettered on its spine 'Kant's Theory of Ethics'. It was Abbot's translation of the *Grundlegung zur Metaphysik der Sitten*; and as I began reading it, my small form wedged between the bookcase and the table, I was attacked by a strange succession of emotions. First came an intense excitement. I felt that things of the highest importance were being said about matters of the utmost urgency: things which at all costs I must understand. Then, with a wave of indignation, came the discovery that I could not understand them. Disgraceful to confess, here was a book whose words were English and whose sentences were grammatical, but whose meaning baffled me. Then, third and last, came the strangest emotion of all. I felt that the contents of this book, although I could not understand it, were somehow my business: a matter personal to myself, or rather to some future self of my own. It was not like the common boyish intention to 'be an engine-driver when I grow up', for there was no desire in it; I did not, in any natural sense of the word, 'want' to master the Kantian ethics when I should be old enough; but I felt as if a veil had been lifted and my destiny revealed. (*An Autobiography*, pp. 3−4)

There is, in the piercing and appealing book of which this passage is typical that felt sense of authority and intense conviction which characterizes intellectual heroes, and makes them, for better and worse, subject to such veneration from their pupils. To his peers, by report, Collingwood was haughty, irascible, disdainful, withdrawn − he had cause to be all of these. For all that he held the Waynflete chair in Metaphysical Philosophy, the senior office of its kind in the country, he remained isolated and neglected in it, while the enormous energies of men's minds were poured assiduously away into what Collingwood was convinced was rock and no water and the sandy road.

It is always important to suggest reasons for the neglect of a man you believe to be a mighty mind. There are routine ways of accounting for such isolation, or for neglect and abuse. You can blame other people's hypocrisy and stupidity; you can blame jealousy or suspect that a plot has been laid to put down a newcomer of genius whose ideas will upset the old-stagers' comfortable despotism. All these explanations hold good there is no doubt, when we think of Collingwood — and he was, as I have said, a difficult man. But these are hardly reasons enough to explain his isolation, the lack, until very recently, of any followers of his procedures and his ideas, his absence from present day bibliographies.

In the first instance, he set himself against the mainstream of contemporary philosophy. He did so in an effort to hold continuity with his intellectual tradition and that rich, dense, complex structure of practices, dispositions, customs, habits, ceremonies, which constitute a way of thought and its modalities of speech, and so much more saturating and pervasive than the word 'intellectual' connotes. Collingwood was another pupil from Rugby, who went up to Oxford, read Literae Humaniores at University College, and was a pupil of pupils of T. H. Green. As we saw, he deeply admired the tradition which trained the higher civil servants for Balfour and Asquith, and which provided a collaborative intellectual minority as critics and creators of public and cultural life.[4] But he also saw that resituating idealism in post-1918 Britain would be a drastically difficult and ambitious process.

For a start, cultural and intellectual fashions had made such a task solitary and wilful. Now it is possible to over-emphasize these circumstances. Collingwood cast himself head-on and with all his considerable rhetorical dash against the realist school of philosophy which had in his view so thoroughly demoralized philosophy. But the *Autobiography* has remained in print since it was published in 1939,[5] and as the foregoing quotations suggest, is intensely readable, magnetic and illuminating to anyone interested in the intellectual life. Similarly, *The Principles of Art* (1938) and *The Idea of History* (edited after Collingwood's death from his very full manuscript by his pupil T. M. Knox) appear regularly enough in the separate, technical literatures of their subject-matters. But it is just this separation, partly a mere consequence of the divisions of academic labour in the English-speaking universities, partly (as Collingwood roundly declared) their deep, betrayingly philistine habit of mindlessness, which it was Collingwood's whole intention to resist and correct.

His unsparing criticism of the realists was far from a fit of academic pepperiness. It was a necessary expression of his attempt to recover a science of human affairs capable of standing up for human reason in the face of the tides of irrationalism visible not only in the war during which Collingwood worked in the Intelligence Department of the Admiralty but afterwards when he saw the Italian philosophers he admired,[6]

Giovanni Gentile and Benedetto Croce, coax their version of Idealism into the courts of Mussolini's Fascism. He took philosophy seriously enough to think that the complacent *suffisiance* with which H. A. Prichard in a famous paper in 1912 asked 'Does Moral Philosophy Rest upon a Mistake?' was one of the many *trahisons des clercs* energetically carried out by G. E. Moore, Cook Wilson and others Collingwood arraigns; the glittering, cocksure, and entirely evanescent fireworks of A. J. Ayer's *Language, Truth and Logic* (1935) circumscribes the demoralizing of philosophy which Collingwood fought against and is the readiest text we may find to illustrate the dead human end into which Russell and the realists led very clever and dizzily irresponsible students such as Ayer to carol lightheartedly of the death of God and ethics, alike consigned to the fishy-smelling holdall, 'emotive or meaningless', kept for everything not logic or science.

Ayer was a Johnny-come-lately to the philosophy Collingwood dismissed in the *Autobiography*. By then he knew the Enemy clearly and had behind him a pile of books shored up against His advances.[7] For of course more than philosophy had blown apart a believable ethics. After mass slaughter in the name of God knew what nationalisms and pieties, the solemn self-entrancements of Moore's Bloomsbury pupils might seem an amiable preference; the passionately individual vitalism of D. H. Lawrence ('I shall be wary beyond words, of committing myself')[8] was another, more serious rejection of the victory of science.

In the face of these disintegrations, Collingwood was alone among postwar English philosophers in trying to hold together a unity of mind and experience, and the one as only visible (and knowable) in the other. As I noted, the deep disjuncture in moral philosophy initiated by the realist school left the effort to hold together the life of the mind and spirit in a single and morally excellent unity entirely to the poets. Collingwood apart, the philosophers abandoned ethics and politics in England. It was the displacement which gave Leavis, as we shall see, his opportunity. Literary criticism, the reflexive aid to literature, brought to explicit proposition the intuitions by which the poet sought to balance himself in the times. W. B. Yeats set himself the rediscovery of such unity of thought and feeling, and only won it at the cost of abandoning rational thought and inventing an ontology and politics of such Gothic darkness as to drive poetry even further from the centres of intellectual power. T. S. Eliot brought off his success only by litanizing poetic diction. Wallace Stevens, trying to work in a tradition not unlike Collingwood's, made his idealism into his own poetic joke, became tired out with the struggle to affirm monism, and wrote out a garrulous and pluralist old age.

I mention these writers — all of them major figures shaped by the same history of ideas as Collingwood — to emphasize the difficulty and importance of the task which he set himself, while still remaining in the mainstream of European, and particularly Italian and German, Idealism. Around him, the drastic and irreversible movements of twentieth-century war and revolution drove the best of contemporary intellectuals either into the cautious, temporizing and exiguous provisionality of the new scepticism, or away towards the monistic satisfactions of the new churches set up under the stirring bugle-calls and banners of Fascism and Marxism. Croce became a hired mouth of Mussolini; men and women in the German tradition — Kautsky, Luxemburg, Lukacs — became revolutionary Marxists. In the case of someone like Collingwood, the struggle to achieve a monistic view of mind, to resist totalitarianism and the irresponsible realists, to hold a post-1918 line against the dark forces of unreason and the blind menaces of positivist Enlightenment, really was to stand foursquare against every current as the main stream slid widely and darkly past.

But I am not simply praising him for being the only one in step. Collingwood addressed himself to a deep crisis in human knowledge and its structures: not only war, but technology, economics, culture, the social order of Europe itself failed to answer to the old terms, and on his analysis the new ones never engaged with the matter or its heart. In a style unfamiliar to Oxford or Cambridge professors of philosophy since Green himself, Collingwood set out to hold the connection with the tradition of the English Hegelians, especially T. H. Green, in the teeth of the new positivists, both from Vienna and at home. He set out to keep alive the example of Ruskin — cultural critic, historian, painter, theorist, capacious and boisterous man of letters. Now Collingwood was, supremely, an Oxonian and a scholar, but he was also a practical archaeologist, a competent pianist, composer, singer, water-colourist and draughtsman, fluent in both ancient tongues and half a dozen modern ones, a philosopher, a historian, an aesthetician, and an accomplished yachtsman[9] (it is an attractive detail of his life that he was, from their meeting at Rugby and Coniston, a close friend of that remarkable man Arthur Ransome[10]). He was also a convinced Christian and, while I do not suppose he ever put it to himself in such terms, his life's endeavour to revise an Idealist version of the map of knowledge with a proper dose of empiricism, to accommodate within his version of a doctrine of universals the novel demands of relativism, and to create the science of human affairs for which he believed the opportunity was come and the need urgent, this gigantic effort may be read as an English rejoinder to the success and advances of Marxism.

Early in the 1920s when Collingwood was writing his first notes towards his vast project, *Speculum Mentis*, Marxist theory had been revamped by Lenin to justify and explain the Bolshevik victory, and by Lukacs in his support of the Bela Kun government in Hungary: similar triumphs in the name of similar theories looked at least imaginable to the optimistic with Gramsci in Italy and with Kautsky in Germany; nobody had raised the retrograde cry, 'Socialism in One Country'. Now, with another sixty years of blood under the bridge, an idealist science of human affairs looks a more creditable ambition.

'Idealist' however needs instant qualification. It may be a slippery term, it may be for a Marxist a term of abuse. I began this book, however, by noticing that a much needed rapprochement impends between idealism and materialism; Collingwood's work is an essential solvent in this process. For all the approval with which he speaks of Hegel, the fact that it was in the manuscript notes dealing with Hegel in *The Idea of History* (written during 1935–6) that he brought out the central, lapidary doctrine of the *Autobiography,* 'All history is the history of thought',[11] nonetheless Collingwood criticizes Hegel both for the ingenuousness of supposing that politics is the teleology of history (and that therefore the development of the rational state is its ideal purpose) and for failing to see that history should be practised as, in the later phrase, 'total history', and that 'the historian should not be content with anything short of a history of man in his *concrete actuality*' (p. 122, my italics). In going on to deny Marx's claim to have 'stood Hegel on his head' and reasserted a naturalism in which mind is the product of production, Collingwood is not just counterposing the primacy of idealism over materialism, he is rebutting Marx's claim that all history is the history of economics, and claiming once more that understanding human practices, though inevitably a partial activity for each enquirer, is only possible when the part is inserted into the totality. The effort to grasp the unitary nature of the enterprise represents the trajectory of Collingwood's lifework.

That work cannot be readily classified under the heading of any particular school, whatever he owed to English and Italian idealists. For him, as for Keynes and Leavis, morality and experience were paramount points of reference. Collingwood's exemplary Englishness and what commends him to us here as a best version of that frame of mind lies in his determination to hold together in his thought in tense and dialectical play categories which other thinkers have required to be kept separate in order to think at all. And being a philosopher, whose business is thought about thought, he was intent upon bringing to explication and schematizing a process which for Keynes was just the way he worked.

The mode of thought comes out if we dissolve the concept 'category' and even the concept of a concept, and look hard instead along the planes of intellectual vision which shape our meaning (without which there would be no meaning) when we use the words 'practice' and 'cognition', 'apprehension' and 'construction', 'intellect' and 'imagination'. One way of directing attention towards the dissolution[12] is to describe the process as dialectical, but this is often no more than labelling the difficulty: it does little for our understanding. Collingwood's insistence is that it is the nature of human mind to be a part of action; you can't act 'thoughtlessly', although the nature of thought given to single actions can obviously vary in length. But the unbelievably rapid interplay of practice and cognition whereby what you apprehend and the intelligible relations you construct out of the apprehensions cannot be figured sequentially, only dynamically. Nor is this a footnote to launch a psychology of perception — Collingwood is contemptuous of claims that psychology in any of its versions can deal with 'problems of logic and ethics'. Rather he starts from the condition which Mink summarizes very neatly: 'It is that we think forward but understand backward.'[13] The politician does one thing the historian the other, naturally enough. The really intractable adventure is to essay both, and if we play the game of dividing the world into sheep and goats — the thinkers forward, the understanders backward, and those few people who tried to do both — Collingwood is keeping company not according to the schools of thought but with a heterodox elite including Heraclitus, Aquinas, Spinoza, Pascal, and of course Hegel: monists all, but hardly characteristic of the English commitment to 'concrete actuality'. Of course Collingwood is hardly of the stature of those fellow philosophers; but he is of their colour and orientation. The point at this stage is not to make quite such invidious comparisons, but to identify a certain kind of moral and epistemic teleology, that is, a particular way of thinking about the world and the meaning life can be made to have in it.[14] Collingwood sets out to bear the strain of thinking forwards and understanding backwards, and to present the insistent rapidity of thought from apprehension to construction or, as we may say, from intuiting the mass, density, colour, and even forms of experience to explicating its precise detail and shape, its meaning and its significance. As Mink puts it, 'experience, one might say, is the realist, reflection on experience the idealist' (p. 113).

If we set aside what he himself disowned as an early juvenilium, *Religion and Philosophy* (1916), then Collingwood's first, neglected, and surely great statement of his life's plan and of the difficulty of bringing off such a task in his historical circumstances is *Speculum Mentis, or The Map of Knowledge*.[15] Like any other intellectual, Collingwood battled to make sense of his experience in words. The strain for him as for us was a killing one, and there is no need to expect the progression of his thought to be aesthetically gratifying, unfailingly clear, brilliant, and precise.[16]

As I shall suggest, *Speculum Mentis* represents an ambition as well as an argument, and if as we should we give the *Autobiography* canonical status, then by 1938 Collingwood had considerably modified this ambition for theory in order to gain much sineviness and grip so far as intellectual purchase went, at the legitimate expense of much greater ambiguity for any teleology. In writing in *Speculum Mentis* about the lost medieval ideal of a beautiful unity of knowledge, culture, and identity conferred by Aquinas's and Catholicism's epistemology and its concentric pre-suppositions, he knows as well as Morris did that such a unity is irrecoverable. All the same, it may be used as an image of desire against which to test his new tract for the times, a 'new *Treatise of Human Nature* philosophically conceived', in which he seeks, so to speak, to create a developmental spiral of the mind-as-knowledge, a spiral in which art is the first and most essential form, more essential even than religion because men may grow up irreligious but unless they begin in art, they cannot grow up at all. The critical passages of the book, however, come in those pages towards the end in which Collingwood restates for an English audience the Idealist problematic for which Kant and Hegel are the essential co-ordinates. In defining, with his characteristic and patrician self-confidence, the meaning and centrality of a rather more modest Absolute Mind than Hegel did business with, he writes

In knowing my mind, I know yours and other people's; these reveal me to myself and I simultaneously explain them to myself. My mind is obviously a product of society, and conversely the society I know is the product of my mind, as thinking it according to its lights.

The absolute mind, then, unites the differences of my mind and other people's, but not as the abstract universal unites: rather as the concrete universal of history unites. The absolute mind is an historical whole of which mine is a part.

Yet the category of whole and part is false, for the part in its externality to other parts is but a reassertion of abstract difference. The absolute mind is not 'one stupendous whole'. It lives in its entirety in every individual and every act of every individual, yet not indifferently, as triangularity is indifferently present in every triangle, but expressing itself in every individual uniquely and irreplaceably. This is its necessary nature as concrete . . . (*Speculum Mentis,* p. 299).

It is as round a confutation of a classical difficulty as you can find, and its great merit is that you know clearly where you are. The historicality of all such moral and epistemological enterprise is Collingwood's main contribution to our intellectual primers. He veers, perhaps unnecessarily, between crowning philosophy or history queen of the sciences, and he may be found in later works not only modifying but in detail contradicting in a no less self-confident way some of the arguments in the earlier book.[17] Substantially, however, the programme he set himself with *Speculum Mentis,* he carried through unwaveringly until the first haemorrhages of the cortex in the mid-1930s told him that he could not complete his giant ambition to place a distinctly pragmatic Kantian and Hegelian idealism in an English context.

The strong example he adduces for illustration of this particular doctrine of absolute mind is the hardly Hegelian but thoroughgoingly liberal instance of the individual personality itself. The personality persists through time; it varies incorrigibly with circumstances, it is hugely unpredictable; but it is incomprehensible except in relation to itself, and itself as a type of others. This brings out in a quite untheoretic and experiential way the interconnectedness of part and whole, and shows thereby that the label 'idealist' is no greater help than the label 'realist' in dealing on Collingwood's terms with man as a subject for science. As he went on to write in *The Idea of History*, 'Philosophy [let us say, the sciences of man] is never concerned with thought by itself; it is always concerned with its relation to its object, and is therefore concerned with the object just as much as with the thought' (p. 2). In *Speculum Mentis* the truistic nature of this dictum gets its force from its close pursual through the five stages or levels of knowledge-as-knowable-by-the-agent: art, religion, science, history, philosophy.

It is important to stress that this is a progression, both in terms of historical development — art and religion were the dominant thought forms of the thirteenth century, science of the nineteenth and early twentieth — and also as a movement from lower to higher. It is also important not to misunderstand the proposed order. For while he undoubtedly argues about the limitations of art as dangerously autotelic, about how its vehicle the imagination is far too apt to be lost in fantasy and unattached to reality, and warns against a too heavy and continuous saturation in art as destroying its inherently occasional nature, yet Collingwood affirms art as the ground of being and the necessary origin of child's thought and man's education. By this token art is not only fundamental to an individual life, but to a culture's; subsequent thought can only build on that social as well as personal foundation. Within an individual life, moreover, aesthetic life continues alongside the religious, scientific, and if a person gets that far, the historical and philosophical lives. Each has its distinct mode of being; the aesthetic is not superseded as a man or woman develops, instead it prefigures the grasp for what, in Blake's words, may be proved but as yet is only imagined. Thus, for a child, for a culture, art embodies a deep contradiction: it is not factually true, 'only imagination'; yet it is a supposal, a theory about how things might be.

The value of art as a form of experience is thus its self-transcendence. Art is not attacked and destroyed by philosophy as by an external enemy; it destroys itself by its own inner contradiction, by defining itself as at once pure intuition and also expression, imagination and thought, significance without definable signification, the intuitive concept. This contradiction is not irreconcilable. On the contrary, its reconciliation is the whole life of thought.[18]

Given Collingwood's gifts and his education in art, no one will think that he underrated its sacredness and significance. He speaks briskly against the Romantic over-valuation of art (with its dire consequences both in the market and the mind), and does so in order to move towards what in *Speculum Mentis* he saw as the philosophic maturity of intellect, bringing to explicitness (though not to paraphrase) what has been intuited — 'hence the paradox that the content of the work of art is its own form in an intuitive guise' (p. 95). Art, then, is 'the cutting edge of the mind' (p. 101) but the complex accretions of culture and its attendant increases in self-knowledge require historically responsive epistemologies and produce different frames of mind for the transformation of the data of inquiry into what may properly be called knowledge.

These processes, co-present in all self-conscious civilizations, encourage the gradual predominance of certain modes of knowledge over others. Hence, thought *may* advance to history and philosophy, via religion and science, each cast in the same conceptual dialectics as art — intuition and conceptualization; supposal and assertion; truth and error; supremely, question and answer. In a rough sketch of progress, Collingwood then notes that 'critical history is the child of the 18th century'.

At this point we touch the twistpoint of Collingwood's thought, the tense scrutiny of definitions that brought him to an account of a truly critical philosophy which at the same time satisfied the exacting demands of his historicism. He turned and returned to this serpentine question. In *Speculum Mentis,* he plumps a bit rhetorically for the philosophy of philosophy as the highest level of knowledge. Although, with his seductive habit of using quotations as glancing facets of his argument, he admits that 'to see in a glass and to see darkly are the same' (p. 314) he leaves the reader in the last paragraph with the assertion that the purpose of philosophy is to draw a map of knowledge which provides for the mind 'its self-recognition in its own mirror'.

Well, it will do as a flourish. And the book itself is an unbeatable summary of Collingwood's ambitions and intentions, as well as a transparent realization of the difficulty of bringing off such a scheme in 1924. *The Principles of Art*[19] and *The Idea of History* were written more or less consecutively between 1935 and 1937. They follow the programme in so far as he works out in each the particular form on the scale of forms which the knowledge in question takes in the growth of mind and its expression, civilization. Each however represents a large enrichment of the initial scheme, as well as a distinct movement towards the radical historicizing of all the maps of knowledge, a movement which, as we shall see, led him towards the deep recalcitrance of relativism.[20] Both books affirm, in Collingwood's beautiful and limpid prose, the largest possible definition of self-knowledge (and its consequences in action) as the disinterested purpose of thought, and the ground of freedom.

Theoretically, the artist is a person who comes to know himself, to know his own emotion. This is also knowing his world, that is, the sights and sounds and so forth which together make up his total imaginative experience. The two knowledges are to him one knowledge, because these sights and sounds are to him steeped in the emotion with which he contemplates them: they are the language in which that emotion utters itself to his consciousness. His world is his language. What it says to him it says about himself; his imaginative vision of it is his self-knowledge.

But this knowing of himself is a making of himself. At first he is mere psyche, the possessor of merely psychical experiences or impressions. The act of coming to know himself is the act of converting his impressions into ideas, and so of converting himself from mere psyche into consciousness. The coming to know his emotions is the coming to dominate them, to assert himself as their master.[21]

Writing, as he is here, of criticism and creation, he is able to make the criterion of good art and of good art criticism its truthfulness to feeling. In a powerful conclusion to the finely named chapter, 'Art and Truth', he goes on to press for the increasing convergence of good poetry and good philosophy and concludes, in a flashing aphorism; 'Subject without style is barbarism; style without subject is dilettantism. Art is the two together' (p. 239). The clarity and beauty of Collingwood's prose, when he overcomes his tendency to assert at the expense of argument, are their own example of art as subject and style together. In so far as they do come together, then the philosopher-poet discovers the truth of truthfulness. His way of saying what has to be said about the knowledge which is both subject and object in hand is as true as he can make it. The discipline of art and thought is so to attend to what is said, that the saying is as complete as you can make it.

The trouble with the style is that it is so quotable, that it is easy to overlook the place of such admonitions in the larger scheme. *An Autobiography* in its poise and succinctness, its decided air, represents the terse synopsis of his thinking to that point, and the version of his revisions of his own and English historicism which will serve our contemporary purposes as a primer in social theory. Much is implied by his last book, *The New Leviathan*,[22] for the relativism which is not so much argued through as put down by assertion in the *Autobiography*, but the lines of procedure and its justification are all there in the story 'of a man whose business is thinking' (*Preface*). He wrote the *Autobiography* in a few months of sick leave during 1938 in case the illness whose victory he knew was never far away cut him off before the project was within reach of its end. In the event, two more terrific strokes followed in 1941, and even though his boundless energy drove him through to the completion of *The New Leviathan*, broken health made him an easy prey for pneumonia, and he died at the age of fifty-three in 1943.

The energy however is infallible. As is clear from the earlier quotations in this chapter the force and style of his best book are immediately recognizable, and the confidence, even when he puts down his own work, perfectly olympian. It is also a book of great moral courage. As Stephen Toulmin points out in his introduction to the new edition, once one considers the record of evasiveness, indifference, cowardliness, and brutal reaction in the Oxford of the 1930s, Collingwood's fierce attack on the frivolity of much of intellectual life no longer looks overdone. Collingwood knew the social affront he would be bound to cause; he had lived in Oxford and London all his working life. Once again, however, his scathing asperity and what the genteel tradition of Oxford and Cambridge would want to call his arrogance is, first, a part of his painful honesty, and, second, a necessary consequence of forcing his theory through into the practice of everyday life. For after he has recorded the strong, vivid formation of his intellectual origins by his father and mother, and his determination to make his own intellectual fortune, and after going on to describe the disintegration of a believable moral philosophy as an honourable subject for study at Oxford, the war forced on him the realization that 'a young man's expectation of life was a rapidly dwindling asset' (p. 43), followed by the hardly less frightening discovery not only that the war could have no victors 'in the sense that no party could be enriched by it', but that 'it closed in a peace settlement of unprecedented folly, in which statesmanship, even purely selfish statesmanship, was overwhelmed by the meanest and most idiotic passions' (p. 89). And he concludes, as we have seen, that since the enormous triumphs of science were quite incapable of doing anything to prevent warfare and did much to augment its most dreadful effects, an entirely different form of knowledge and inquiry was needed to control human affairs. That form was history.

This was no case of the scholar loyal to his own subject simply declaring its power of redemption. Collingwood was foremost a philosopher, and we know what he made of contemporary philosophers. Nor did he think much better of much of the history as practised round about him. After all, he had had to work out in the intellectual and practical niceties of archaeological digs[23] how not to waste his time. The bookish historians could get by with 'scissors-and-paste' work, that is, by patching together bits from other people's records; if an archaeologist just dug vaguely, he could make no sense of anything. Hence Collingwood developed his 'logic of question-and-answer', a method of inquiry founded absolutely on his premise that the past, in the form of 'traces', has to be something which exists in the present.

His strictures against scissors-and-paste intellectual history stand ominously over my desk. The temptation simply to summarize each figure on an idiosyncratic reading-list and hand over the summary to students is strong because the procedure is familiar and academically respectable. But the point I wish to press home is Collingwood's, like Keynes's, usability in the present condition of the world. Keynes's indeed is the mode of thought which has dominated the more rational discussions of political life since 1945. Collingwood's is one essential complement in a hermeneutic revised to include high unemployment and high inflation, the vertiginous gamble of nuclear armaments, and the entirely doomed attempt of all the social formations in Britain to regain a familiar order which has gone for ever.

So, as Collingwood says, if 'the past is in some sense still living in the present' (*Autobiography*, p. 97) and is still alive and active, the historian can provide both rules and insight for the diagnosis of situations ('how did we get to be in this mess?'). He also provides for action and acting even when the situation is unprecedented, when you conclude that the existing rules will be no good to you in the situation you are faced by, and have to improvise.

Rules of conduct kept action at a low potential, because they involved a certain blindness to the realities of the situation. If action was to be raised to a higher potential, the agent must open his eyes wider and see more clearly the situation in which he was acting. If the function of history was to inform people about the past where the past was understood as a dead past, it could do very little towards helping them to act; but if its function was to inform them about the present, in so far as the past, its ostensible subject-matter, was incapsulated in the present and constituted a part of it not at once obvious to the untrained eye, then history stood in the closest possible relation to practical life. (*Autobiography*, p. 106)

In the present world the necessity for a mode of thought capable of forestalling piracy, bullying, lunacy, or suicide hardly needs urging upon even the most zealous of liberation fronts, world bankers, or harmless trade unionists. If a new kind of history is to be a help, what will it look like?

Any such history 'will be a history of thought' (*Autobiography* p. 110). In order to recover a past thought, the historian, working from its 'traces' must 'be able to think over again for himself that very same thought, not another like it' (p. 111). To do this, he must first stick to what the original thinker expressed in language (and not its scissors-and-paste synopsis) and at the same time, recover what question the original had posed to which the expressed thought was an answer. Although Collingwood argues firmly for a logic of question-and-answer, the word 'logic' seems to fit rather ill; we would do better to speak of a theory of interpretation, or hermeneutic. It is, however, quite satisfactory to set it out, with its author, propositionally: 'So I reached my third proposition: "Historical knowledge is the re-enactment of a past thought incapsulated in a context of present thoughts which, by contradicting it, confine it to a plane different from theirs." (p. 114).' This is much more than a matter of words on the page; sometimes, in spite of the insistence on expression, the object of inquiry can't be linguistic in form. An action is no less a form of expression, and *The Principles of Art* make it clear that an artefact is an expressive action; hence the bits and pieces of stone and shard which an archaeologist digs up are, if he finds in them the questions to which they are successful answers (for Collingwood asserts disputably that no one can reconstruct history from failure), the intentional and purposive expressions of thought available for his rethinking.

The recovery of historical intention takes us close to relativism.[24] For if it is a necessary condition of understanding an action that we ask what it could have meant to its agent, we have to take his intentions and purposes as valid.

Collingwood sketches out the process in chapter X of the *Autobiography,* insisting as he always does on intellectual endeavour as essentially practical, and on all human minds as resolutely interrogative of their experience. All thought is an effort to answer specific questions; understanding the thought of others is a matter of understanding the questions they put to themselves about the intractabilities of their lives. To understand Plato or the uses of a fort on the Roman Wall we must recover the intentions of the original agents, and re-imagine the questions and problems to which *The Republic* and 'a rotten little fort' were offered as answers. Such a procedure is comfortably held by literary students to fall into the Intentional Fallacy (rejected in the formula 'A man does what he does, not what he intends to do.') But it is surely true that you cannot be said to have understood any action if you mistake what it purposes. The question What does it mean? is only answerable by our trying to imagine what the agent intended it to mean, and this in turn is a matter of knowing what questions he could have been hoping to answer. The relativist trap is then to suppose that that is all there is to do. But the act of interpretation (which is by definition an act of evaluation) returns the source of energy and purpose from the past to the present. Collingwood emphasizes this in the reconstructed notes of *The Idea of History* (p. 247).

Historical thinking is an original and fundamental activity of the human mind, or, as Descartes might have said, the idea of the past is an 'innate' idea.

Historical thinking is that activity of the imagination by which we endeavour to provide this innate idea with detailed content. And this we do by using the present as evidence for its own past. Every present has a past of its own, and any imaginative reconstruction of the past aims at reconstructing the past of this present, the present in which the act of imagination is going on, as here and now perceived. In principle the aim of any such act is to use the entire perceptible here-and-now as evidence for the entire past through whose process it has come into being. In practice, this aim can never be achieved. The perceptible here-and-now can never be perceived, still less interpreted, in its entirety; and the infinite process of past time can never be envisaged as a whole. But this separation between what is attempted in principle, and what is achieved in practice is the lot of mankind, not a peculiarity of historical thinking. The fact that it is found there only shows that herein history is like art, science, philosophy, the pursuit of virtue, and the search for happiness.

Having started his account of reconstruction from Hadrian's Wall ('What was it for?' 'To keep out the Picts.' 'No, it was "an elevated sentry-walk"'), he goes on to draw the moral for fields of history as varied as statistical demography and popular songs, not only keeping steadily before us the necessity of knowing the past only from the present, but also of accounting for historical continuity not on a linear scale but as something more like the stratifications of archaeology, and limning archaeologies of consciousness which recognize the strange 'encapsulations' of human thought and experience.

There are important criticisms to make, of course.[25] Collingwood's method too much confines us to individuals; he doesn't allow for the power of ideological structures and tradition, for convention in its widest sense (Quentin Skinner, as I show in the last chapter, puts this right). Collingwood makes too much of thought and not enough of brute, contingent facts. He confuses 'thick description'[26] with causal explanation. And in spite of his hopes of providing us with a means of thinking forwards, all we have is his recipe for understanding backwards.

His answer to these criticisms comes, at least in the *Autobiography,* in a stirringly knockdown form. He has spent the book of his life insisting on the presence of the past. The last chapter rouses us in turn by telling how the present broke into his absorption in the past, and first roused him to see and understand the craven duplicity of the British Government's policies in Spain and Munich, the horrible irrationalism of Fascist movements all over Europe, the leaden ignorance of a British people kept stupid by its means of communication, lied to and despised by its leaders, including its intellectual leaders.

It was all true. And it is further true that his method, if it is to be faithful to its own claims on logic and certainty however defined, on purpose and intention, on freedom and reason and truth above all, must be constantly rewriting the present according to those claims in order to interrogate the past at all. To answer the question, 'How did we get to be where we are?' it must first be possible to say where we are. However relative a position that must historically be, it is the only place we have in and for which to live, and if necessary, to fight. Collingwood offers us a science of human affairs in which history is now, and always, and the word science centrally betokens the activity of enlightenment. The gap between theory and practice is closed by switching on the sunshine. As he ends his great book,

I am not writing an account of recent political events in England: I am writing a description of the way in which those events impinged upon myself and broke up my pose of a detached professional thinker. I know now that the minute philosophers of my youth, for all their profession of a purely scientific detachment from practical affairs, were the propagandists of a coming Fascism. I know that Fascism means the end of clear thinking and the triumph of irrationalism. I know that all my life I have been engaged unawares in a political struggle, fighting against these things in the dark. Henceforth I shall fight in the daylight. (*Autobiography*, p. 167)

5

Resistance and Social Decline:
F. R. Leavis

F. R. Leavis (1895 – 1978) is the third great figure in the triangle of forces which I propose for an English hermeneutics, and as a basis for understanding displacements and reconstruction necessary to radical earnestness and its theorists after the first world war. Understanding that reconstruction, as any Collingwoodian history of ideas will conclude, is to make the first essential moves towards understanding the conceptual structures we have in the present as consequences of the past, available for controlling or at least thinking ourselves into the future.

So, Keynes is the engineer of the economic structures which, in at least a weak sense of the verb, determine the texture of the social and political order. Collingwood is the methodist of ideas (and, if you like, ideologies) and their essential history which give us purchase on the agents of that social and political order, and some way of recovering the motives, intentions, and purposes of their urgent voluntary errands. Leavis concentrates himself and us on the meaning and value of the errands themselves.

This completes my first trigonometry. But the three men pull away from one another as much as they prompt us towards a convergent human science. Leavis, who deliberately and wilfully resisted any recognition of economic forces in his theodicy all his life, was harsh also, as we have seen, upon Keynes's early beliefs and Keynes's continuing enjoyment of enormous public prestige and power combined with, according to his pupils, a sometimes teasing moral nonchalance and a genuine libertarian insouciance. Leavis powerfully disliked the upper-class fecklessness and dilettantism which the Bloomsbury set at times delighted in.[1] To place Keynes and Leavis on the same intellectual axis is to oblige oneself to live with a tense and resistant polarity.

Yet both are products of and spokesmen for a grandly imaginative restatement of English liberalism in the uncharted turbulence of postwar Britain. Both speak, across drastic differences of temperament, status, conceptual categories, key and cadence, mind and language, for the Romantic individual as the realm and fount of value, for the great epistemes of human being, freedom, fulfilment, and self-awareness,[2] for art as actualizing the highest aspiration of the human mind, and for the strong system of denials and resistance — denials of privilege, injustice, arrogance of caste or church — in which the balancing positive was the freely choosing, morally autonomous and grown-up hero. This was the liberalism of Mill and Green and their successors. Collingwood, Keynes and Leavis committed themselves, with all the immense freedoms and reputation of Oxford and Cambridge at their backs, to giving that individual, in the phrase, a land fit for heroes to live in. All three acknowledged, without taking for granted, the peculiar richness and satisfactions, the reality of momentous continuities in a British culture and history without revolution and without a war of occupation in half a millenium. England, in particular, has never been a good place for those sensitively disposed towards the more candid expressions of chauvinism, and even after the war to end all wars, ruling-class Oxford and Cambridge were still deeply poisoned by the playboys of Brideshead. At the most everyday level, finding serious-minded fellows and not having too shamefacedly to conceal either a lively interest in the life of the mind or the life of the urban proletariat remained difficult until the genuinely transfiguring consequences of a second wartime university generation and its special 1945 membership of the demobilized and the wounded and the now politically wideawake opponents of Fascism. For the first forty years or so of this century, serious intellectual activity in what are complacently called the ancient universities was confined to the very clever in small enclaves and masked by the insistent narcissism of the bright young things.

Keynes, we have seen, was one such thing himself, and his practice as the greatest economic policy theorist of the century hardly touched the quite other practices of King's College. Collingwood won the devotion of a large following, of students certainly, and — so it is reported — of archaeologists, but his intensive programme of work and thought was very much a solitary one, at least in virtue of the contrast he affords to Leavis. For Leavis is centrally important to this part of the book and to social theorists of our day on three grounds: first, as I have said, in that he insists upon the strictest moral responsibility to the social experience shaped by Keynes's schemes and interrogated for its significance by

Collingwood's method. Leavis insists not only on having out the deep matter of significance, but also on determining its life or deathliness. Much, after all, may be significant, and much of it may be dreadful. Leavis's life's work was to search out the significance which made, on his terms, for life itself, for creativity, in the famous phrases of *The Great Tradition*,[3] for 'a vital capacity for experience, a kind of reverent openness before life, and a marked moral intensity'. Secondly, he is important for his working out through the study of literature of a historical sociology in which to place and value the cultural objects he selected for study. Thirdly, his name focusses a range of texts which bring us up to the present day and embody a complex range of intellectual practices which not only identify a community of inquiry but whose clear intention was to oppose and subvert the system of social relations within which it lived and grew. The key to understanding this history of a critical practice is Leavis's famously transparent exchange which prefigures the mode of his intellectual procedure — his courteous query to a collaborator, 'This is so, isn't it?' anticipating the reply, 'Yes, but . . .' The proper study of Leavis begins from this model of critical practice.[4]

Social theorists have been puzzled by the fact that the discipline of English literary criticism should have been the ground upon which a secular and critical theodicy was built. On some arguments, Collingwood's perhaps, that task is really the historian's; on others, Perry Anderson's for instance, all indigenous cultures require a classical sociology. Some latter-day Marxists,[5] irritated by what they take to be the provincial displacements of a necessary hierarchy in intellectual power, have admonished English culture for allowing interesting social theory to appear in a subject marginal to politics. I do not think we need agree. For one thing, it makes sense in the sciences of man, as in the natural sciences,[6] to speak of a certain mobility and fluidity in the sources, resources, and styles of intellectual energy and its production. The dominance of Viennese and Cambridge positivism, of Schlick and Carnap, Wittgenstein and Russell, caused, as Collingwood laments, the virtual closure of moral philosophy for a generation. The triumphant anti-intellectualism of Lewis Namier and the scientistic attractions of his empirical sociology led to an academic history without a historiography being practised at Oxford and Cambridge. The first seepings upwards of 'history from below' were to be found in Barbara and Lawrence Hammond's classic study, *The Village Labourer*,[7] which so stirred Fabian circles. They were followed by a fellow Fabian, R. H. Tawney,[8] who sought both for the present and the past to return a political economy to the heart of history. But it was Leavis who drew these writings into the cultural problematic he made his own and *Scrutiny*'s. Academic history continued to leave out the discomforting questions of politics, just as philosophy moved away from ethics and ontology.

The operation of these two disciplines, together with the failure of the LSE and the sociologists to theorize a sufficient politics of English culture in the years between the two wars left Leavis with everything to do for himself. This is, once more, to take a notably voluntaristic view of what one man and his wife could do for themselves and their friends. Well, truistically, men make their own history of ideas, but not in circumstances of their own choosing, and in any such manufacture, it is simply if tautologically stupid to count personal intelligence out of it: Leavis, as I say, was a genius, the third of our second part, and whereas Keynes was so dazzlingly clever, we may say that Leavis was by far the most complex, subtle, profound and voluminous of our three worthies. But to understand the decisiveness of his intervention, we must turn back to a rather different version of the historical conjuncture at which all three began.

I have ventured more than once that a blank supervened at the heart of the moral sciences of the 1920s. Keynes merely filled it with a decent consumer, Collingwood with himself. But if it is plausible, or even true, not that all men, but serious and idealistic young men and women at Oxford and Cambridge in the 1920s, naturally sought a field of studies with a heart, capable of inspiring them to live well and do good, they did not find it in philosophy or politics or history, and there weren't many other places to look. It isn't necessary to take the *geist* of *Geisteswissenschaften* with Hegelian literalness, to think of intellectual energies and production as naturally seeking and asserting meaning: the naturalness, in a short time span, is a result of there being a tradition of radical earnestness. Once its language was no longer spoken in its customary homes, that language displaced itself and sought out a new set of materials for its attention. Recruits to the English intelligentsia have always used literature as a ready stock of reference, as I have said; the new recruits in 1925 or so found 'modern Greats', or philosophy, politics, and economics, in modish disarray at Oxford, but a drastically revised and marvellously tonic and invigorating version of English studies at Cambridge. The usual currents of intellectual life in the human sciences having dwindled to rather narrow and shallow rills, the real force of things broke out elsewhere.

The process illustrates Berlin's fluent summary of the life and death of ideas quoted on p. 13. It is always important to ask of one's father's house, what intellectual mansions it contains, and where their real action is, even if it is only to be found with the bats in the belfry. In Oxford and Cambridge, which dominated then as now the production of ideas in England, the centre of the action was with Leavis and English studies, and remained there until he left the university's employment in 1964 (to pick a date for convenience). By that stage, Leavis, though about to enter one of his most prolific flowerings of ideas and writing, had pulled clear away from the main institutions of English studies, and they had settled into what William Empson approvingly called their 'sturdy placid way',[9] and what others less indulgent may think of as a dullness, a lack of gaiety and sagacity, unrivalled since Pope finished the *Dunciad.* Since Marxism reawoke, the force lines of a new energy have been pushing through the old dustheaps of philosophy, history, and political science, and are running them, as we shall see, in new directions.

Leavis's first advent, however, came at a moment when cultural authority had obviously broken down, when a ruling class had lost all claim to justify its rule by grossnesses of incompetence and stupidity at war, and when the continuing of the English social order was threatened by the slaughter of its best young men in every social class, and by the destructiveness and blind vengefulness of revolutionary movements all over Europe. Religious belief was incapable of making a way in the world: it had and has no social reality. The great class compromise patched up by the Liberals, treatied with by the new Labour party, threatened by revolution in 1913, but re-confirmed in 1919 by weariness, by a natural desire to return to the peaceful summer and the garden of England they had left behind in a hot August before the Dynasties broke up, all this left a potential intelligentsia disgusted with the lies and cowardice of politicians, sceptical of the new gods of secular religions,[10] and with no way of translating highmindedness into action. Leavis pointed such a way.

The first form of his threefold importance for our social theory was more a matter of the innovation he made possible in the social relations of intellectual work. In a manner alien to Keynes and Collingwood, he changed the site on which the work took place. Partly this was a matter of his contempt not only for the obviously contemptible versions of *jeunesses dorées* who decorated King's Parade with two-seaters and the Misses Runcibles, but also for the genteel aestheticism of the entirely unshocking Bohemia living in great comfort in Mecklenburg Square.

Indeed, and less ingenuously than it sounds, Leavis put down the trivializing of metropolitan letters to the dominance of the weekly organs of cultural mass communication — the *Times Literary Supplement,* the posh weekly reviewers — by these frivolous and deracinated exquisites. What this at times reflex vituperation correctly identified was the continuing rule in culture of the old ruling class, but this time without either confidence in progress or in the significance of culture: they were the early representatives of a now impressively coherent social formation, the meaning minders of the symbolism industry who represent a cutting edge of modern capitalism[11] honed by the production systems of the electronic media — print, photography, broadcasting, storage, retrieval. Leavis spotted this tendency first and early, and he counterposed to it the determined respectability, the probity and intransigeance, the careful virtues of hard work, frugality, decorousness and unostentation allied to a flaming, darting vitality, astonishing quickness of perception, a swift and understated wittiness, and a fierce intensity of commitment to whatever human encounter was immediately before him which thrived rarely in the life of Cambridge Leavis was born into.

He was the son of a successful Cambridge piano and musical instrument dealer who held family readings of Dickens and Shakespeare on Sunday evenings. Leavis was a pupil at the Perse grammar school, Cambridge; he spent his whole life in the city. But he came to the university with a different experience, from a different social formation from that of Keynes and Collingwood. For a start, he spoke with a different class accent: not Eton, nor Rugby, but the grammar school. It is too pat to say that class simply explains this other accent, but it is a proper beginning. What is more, at the outbreak of war when Frank Leavis was only nineteen, he had shared Keynes's bravely pacifist views, but became a stretcher bearer with the Quakers' ambulances, and worked at that unbelievably grisly task with Milton in his pack until severely gassed and shell-shocked, when he moved behind the front lines to deal with clearing the wounded at the railway stations. So he came as an undergraduate with a developed sense of the emptiness of certain claims to gentility and cultivation on the part of those whose authority commanded both Cambridge and the Somme. He set himself implacably against what he knew for certain as this deathliness all his life, and he absolutely refused all the habitual and conventional politenesses of a ruling-class culture which has taught itself how to soften, blur, and incorporate all angularities and recalcitrances for over a century.

It is this resistance in the name of a quick, vivid, apprehensive intuitionism which holds together the contradiction, idiosyncrasies, wilful blindness, and self-immolation which disfigure not so much Leavis's intellectual as his social biography. The intellectual biography we may approach by way of Edwin Muir's fable:

It is clear that no autobiography can begin with a man's birth, that we extend far beyond any boundary line which we can set for ourselves in the past or the future, and that the life of every man is an endlessly repeated performance of the life of man. It is clear for the same reason that no autobiography can confine itself to conscious life, and that sleep, in which we pass a third of our existence, is a mode of experience, and our dreams a part of reality. In themselves our conscious lives may not be particularly interesting. But what we are not and can never be, our fable, seems to me inconceivably interesting. I should like to write that fable, but I cannot even live it; and all I could do if I related the outward course of my life would be to show how I have deviated from it; though even that is impossible, since I do not know the fable or anybody who knows it. One or two stages in it I can recognize: the age of innocence and the Fall and all the dramatic consequences which issue from the Fall. But these lie behind experience, not on its surface; they are not historical events; they are stages in the fable.[12]

Leavis's life is striking even among those lives summarized in this book for precisely this quality, that it may be understood as fitting unusually closely to its own, always unknowable fable. Or perhaps we may say that the history of ideas which attempts, as does this book, to reproduce the vivid aura of experience which vibrates about the ideas and brings them into visibility out of the darkness of massed events, finds in Leavis a peculiarly apposite subject. All my subjects are intended to embody, in Muir's sense of the adjective, fabulous possibilities; Leavis's fable, reconstructed in the terms made possible by the great length of his life, by its exceptional purity and intensity, by the explicitness and directness with which he faced the facts of twentieth-century life, puts him at the very heart of our mystery.

A photograph of the man in old age makes this clear. There are many of them, and in the smallish circle of what would be, in a good society, the English intelligentsia, his face is at once known from its photograph. The explicitness and directness are immediate, the gaze is intent, attentive; it is a face of piercing and instantaneous authority, more than a little frightening, as any great teacher is frightening. In the deep, resolute markings of a strikingly noble head are signals which are quickly, perhaps by some too quickly, to be understood as denoting severity, fierceness, determination.

No doubt these are all qualities amply to be found in his writings. And yet anyone who was taught by Leavis remembers him in movement, 'brushing out the door with a step characteristically sinuous, lithe, and unheeding . . . That a literary critic should have done so much to re-shape the tenor of spirit in his time, that he should have enforced on the progress of feeling much of his own unrelenting, abstract gait — the man walks in the outward guise of his thought — is, of itself, an arresting fact.'[13] And yet George Steiner, in this stylish, vivid essay on Leavis concentrates his attention on the mere unconviviality implied by Leavis's rapid walk, and the decisive march of his thought. It is as though Steiner, in spite of his own undoubted fight and his great gifts of intelligence and scholarship, cannot get over the fact that in its contained, polite way the class universities of Oxford and Cambridge gave him refuge and some respect, and having a voluble, generous nature, he took the deed for the will. He doesn't see, or doesn't name here (and elsewhere) the killing philistinism, the deadly coldness and complacency, the grim, biting graspingness of the culture whose properties include the Fellows' garden, the Chapel, the college cellar, and the Senior Common Room. And so Steiner, who ought to know so much better, fixes Leavis in the grainy stereotype of the photograph: solitary, punitive, damning, exclusive.

It is by this version of the fable that its authors sought, and largely failed, to exclude Leavis himself from, in Steiner's phrase, 'altering the inward cadence of intelligence'. To understand the peculiarly massive architecture of Leavis's achievement, we need to go back to the specific history of the Cambridge in which it was built, and the motion of the man himself in and through its groundplan.

At twenty-three, he was gassed and shellshocked; he came back to Cambridge in 1918 to write his Ph.D. on the early history of journalism suffering, like many of his contemporaries,[14] from some of the symptoms of neurasthenia, from a ruined digestion, and from acute insomnia. The digestive difficulty gave Leavis his widespread reputation for extreme austerity at the dining table, the insomnia brought from his doctor a prescription for nocturnal distance running, a sport at which Leavis had been good as a schoolboy and which was now to absorb the extreme high tension, the restlessness and the tremendous excess of nervous-physical energy which were the consequences, no doubt, both of his personality and his wartime experiences. Long-distance running is also and obviously an admirable expression of all that Leavis is;[15] it demands grace and fleetness, extraordinary dedication and stamina, an unusual fitness and the endurance of great solitude. Distance running for Leavis is indeed 'the outward guise of his thought'.

His biography for our purposes, then, begins in the trenches, and proceeds along the miles of flat, untrafficked road around Cambridge in the 1920s. It is to the point to note that he had lived there as a boy with his family and at the Grammar School, and had come neither from Eton nor from Rugby. But what is much more at issue is to recall the drastic breaks in intellectual, cultural, historical continuities which Leavis had the genius to see and the courage to force himself directly up against. Keynes saw them also, of course, but insouciantly: he patched up his economic policies precisely to tide people over the break; Collingwood saw them as well, saw them much as Leavis did, but sought to effect the repairs by a mammoth act of single-handed idealization. From the start, however, Leavis understood − or rather, saw that he would have to understand − the directly social nature (and personal because social and historical) of a momentous series of lesions in the experience and identity of culture.

Remember the circumstances. Six million dead between the ages of eighteen and thirty-nine in France. Revolution and dreadful civil war in Russia, insurrection, strikes, street warfare, as defeated Germany tried to balance the army, the social democratic party, and the revolutionary Spartacists. The chaos of the Italian economy drove Mussolini's factions more and more wildly to the right. The Balkans remained as precarious, factious, and inflammable as in 1914. The faultlines had opened wide across the great old empires − Austro-Hungarian, Ottoman, even, at the point of its widest geographical reach, the British.[16] And within a popular historiography of remorseless Eurocentrism, the modest social upheavals of Britain herself made the view plausible that the loosing of the blood-dimmed tide was indeed waiting at the next lockgate along the line. There was starvation in Scotland, northern England, Wales; there were the vast beginnings of enormous, structural unemployment; there was also the abrupt and considerable extension of the powers of government made possible by wartime production which coincided with the necessity on the part of capitalism to create the corporate industrial machine and the consumer culture to feed it, and to feed off it.

These latter processes may be said to characterize the fifty odd years up to 1975 or so;[17] they are now faltering badly, and a different crisis supervenes. After 1918 the political crisis registered itself in cultural life as an irretrievable rupture in authority. This was the profoundest disjuncture which Leavis encountered: it was the focus then of his amazing energies, energies as much of organization as inspiration, and we may use it as one key with which to unlock some of the main doors into the mansion of his thought.

To place the emphasis on 'authority' gives us a way of pushing past the obstacle so many people have found placed in their way by Leavis's determined insistence on precise and explicit judgement, and by the rhetorical mode in which he worked and which affirmed its own standards at least in part by putting down those who spoke from different standards in other camps. Historical circumstances, of which Leavis was always so profoundly conscious, required such explicitness in the conditions of the twenties. The breakdowns and disjunctures I have described initiated a loose individualism which the forces of production were rapaciously fast to capture and corral within their own, consumer fencing. Where no court, no jury, and no judge of appeal were commonly acknowledged in moral and cultural life, it followed that those who claimed for themselves both rightness and right of judgement, had to win that claim in open competition with other claimants. In part the claim was asserted by Leavis and then by his collaborators and pupils in *Scrutiny* in terms of the obvious triviality, irresponsibility, unseriousness of the opposition. It was thus and thus that the Bloomsbury group of writers — Lytton Strachey, Virginia Woolf, Bertrand Russell, the Bells, even E. M. Forster and, as we have seen, Keynes, at times — were put down. And there was justice in the judgements. For the Bloomsburyan ideology itself repudiated the notion of any larger authority than the fine cobweb of individual response to personal relationships.

In so far as Leavis's and *Scrutiny*'s commitment was to the re-establishment of a community of values, sanctions, and pieties capable of commanding the individual's allegiance as well as answering his intelligence, then it was inevitable that he should attack with such fierce courage the greenery-yellery offspring of Bloomsbury's and Cambridge's graduands whose class and property privilege gave them columns in genteel journalism where they could celebrate their own subjectivity for a modest public salary.

Given his view of a responsibility to a life larger than the individual's own, he was bound by the integrity which was such a main principle of his mode of inquiry to name mere cultivation as the pretentiousness, strictly, it is. To advance cultivation, civilization, and other tokens of the aesthetics of consciousness as authoritative standards in the cultural life, is to dignify as values the surface advantages of class position. This was not, however, how Leavis rebutted the claims of Old Corruption at Oxford and Cambridge. Even Mrs. Leavis, when she scoffed at Virginia Woolf, in a memorably biting review-article[18] was not primarily making a point about class. '"Daughters of educated men have always done their thinking from hand to mouth . . . They have thought while they stirred the pot, while they rocked the cradle. It was thus that they won us the right," etc. I agree with someone who complained that to judge from the acquaintance with the realities of life displayed in this book there is no reason to suppose Mrs. Woolf would know which end of the cradle to stir.'

Mrs Leavis is intent far less upon the social structure and all, than upon the relations of intelligence to experience, and of both to that elusive but essential standard of authority in the Leavises' work, 'life'.

For Leavis knew, as a function of the really astonishing vitality of his intelligence, that somewhere in the dense arrangements of social life, a thinker would touch the mystery by which culture and structure, consciousness and being, issued in new, vivid life. His strenuous, sixty-year search was for the strong shaping spirit which informed that life, and to pursue that search he insisted on rejecting all the conceptual frameworks which had about them the look of the readymade, the mechanical or the partisan. Hence his rejection of a world of Bloomsburyan personal relationships, precisely because it seemed to him poisoned by all that is meant by the accurate word, modishness. Hence also his no less fierce attack on the mechanical and deterministic vocabulary of Marxism, or Marxism as thought aloud by Trotsky in his pamphleteering vein and by the private-school communists at Oxford and Cambridge. Leavis, we may say schematically, built together a Romantic metaphysics, a Kantian ethics, and a liberal politics, but in doing so he proscribed vehemently the terms we might too readily advance in order to understand and order this assemblage. He will have nothing to do either with the drawing-room implications of exquisiteness and cultivation (nowadays translated into the strident status-symbolisms of Harrod's window-dressing) nor with the larger and more terrible depredations of what he elaborately reformulated not as 'consumer capitalism' but as 'technologico-Benthamite civilization'. He refused the former term because its earlier provenance was the Marxism he hated for its narrow, self-righteous determinism, its simplifyingly mechanical cranking out of a social analysis, the murderous brutality Leavis saw first and clearest in its most powerful advocacy, Bolshevism. The analysis and the resistance began, he understood, from unprecedented historical conditions; if the enemy was not to be victorious, a novel historiography had to be constructed capable of bringing a new past to bear upon an unintelligible present. The lesson, as we have seen, is Collingwood's; but we may relevantly understand Leavis's achievement if we think of him, rather than Collingwood and quite without incongruity on either side, as the English Hegel.

What does such a claim intend? First, it confirms Leavis's profound historicality of mind; as I say, he knew that in the new century, the recovery of continuity could only be won by a different account of historical development and by devising a new theory of action for individual intelligence. He placed personal creativity in a tragic social movement. Second, Leavis may be compared to Hegel not in his ardent idealism, which is unimportant for our purposes, but in making the infinite practices of language the ground of being; and taking literary language as his tiny segment of the totality of linguistic practices, he developed a mode of analysis capable of application to all others. In this, of course, he was part of the mainstream of the human sciences in the twentieth century, but the large coherence of his work was such that his learning and borrowing from I. A. Richards and William Empson as well as from the more informal asides in T. S. Eliot's critical notebooks were integrated into a praxis whose grand ambition was to understand social action as a text in which value was created or destroyed inasmuch as the language of the text sprang from sources of being either quick or dead.[19]

Thirdly and as a consequence of the central place given to language not so much as a methodological category nor as a medium of expression but rather as the terrain of intersubjectivity, or what Leavis came to call 'in my unphilosophical way' 'the third realm',[20] Leavis was obliged to develop his own phenomenology of being, one capable of embodying the vitalism which was the cue to life.

Heidegger's terminology — in *Being and Time* above all — comes readily to mind when thinking of Leavis, and it is true that Leavis faced as absolutely and nakedly as he could the existential questions which Heidegger searched to answer in his great essay. But Leavis cuts right across either the Heideggerian or the Hegelian forms of definition and thought by the closeness and particularity of his attention to the concrete. It is this which makes him central to the hermeneutic of twentieth-century social inquiry and directs us, ultimately, towards its post-liberal forms. One version of this particularity of attention comes out in an example of his many attempts to demonstrate (either by definition or by assertion, but still validly) creative life in example.

What Blake represents is the new sense of human responsibility that we may reasonably see as the momentous gain accruing to the heritage — to be taken up (that is) in the creative continuity — from among the diverse manifestations of profound change that are brought together under 'Romanticism'. The Blakean sense of human responsibility is as much the antithesis of the defiant Byronic hubris as it is of the hubris of technologico-positivist enlightenment. It goes with a realization that without creativity there is no apprehension of the real, but that if experience is necessarily creative, the creativity — as every great artist testifies — is not arbitrary; it is a Doyce-like self-dedication to a reality that we have to discover, knowing that discovery will at best be qualified by misapprehension and certainly incomplete. Our reality couldn't be 'there' for us without collaborative creation, but it is not an achievement to be credited to creative human selfhood (an essential contradiction) — or to coagulated egos.[21]

In a characteristically local and perhaps parochial way, he goes on to counterpose Blake not to capitalist (or consumer) society, but to 'technologico-Benthamism', to those immanent tendencies of industrial processes which reproduce in individual lives the hateful, trivial, inhuman mechanization of response, thought, and value inscribed ineradicably in the systems of production themselves. The diagnosis in this foreshortened form is shared with Marxism, and so is Leavis's *totalizing* of the social field of force under research. Each individual life is caught up in the structure of the dominant cultural energy. But it is precisely by his use of the word 'culture' that he opposes Marxism, and this 'because of the need to dwell on what it is that makes Blake so important'. He goes on (p. 14)

The sense of human responsibility as he represents it is inimical to what is commonly meant by 'humanism' in our technologico-Benthamite world. Genius for him is a peculiar intensity and strength of representativeness: the artist's developed, conscious and skilled creativity is continuous with the creativity inseparable, he insists, from perception itself, and from all human experience and knowledge. Of its nature it can't be wilful and gratuitous — that is, irresponsible; though it may (or will) in this or that way fall short, achieving at best a limited rightness, it is always concerned for the real. To be creative in the artist's way is implicitly to assert responsibility, and Blake's distinction is to be fully conscious of that — to recognize unhesitatingly the nature of the responsibility resting on man; resting on himself.

Yet, while he was so far clear in his certainties, and though he was incapable of hubris, his thought ran out into a region where thought and imagination must necessarily incur defeat; he undertood what couldn't be done, and, in attempting it, was lost in the wordy generality that covers contradiction and confusion.

Marxism is rejected in the name of that representative creativeness which Marx's predecessors in the Romantic movement spoke for, but which in Leavis's analysis is destroyed by all the deadening and herded associations carried by the mechanical vocabulary of politics, whether politics is a matter of the power of classes, masses, or tyrants, or whether it is a matter of the grim exigencies of production.

Leavis, I am arguing, dissolved the category of politics.[22] He did so in order to insist upon the domain of morality as coterminous with that of both politics and aesthetics, and further as conceptually superordinate to both. His project was to vindicate a politics of letters as the type of the city of reason. Newman's idea of a university was rewritten as a republic of culture. Politics as a category is expelled under the high pressure of a dual voluntarism. On the first hand, Leavis wishes to assert the paramountcy of the Blakean-Wordsworthian-Dickensian-Lawrentian individual, brave, free, responsible to life and life's integrity, and to acclaim such a hero against the threats of acquisitive practices, mechanical structures and bureaucratic institutions. On the other hand, he wants to reimagine for the present a community of values and beliefs in which common destiny and not private interest is the measure of significance, and in which meaning and significance transpire from actions not in a social (and therefore class) dimension, but in a metaphysical one. Hence his lifelong preoccupation with the nature and conditions of 'community' itself, a preoccupation shared in one language (or discourse) after another, as the serious thinkers of Europe — Tönnies, Simmel, Marx, Durkheim, Dickens, Proust, Weber, Tolstoy — all addressed themselves to the mammoth displacements of the new industrial order, and its twin, mighty engines of production and capital.

Leavis is no innocent. In his early attention to the conditions of community, he invokes the self-explanatory order of pre-industrial society in the broad simplifications appropriate to a sixth-form textbook:[23]

Sturt's villagers expressed their human nature, they satisfied their human needs, in terms of the natural environment; and the things they made — cottages, barns, ricks and waggons — together with their relations with one another constituted a human environment, and a subtlety of adjustment and adaptation, as right and inevitable.

This brief cartoon of community in which all members are, in a key word, 'organically' related, may serve to signal a subject and object to which Leavis returned again and again exactly because the image and symbol of community were central to his social theory and to his method of inquiry. He knows, as did the William Morris he has read many times, that medieval or Elizabethan world-pictures and social orders are irrecoverable (*'Don't mistake me'* [he says] 'I am not preaching that we should defy, or try to reverse, the accelerating movement of external civilization . . . that is determined by advancing technology'[24] — my italics.) Their significance is that they provide a ready structure of reference against which to test the present.

There are numerous critics of Leavis's use of the notion of 'organic community', and it is not my business to rebut them here. An inevitably dominant feature of industrial capitalism has been its placelessness and the helpless mobility of its labour forces. When this deracination is allied to the collapse, at least in capitalism's heartlands, of a credible theology and to the disappearance of God, it is hardly surprising that the social theorists who sought, as we have noted, to understand the world scientifically in conceptual relation to enabling men and women to live good and just lives in that world, turned and returned to the theory and practice of community.

Leavis's examples of community are many, and immediately practical: it is in his strong sense of and feeling for many different varieties of English provincial life that he most successfully allies idealist to materialist analysis, and insists not on the reconciliation of an antinomy but on the mutual embedding of the two in the practical, social relations of culture and being, value and experience. His examples of a strong culture working through a community go well beyond the use he and Thompson make of George Sturt[25] in *Culture and Environment*. The communities he instances include Bunyan's Puritan congregation in Bedford, the irresistible pull of the Mercantile Marine and the training ship *Conway* for the nomadic, Francophone Polish exile Joseph Conrad, the 'comfort, well-being, and amenity'[26] whose solid domesticity is part of the larger, rich and robust Mississippi culture which Mark Twain celebrates in *Pudd'nhead Wilson*. And elsewhere, naturally, Leavis examines the conditions of court, city and country which gave the two greatest periods of English literature their distinctive language and form, and issued in the work of that literature's two greatest writers: Shakespeare and Dickens. But it is perhaps in his championing and exposition of the work of D. H. Lawrence that he most brilliantly locates a special and representative genius in the process of social formation which made Lawrence what he was, and without which the novels and poems are only partly intelligible. He speaks indeed of our immeasurable good fortune that Lawrence was born in Eastwood, Nottinghamshire, in 1885, at just the moment when members of a newly self-discovering working class were still countrymen enough, living on their untidy mixture of farmland and coalmine, to know in detail the garden flowers and vegetables, the bees, wild life and wild flowers, the bits of farms, of a once agrarian way of life, at the same time as they began to understand and organize the demanding, dangerous, poverty-racked but close-textured, fraternal life of men at work down in the coalpits. Refusing the language of either Fabian or Marxist, Leavis is under no obligation to name the Lawrence family as members of an oppressed proletariat. Thus he can describe[27] the local culture and domestic way of life as intensely civilized in terms of its natural piety (the Nonconformist church), the seriousness and relevance to living of its education (the Miners' Institute library, the University of Nottingham and the passion for literature Lawrence recollects among cultivated local friends in his letters), the closeness of work to home and of both to hardship, to the natural mutual interdependence of the working poor, to the presence of danger down the pits.

Leavis makes very active play with this perfectly unsentimental contextualizing of Lawrence's art and thought. It is not to rebut such claims to point out Lawrence's own hatred of the ugliness of Nottingham and the mining countryside[28] or his hot, scathing animus against chapel sanctimonies and the genteel traditions of his womenfolk. It is Leavis's view that the essential structures of his culture made such an expression of it as Lawrence's (even in, perhaps most of all in, his fierce criticisms of it) what it was. For Lawrence, like the very different but incomparably great writers to whom Leavis links him — Shakespeare, Bunyan, Blake, Dickens, Twain, Conrad — found a 'knowable community',[29] a living language, an infinitely delicate balance of purity and danger[30] for the life of the spirit and of the body, and the unification of all these in a morality whose peculiar grounds cancelled the necessity of politics by making its creative individuals members one of another, and examples of potentiality to a whole society. Working from these examples of cultural health ideal for the expression of creativity made it possible to escape both the narcissism of Bloomsbury's personal relationships and the ponderously mechanical forms of Marxist determinism as argued in England in the twenties and thirties.

Leavis, we have noted, experiences right through his being and biography the lacerations of discontinuity. He saw that the grounds of morality were hugely shifted by the advent of Romanticism, and that the piercing beauty of personal spontaneity and the solid strength of communal and religious values were for ever set at odds. He also saw that happy accident and human will could create a moment in which culture and creativity moved in a common rhythm, and reanimated the promise of happiness: his great spokesmen had found and made such moments. That is why Leavis's attention turned so closely to the novel. Leavis's novelists spoke both the language of science and the language of religion. The careful, expository mode which prose enforces required them to exhibit in great detail the phenomenology of moral puzzlement and self-examination. That is, they have to recognize the loss of a moral framework which would make possible prescriptive and universalizable maxims, and follow the moral agent through doubt, and often tragedy, in all the immediacy which a fiction enforces. At the same time, the moral agent who is the hero or heroine of the novel picks a way through the intersubjective reality which it is the novelist's business as scientist to record as objectively as possible. The epistemology of such a process hardly answers some of the more glib classifications enjoined upon Leavis. They include, of course, 'idealist' and 'petty-bourgeois', but they also, and more confusingly, include both empiricism and logical positivism.[31] Set aside for the moment whether these terms are quite so straightforwardly the swear-words their authors suppose them to be, and it remains true that the connection between his ontology and his ethics, while essential to his picture of the real — he certainly seeks for a valid historical naturalism, but then so do many intelligent men — does not answer quite so ingenuously to this rollcall of intellectual misdemeanour. One of the strengths of his doughty refusal to practise technical philosophy is that he requires himself to think without the terminology and its defining concepts of any one too decisive an epistemology. As I have argued, Leavis collapses politics into morality, and grounds both on a naturalist field.[32]

It is my argument here, however, that this dissolution is not, as

Mulhern would have it, an intellectual evasion and a conceptual impossibility, but is precisely the meaning of Leavis's significance for the human sciences. The triple movement of his thought starts from its epistemology as set in the concrete encounter with the text, and proceeds to the insistence that this encounter perpetually re-enacts the essential process whereby human values recreate, criticize, and confirm themselves, a process without which a society's spirit can only wilt and die; thirdly and lastly the spiral of this dynamic carries on in the best individuals the search to establish the continuities and the disjunctures between educated and customary forms of life.

To describe both the structure and energy of Leavis's thought in this way is to push his significance well beyond the limits of English studies in the university. And this was indeed his ambition. His system of interpretation was intended to pose literature as the type and supreme example of 'methodological self-consciousness'[33] in order to connect the means of intellectual understanding with the discovery of meaning in the totality of our experience of the world.

To do so, in the world as he found it, was to return to the domain of politics, although according to his own, highly idiosyncratic version. (It is the last, clinching point of comparison with Hegel.) For at the heart of his theory of interpretation — the unremitting interrogation of experience for its meaning — is the celebrated exchange, 'This is so, isn't it?' 'Yes, but . . .' And even if the interlocutor rejoins, 'Well, no . . .' the necessary politeness has, as always, its political cadence. For what Leavis inspired and inspires was membership of a party; like any political visionary, he drew a picture of the ideal community, and his collaborators and vanguard — in Mrs Leavis's stirring phrase, the 'armed and conscious minority' — saw themselves as an intellectual guerrilla, working to keep such a vision and the hope it nourishes alive in a bad age.

The tense of Leavis's hermeneutic is imperative. To practise the study of human behaviour according to its method, it is necessary to do something. That 'something to do' has logically turned out to be, 'teach'. To teach according to *Scrutiny's* procedures and methods is, therefore, to do more than pick up a legacy. It is to seek not only to take part in, but radically to inflect the entire conversation of a culture. The human encounter — 'This is so . . .' — implies a radical equality and a no less radical range. The material (*sic*) upon which the conversation plays is the material of a whole culture, and a whole culture is interrogated for its meaning, popular and elite, live and dead.

INTERVAL

6

Practice Against Theory: George Orwell and Adrian Stokes

In the first chapter I summarized certain main habits of the English mind, which included an instinctive recourse to concrete examples in argument, a calm refusal of formal metaphysics, a sometimes reflex resistance to other people's 'over-abstraction', and a general preference for non-systematized or pluralist theories of political life. I offered these in no spirit of chauvinist self-congratulation; for all that they have been examined as they transpire in the work of deeply impressive and original native thinkers, their weaknesses signify more than a matter of a stylistic tendency to philistinism or provincialism. In Leavis's case the personal biography intrudes much too deeply into the method: his insistence on excluding formal theory from literary criticism, on thrusting philosophy out of its doors, on so bitingly repelling the genteel advances of literary history as professed by the Oxford stepsister to *Scrutiny, Essays in Criticism*, are all intellectual manoeuvres twisted out of shape by Leavis's battle to establish *Scrutiny*'s procedures as a discipline, and by the consequent depth of his subject-loyalty and its irresistible power to form intellectual and personal identity as enjoined by the discipline. The extraordinary compellingness of this process — given the central personality and the historical occasion, its inevitability — worked with a strange, contradictory force, which can in one diagram be ingenuously but fairly represented as a political contradiction. That is, Leavis's work and the 'moment' of *Scrutiny* energized two opposite political pulls — to the Left and to the Right. Cultural theorists on the right took, comfortably enough, to the theory of deturpation, to the long slide of cultural standards, to the exploitation of folk aesthetics, above all to the defence of themselves as minority defenders of Arnoldian faith. Theorists on the left, whom we shall follow later took to heart the radical critique of mass culture, the phenomenology of alienation from self and meaning brought about by industrialization and the ruin of a speakable language, the commitment to and absolute, continuing identification with what, in one of his best and most bracing phrases, he called 'the inevitable creativeness of ordinary everyday life'. It was the deep contradiction of his life that its conditions in the peculiarities of English class and academically stifled life at Cambridge sent him to find that 'inevitable creativeness' only in great books (where it undoubtedly is) and not also in everyday (where it also keeps unrepentantly on).

The theorists of the Left took his admonition. The quick and the dead are divided in everyday life much as they are in books. But in seeing the method that way, they walked too much in parallel with as well as in negation to their enemies. What became the issue was who was in and who was out, and although a particular way of organizing such a competition — Blake not Swift, Dickens not James, Lawrence not Eliot — itself adumbrates the larger cultural meanings and their ontology, it has been the competitive judging which has been absorbed into the practices of our cultural life.

It is not this method and its truthfulness which the last chapter was concerned to establish. The heroes of a new hermeneutics followed Green and Morris (and by implication criticized both Mill and Marx) in breaking with the old, massive thought-forms of Cartesian and Kantian epistemology. Keynes grounded his working instruments in his brilliant sketch of a moral science, *The Treatise on Probability.* Collingwood rejected the positivists' and realists' history in the name of a dialectical historicism. Leavis clinched these advances by refusing the theory of knowledge as his domain, and moving ultimately to the recognition that the mode of thought he sought to recover from his choice of great writers in their works acted as radical dissolver of the epistemological thought-forms shaped decisively by the drastic changes of the seventeenth century, to determining whose significance he had given his life's thought, and for the complexity of which one name is that of Descartes. He brings this out in one classic statement in his last book but one, a statement whose clarity and finesse together with the plenitude of its utterance has about it something of the kind of great poetry he commends as a way out of the dead end into which scientism in the service of the market has driven us — the deadly 'technologico-Benthamism'.

All major literary creation is concerned with thought. That is a constatation the force of which I have tried to make plain in a discussion of one of the world's great novels, *Little Dorrit.* In that work, as the challenged critique must aim at bringing out, Dickens, making a characteristically profound, and necessarily creative, inquest into society in his time, tackles in sustained and unmistakably deliberate thought the basic unstatable that eludes the logic of cartesian clarity — and of philosophic discourse too. Taking it as granted that life is the artist's concern, he develops in full pondering consciousness the un-Cartesian recognition that, while it is 'there' only in individual lives, it *is* there, and *its being* there makes them lives: what the word 'life' represents, and evokes, is not to be disposed of under the rubric of 'hypostatization', or collectivity, or linguistic convenience.

Emphasizing the affinity between Dickens and Blake, I point out how the scheme implicit in the cast of sharply different main personae who interact in *Little Dorrit* applies an equivalent of Blake's distinction between the 'selfhood' and the 'identity'. Making and enforcing this point is inseparable from observing how Dickens' art insists on creativity as the characteristic of life. The selfhood asserts its rights, and possesses, from within its egocentric self-enclosure; the identity is the individual being as the focus of life — life as heuristic energy, creativity, and, from the human person's point of view, disinterestedness. It is impossible to doubt that Dickens, like Blake, saw the creativity of the artist as continuous with the general human creativity that, having created the human world we live in, keeps it renewed and real. This day-to-day work of collaborative creation includes the creating of language, without which there couldn't have been a human world. In language, as I have said, the truth I will refer to as 'life and lives', the basic unstatable which, lost to view and left out, disables any attempt to think radically about human life, is most open to recognition and most invites it.

One can say with pregnant brevity that the achievement of the aim in vigorous established practice would be a potent emergence from the Cartesian dualism. 'Potent' here means fruitful in positive consequences. A new realization of the nature and the pervasiveness of creativity in life and thought would be fostered; there is nothing that the world in our time more desperately needs.[1]

This remarkable passage may be seen to connect this second part of my book with the third by means of a short excursus. For Leavis summarizes much of the previous twenty years of his work — the quoted chapter is sprinkled with examples from earlier essays. What that summary connotes is the explicit refusal to practice the conventional modes of philosophy, particularly as that has concentrated on epistemology. What Leavis insists upon is a theme which, on the view of this book, richly transpires from the best intellectual-cultural discourse of his society as well as, on a less fervently patriotic basis, from the best such discourse spoken latterly in German by Jurgen Habermas, in

French by Maurice Merleau-Ponty, and in American by (among others) Wilfred Sellars, Donald Davidson, Lionel Trilling, and — on whom so much of what I say reposes — Clifford Geertz.[2]

Leavis's theme has been orchestrated by many disciplinarians in a number of academic centres for the past half a century. It states that the wholesale revision of intellectual frames of mind which took place in the seventeenth century sundered inquiry from evidence and fact from value; that this established the methodological dualism of which Leibniz and Descartes were the first, tremendous theorists; that the first stages of the road towards the enormous and irresistible success of technology and pharmacology were then constructed; but that the very high cost of this grand new intellectual structure was that the field of universals shrank into the tiny corner allotted to the human sensibility, and that the consequent treatment by scientists of human beings as so many physical objects among others prevented the sciences of man from keeping any kind of pace with the conceptual advance of the natural sciences. If Collingwood's 'science of human affairs' had used the past century adequately, there might have been a political economy capable of forestalling world wars.

To blame Descartes for the human world so signally failing to take the right and royal road to reason when Galileo and Harvey and Bacon and company launched the new advancement of learning is to foreshorten history, simplify individual will, and flatten the real corrugations of ideas with an awful vengeance, and real history always does take vengeance upon the simple-minded, since they never know when to get out of its way. Nevertheless, the importance of being radically earnest is that to be so is a way of avoiding even the most impressive formulae of physicalism, behaviourism, or other versions of the treating of human experience as scientific object. Don't mistake this. There have been indispensable gains from such treatment; medicine and its associate, dietetics, are only the most obvious fields. But the success of the method has convinced human scientists too readily of its universalizability; the English school of cultural theorists is not the only, but it is the most accessible, the most detailed and attractive of those who have spoken for a different model of inquiry.

It is no accident that Leavis is a literary critic and (however he would have disliked the designation) an aesthetician. Keynes, economist, Collingwood, historian, Leavis, critic, all deal unmistakably in the concrete practices of social life, but as we have seen, Leavis drew idealism and materialism tightly together; he most of all insisted upon the livingness (spirituality, if you like) of the cultural object, its concrete actuality. His insistence on confronting the object as living can go, no doubt, the wrong way. You may, for instance, in a fashionable but useful expression, 'deconstruct the practice',[3] or you may meet it as a living individual, and, as Leavis did, seek to listen to it and understand it in much the same way.

The attempt to live intellectual practice, and to transcribe experience directly into theory is always open to charges of ingenuousness, at best, and at worst leads to the worst of English casual academic rumination, a form of writing which may possess the merit of intelligibility and informality but which is disastrously apt to exclude any more technical, ambitious or even rhetorical language as windy metaphysics or mere jargon. Lived experience, to say it again, is not something you can even identify without some conceptual focus capable of bringing events within a signifying frame. Conversely, as in Marx's phrase on Darwin, the 'crude English' practice has always insisted, to theorize in direct relation to experience is at least to avoid the arid frightfulness of certain of the more abstract social theorists across the waters of both Channel and Atlantic. The difficulty is successfully to mix all metaphors, to tread the line between, to eat both cakes and have them.

George Orwell (1903–1950) serves both a chronological and a structural purpose. His best essays, written between about 1936 when he returned wounded in the throat from the Spanish Civil War and an essay like 'Decline of the English Murder' published in 1946 just after the Labour party came triumphantly to power at the end of the war,[4] coincide with and then succeed the best years of *Scrutiny,* and the years in which the three champions, Keynes, Collingwood and Leavis, brought some of their main theories to completion. Orwell serves neatly as a hinge to join the political economy and the cultural theory of the three giants of liberalism to their post-second-war successors, and the very much more exiguous and attenuated models of man with which the latecomers had to make shift. Orwell's chronological significance anticipates his structural one. Setting his cultural insights in an explicitly political and economic context, he exemplifies exactly the procedure Collingwood and Leavis enjoined: he inquired after the meaning of an unusually wide range of important but intellectually neglected human activities and asked for that meaning so that he could ascribe to it, or better, discover in it, a human value.

At that point political and moral economy coincide. I do not claim that he was influenced by *Scrutiny,* and his primitive fair-play economics could not begin to engage with the subtleties of Keynes's machinery. All the same, the simplicity and power of Orwell's method was that he was able to situate his cultural inquiry in a frame of values whose provenance was both political and economic, and the one because the other.

It is, at first, the simplicity which is so attractive. Orwell has not so much taken to heart as taken for granted that social theory and social criticism are one and the same practice, and that there need be no long expository detour through theory, nor even what I have understood as Leavis's highly theoretic refusal of theory in identifying the sources of life and death in the culture. He begins from the facts of oppression and the complementary motions of cruelty and passivity which those dry facts endlessly reanimate. He goes on to search for the occasional but inextinguishable surges of resistance, libertarianism and creativity which continuously prevent power having everything its own way. He identifies these in the small endearing practices of everyday life, in both work and home. Momentarily, he experienced his brief service with the volunteer and communist workers' militia (the POUM) in Spain as one inevitably shortlived but vaster movement of creativity and resistance to the flattening irresistibility of totalitarian power rolling across the twentieth century. Later, he saw the best of England herself, of British luck and culture, as a mysterious, opaque, and compelling image, inspiring both reverence and courage in the fight against the two dreadful wings of the bird of the future, Fascism and Stalinism. By Orwell's end, the shadow of the bird settles over all, until and beyond 1984.

He came to this end from beginnings whose central contradiction prefigured the simple, telling diagrams which he drew of politics during his best years. His importance for this interlude is the clarity with which he derives valuations from values, and sets both in the bodily world. His shortcomings are as personal as they are intellectual: he starts from the exceeding simplification of his autobiography and supposes that of itself it will generate a theoretic understanding capable of being carried by the vocabulary, the honest, direct, barbarian and class-bound diction of the public school sweatroom.

His biography[5] is even more plainly the key to his thought than usual. And yet to say so is in this book likely to cause misprision. The really astonishing singularity of men as unalike in intellectual style and personal experience as William Morris or Robin Collingwood is the strength of selfhood which is made manifest in their writing. It is the strength of which Wallace Stevens writes:

Three times the concentred self takes hold, three times
The thrice concentred self, having possessed

The object, grips it in savage scrutiny,
Once to make captive, once to subjugate
Or yield to subjugation, once to proclaim
The meaning of the capture, this hard prize,
Fully made, fully apparent, fully found.[6]

Even this, in its vigorous, innocent representation of the all-powerful mind seizing the recalcitrant object is altogether too Cartesian an image for comfort. Orwell is certainly a strong corrective to that opposition; where he fails is in supposing that the intuitive truths of his experience will do the work of thought for him.

It is easy to see why he did, for he began with inestimably awful advantages. He was born in 1903 to a family whose father was in the Indian Civil Service and, as Orwell mentions, one of the genteelly impoverished middle class, much of whose life in England was an always faltering effort to maintain the maidservant, the bric-a-brac, and the prestige which only the vacant, transplanted Wimbledons of the plains of India made possible. He went to Eton, but as a scholarship boy, and he joined the Imperial Police at the age of nineteen.

He left it after five years service, largely in Burma. This, and his subsequent response to his experience as a policeman of imperialism is a well-known and honourable part of the subsequent mythologizing of Orwell in official English culture. In a strong movement of revulsion from the system of imperialism, he resigned his police commission, and went slumming. The phrase offers itself. Boys from Eton had gone to work with the poor in East End settlements backed with College money for several decades. They had gone, doubtless, with many and mixed motives, and the help was needed anyway. Orwell went, characteristically, further than any of them, and went not to help, but to find out; and less, perhaps, to find out, than in a literal sense to be impressed, to receive impressions, hence his calculatedly impressionistic writing. Above all, he went to experience the same sort of oppression and poverty as those whose poverty he had himself confirmed and oppressed while an imperial policeman, and done so with an ambivalence not without relish.

It is too pat a piece of kitchen psychoanalysis to say he sought to exorcise his guilt at having held what he judged by then to be an entirely demeaning office. Indeed, he recognizes this likelihood himself more than once, quite apart from *knowing* how strongly he felt guilty, as he admits in the essay 'Shooting an Elephant'. It seems more accurate to say that he became a destitute in order to live as intensely as he could the degradation, the noisome, smelly helplessness of those which something in his class formation prevented his ever quite exonerating, not from responsibility for their own condition, but from being quite so horribly impervious to it.

The open contradiction is obvious: the old Etonian imperial police officer becomes first a temporary derelict and then a worker militiaman. The deeper contradiction strains all the plain, blunt prose to breaking point: it vibrates in the tension between his effort not so much to live classlessly, to confront as openly and directly as he could (as Leavis at his greatest could), the experience of others, but rather to enter the lives of the wretched and oppressed while still pitilessly drawing back from them. This is the contradiction which, Orwell being a serious and honest man, is the source of that unlikeable remoteness recollected by all those members of the working class on whom he came to report — in, for instance, the unforgettably titled *The Road to Wigan Pier*.[7] Many of those who knew him on his visits to Lancashire still speak of his humourless distance from other people, his taciturn gloom, his solitariness. And this angularity, this reluctance to commit himself to friendship or even to passion, reappeared in his more everyday relationships.[8]

The moments at which this natural solitariness rises to direct, glad warmth are those at which Orwell feels, and makes us feel, his always transient entry into forms of historical life or cultural expression in which the shape of this immense, yearning desire for membership of an institution which is not irrevocably poisoned by the English class wounds and obstructions, finds its fulfilment in actuality. Such moments do not really transpire even when he stands admiringly before the physical splendour and stamina of the coal-miners in 'Down the Mine'[9] since although the admiration is given readily, it is given obliquely: Orwell's characteristic, willed failure of membership leads him to start from a comparison of his own flabby and puny strengths with the beauty of the stereotypical hero-worker:

They really do look like iron — hammered iron statues — under the smooth coat of coal dust which clings to them from head to foot. It is only when you see miners down the mine and naked that you realise what splendid men they are. Most of them are small (big men are at a disadvantage in that job) but nearly all of them have the most noble bodies; wide shoulders tapering to slender supple waists, and small pronounced buttocks and sinewy thighs, with not an ounce of waste flesh anywhere. (p. 25)

It is idealized, perhaps rightly so; it has something of the memorability of a statuesque, political cartoon or poster, as has this, the weakness of which comes out if we compare it with the much drier, more inward and knowledgeable manner of Richard Hoggart describing the working class interiors he remembers. Orwell's working-class kitchen is as yearningly admired from outside as his pitman.

In a working-class home — I am not thinking at the moment of the unemployed, but of comparatively prosperous homes — you breath a warm, decent, deeply human atmosphere which it is not so easy to find elsewhere. I should say that a manual worker, if he is in steady work and drawing good wages — an "if" which gets bigger and bigger — has a better chance of being happy than an "educated" man. His home life seems to fall more naturally into a sane and comely shape. I have often been struck by the peculiar easy completeness, the perfect symmetry as it were, of a working-class interior at its best. Especially on winter evenings after tea, when the fire glows in the open range and dances mirrored in the steel fender, when Father, in shirt-sleeves, sits in the rocking chair at one side of the fire reading the racing finals, and Mother sits on the other with her sewing, and the children are happy with a pennorth of mint humbugs, and the dog lolls roasting himself on the rag mat — it is a good place to be in, provided that you can be not only in it but sufficiently *of* it to be taken for granted.[10]

The failure is more than personal; the trouble with this method is that it isn't sufficiently methodical. It lacks the inexhaustibly patient attentiveness which, on Leavis's account, transpires as 'sincerity'. Sincerity is the guarantor of reality, and neither Orwell's kitchen nor his pitman are real.

Attentiveness is itself too tricky a thing to define a method. In conventional usage, it betokens a cast of mind and face of a rather bespectacled, heavily gazing and portentous kind. Here it portends a way of seeing (after looking) and of faithfully transcribing what is seen. In Orwell's case, he looks determinedly for those things which the class from which he has resigned is determined not to see. He is looking for the negation of his class culture.

This looking frames what counts for him as experience, and inasmuch as culture defines itself, at once materially and spiritually, as the formal practices and expressions of a society's productions and creations, then Orwell writes defiantly from his experience of the cultures of the working class, the oppressed, the poor and wretched, the unofficial and unheroic.

Consequently he has, partly in spite of and partly because of his partiality, a heroic place on the fulcrum of this book. He understands intuitively the dialectical nature of any cultural or aesthetic inquiry; that is, it is only possible, as Collingwood's 'question-and-answer logic' shows us, to understand actions if you ask what they were reactions to. Like any strong, original mind, he knows he must re-interpret what is in front of him to suit the relatively new history which swirls all about him. Under the bent to this tendency given by his simple political economy, he commits himself to the re-interpretation of a potentially socialist culture, taking as examples whatever came to his hand. The enterprise is something like Trotsky's in *Literature and Revolution,* where Trotsky argues for the necessary re-interpretation of the splendour of Russian literature, and against the hard new men's tearing down of the giants from Pushkin to Mandelstam. But Orwell had none of Trotsky's all-confident theory, and had seen and judged before anyone else the foulness and lies which that theory had instructed art to tell. So he turned back, with deliberate limitedness, to what he had seen and lived, and made it tell a simple story.

That story is best told in *Homage to Catalonia,*[11] his account of the Spanish Civil War and his time there as a militiaman. In writing of that episode, Orwell is able to bring together his brave resolve to embody socialist practice and to find a membership in which that practice may be mutually believable, as well as his determination to resist the conventional political history as written by the rulers. The Spanish Civil War gave actuality to his desires, and briefly offered a bright, white-and-black silhouette which fitted neatly over Orwell's naive politics. That is what it is like to find a subject. Working from the grain of his life as a soldier in an always ill-equipped, incompetent, but deeply fraternal army, he reports in vivid detail the sporadic, badly organized engagements, the beauty of the landscape, the cold and wet, and, presenting with what is at his best an incomparable truthfulness the facts of the matter, allows those facts to make their own order, and quite without pressing them too hard, to rise into a political exposition. Even when he leaves the front and becomes tangled in the duplicities and brutalities of inter-Left quarrels, Orwell hardly ever lapses into that spiteful vilification of what in other moods he endorses, a lapse which so confuses much of his writing. Ultimately this led him to the undoubtedly powerful but hopelessly over-determined pessimism of *1984; Homage to Catalonia* embodies Orwell at his methodical best.

I cannot really offer it here as the next text book on my syllabus. The terms of the Spanish Civil War, like those of any war, are so apt to the collapsing of politics into morality which liberalism comfortably favours, that (at this safe distance from the bullets) support of the virtuous Left becomes merely pat. Social theory is better exemplified in Orwell's work by such essays as 'Charles Dickens', 'Decline of the English Murder', 'Raffles and Miss Blandish', and 'The Art of Donald McGill'. These are essays in popular culture, and in them Orwell is able to start from the literary provenance by which as a writer and bellelettriste and upperclass journalist, he was intellectually shaped, and then in the name of elementary radicalism, to turn its terms upside down in order to show the real decency and human recognizability hidden in this neglected corner of popular art.

What you are really looking at is something as traditional as Greek tragedy, a sort of sub-world of smacked bottoms and scrawny mothers-in-law which is part of Western European consciousness. Not that the jokes, taken one by one, are necessarily stale. Not being debarred from smuttiness, comic post cards repeat themselves less often than the joke columns in reputable magazines, but their basic subject-matter, the kind of joke they are aiming at, never varies. A few are genuinely witty, in a Max Millerish style. Examples:
"I like seeing experienced girls home."
"But I'm not experienced!"
"You're not home yet!"

"I've been struggling for years to get a fur coat. How did you get yours?"
"I left off struggling."

Judge: "You are prevaricating, sir. Did you or did you not sleep with this woman?"
Co-respondent: "Not a wink, my lord!"

In general, however, they are not witty, but humorous, and it must be said for McGill's post cards, in particular, that the drawing is often a good deal funnier than the joke beneath it.[12]

Orwell, in his very different mannerism, has spotted something which Walter Benjamin, writing only a few years before and with a very similar sense of impending disaster, theorized as fundamental to the imagery of popular urban culture:

To the form of the new means of production, which to begin with is still dominated by the old (Marx), there correspond images in the collective consciousness in which the new and the old are intermingled. These images are ideals, and in them the collective seeks not only to transfigure, but also to transcend, the immaturity of the social product and the deficiencies of the social order of production. In these ideals there also emerges a vigorous aspiration to break with what is out-dated — which means, however, with the most recent past. These tendencies turn the fantasy, which gains its initial stimulus from the new, back upon the primal past. In the dream in which every epoch sees in images the epoch which is to succeed it, the latter appears coupled with elementary of prehistory — that is to say of a classless society. The experiences of this society, which have their store-place in the collective unconscious, interact with the new to give birth to the utopias which leave their traces in a thousand configurations of life, from permanent buildings to ephemeral fashions.[13]

Orwell does not underpin his interpretation of comic postcards with Benjamin's subtle and serpentine mixture of Marx and the Kabbalah, whose theory, sturdy and elegant as it is, has about it a heavy smell of the library shelves. Orwell's less self-conscious account allows him to connect Max Miller to Greek tragedy, Sancho Panza, and Shakespeare without any affectation, and to carry all these associations with a really stirring straightforwardness into the tense and dangerous world of a Britain awaiting the German invasion in 1941.

I never read the proclamations of generals before battle, the speeches of führers and prime ministers, the solidarity songs of public schools and left-wing political parties, national anthems, Temperance tracts, papal encyclicals and sermons against gambling and contraception, without seeming to hear in the background a chorus of raspberries from all the millions of common men to whom these high sentiments make no appeal. Nevertheless the high sentiments always win in the end, leaders who offer blood, toil, tears and sweat always get more out of their followers than those who offer safety and a good time. When it comes to the pinch, human beings are heroic. Women face childbed and the scrubbing brush, revolutionaries keep their mouths shut in the torture chamber, battleships go down with their guns still firing when their decks are awash. It is only that the other element in man, the lazy, cowardly, debt-bilking adulterer who is inside all of us, can never be suppressed altogether and needs a hearing occasionally.

The comic post cards are the one expression of his point of view, a humble one, less important than the music halls, but still worthy of attention. It will not do to condemn them on the ground that they are vulgar and ugly. That is exactly what they are meant to be. Their whole meaning and virtue is in their unredeemed lowness, not only in the sense of obscenity, but lowness of outlook in every direction whatever. The slightest hint of "higher" influences would ruin them utterly. They stand for the worm's-eye view of life.[14]

The best of Orwell, as theorist and practitioner, shows clearly in this essay. He concludes in a bare, moving statement: 'The corner of the human heart that they speak for might easily manifest in worse forms, and I for one should be sorry to see them vanish.' What he has done is to *recognize* a scrap of popular art in such a way as to make this neglected corner of necessary joking rejoin the human community, in the same way that the postcards themselves, sent every summer to tens of thousands of typing-pool offices, factory canteens, heavy lorry cabins, confirm that community — 'Ooh, isn't she awful!' 'That's a good one, Fred, I've not seen it before'. In Rorty's term,[15] Orwell provides us with the means of 'edification' by combining recognition with redescription, so that the two processes blend as understanding. What his crude diction and unacknowledged contradiction cannot do is to connect understanding with actions. With the next writer in mind, one might say that he cannot break out of the passivity enforced upon him by the fractures of his consciousness. Only in Spain did he think with his body.

A phrase like 'thinking with the body' does not connote any impending descent into the dire jargon of body-language, nor even the of course much more considerable attacks on mentalism by such a man (such a genius) as D. H. Lawrence. Orwell sustains the lessons of the predecessors I have chosen; he quite naturally takes no account of narrow Cartesian rationalism, but speaks from the world in which he lived. He looks for means of 'edification' from the materials of everyday practice. His great gift to us is to make the revaluation of the commonplace something sweet and natural; the difficulty with his work is the immanent strain and reluctance which prevents his making the connections fully.

What is missing is brought out and restored by Adrian Stokes (1902−72). Stokes, whose name has always been much cherished by a small, very mixed bunch of the best art critics of the past half century, is only now beginning to grow in reputation. And yet he runs easily enough along the track of my curriculum. He too is a product of the cultural, but in his case non-political intelligentsia, educated (like Green and Collingwood and Tawney) at Rugby, and then at Magdalen College, Oxford, soaked in the prose and the intellectual inheritance of Water Pater, Morris and (also like Collingwood) John Ruskin; a man of striking beauty, a gifted athlete (squash and tennis), painter and poet. He lived the life of the cultivated scholar-aesthete, just too young for the first war (in which his brother Philip was killed) just too old for the second. He lived it divided between London, the Mediterranean, and Tuscany, where he was first taken by the Sitwell family, recoiled from the critic-valuer Berenson's personal vanity and Clive Bell's inhuman aesthetics, talked with Ezra Pound, and quickly dedicated himself to understanding Mediterranean art out of his own solitary, passionate, profoundly intellectual and resistant integrity and intensity.

In London, for all his noble house in the homeliest of the capital's Georgian streets, Church Row in Hampstead (no. 20, for the pilgrim) and his membership of the Tate Gallery trustees, his art and ballet reviews, he remained mysterious, remote, rather corrugated, wearing the elegant gaucherie which English public schools confer upon their scholar-athletes. The public manner was consistent with the private geniality and merriment combined with absolute seriousness and attentiveness which his close friend Richard Wollheim remembers.[16] 'At dinner, sitting at the head of a scrubbed table, presiding over many pots with different vegetables, several bottles with different wines, perhaps one of some grandeur, shirt open at the neck, blinking as though a light had suddenly been turned on, he was invariably high-spirited . . . laughter excited him . . . he loved certain music: Monteverdi, Frescobaldi, Mozart, Berlioz, Schubert . . . He thought the decorative was totally underprized in our culture. He could never see enough tennis or cricket.' And then, most importantly for my purposes, 'he was full of irony, and he spoke and wrote in a language that he seemed to have re-invented'.[17]

Stokes had to re-invent the language of art criticism for his peculiar purposes. To say so takes me back to the theme which runs as ground-base to the book and is the major contribution of this long line of English human scientists to the new, international debate on hemeneutics. Stokes found the forms of discourse and the fine cadences of Pater and Ruskin as the current definition of art speech; he listened to those cadences, coarsened to fit Berenson's bids in the auction room and sugared to match Clive Bell's drawing room civilization in Bloomsbury. Stokes had much to take from Ruskin, more from Morris, but he had to break and remake the language of criticism if he was to think and not merely swim in it.

His deep, peculiar purpose, like Leavis, like Orwell, like all the earnest brethren, was to provide new ways of seeing the ancient, common roots of life and art, of being and culture. His place in this chapter signifies that, unlike Orwell, he saw this as a necessarily theoretic practice, a practice synonymous with the art of living. Given that art is a mode of thought, he wanted both to profane aesthetics by clearing away the sacred incantation of Walter Pater, and to make art-speech capable of re-engaging with the existential project. To do this he needed a language which the hardy epistemologist could not dismiss as merely subjective or emotive, and a language which, while dealing with the great canon of art,[18] grew from the lived and bodily experiences caught in the titles of such of his books as *Colour and Form, Rough and Smooth, Inside Out*, and — in his key concepts — both carved and modelled from a living geography. His language, difficult and dense as it is, had to be the real language of men. His powerful and, so to say, anti-Cartesian insight was to know that a human science must be more than methodologically self-conscious; for the practice to be 'humanly scientific', it must understand its own connection, as lived in its agents, with 'the totality of our experience of the world'.

The formulation is the German's, Gadamer; and in this version[19] it seems little more than a pious admonition. Say instead, that the human scientist (the aesthetician-anthropologist) seeks to integrate his or her self-consciousness into analysis and as becoming conscious of all that is expressed in the human actions under study whether paintings or potlatch, tennis matches or string quartets. This demands above all a linguistic de- and re-construction, a criticism and creation of how it is that language means, is encoded and decoded by a bewildering range of unseen structures. It requires, for very freedom, that the scientist should see how languages are mediated by the use of the human body itself as a signifying centre.

To make this claim is not to idealize all 'field' encounters between an ideally free inquirer and a freely signifying set of bodies. There may be plenty that is well hidden in the actions and their actors in question, and the human scientist himself can only get so far in telling his own, historically relative truth. All the same, if he and she move their solid flesh-and-blood into their language, then they cannot make any mistaken assumptions about dualism (minds and objects) nor about objectivity (and its paramount target, hard, realistic knowledge). Embodiment is the primordial condition of all language, indeed of all expressiveness. It is only in our embodiment that we recognize signs and their meanings, and it is only because the world of signs and gestures by others is *our* world, and we know what it is like to be a human being, incarnated in a subjective tissue of lived behaviours, that we can start to interpret the world at all.[20] The body is the central signifier, 'the cluster of meanings, the mode of expressiveness' which brings a world into being and includes others in its meaningful spaces.

Stokes is a wonderful theorist of this endlessly creative process. His subtlety is to bring to consciousness for the purpose of celebration the intuitive, necessary making of meanings which everyone practises as they move about their world, especially the streets and houses they build and live in, the representations of others' bodies they paint and sculpt and touch and desire.

It is only at first a paradox that Stokes refined his theory of how we experience architecture, painting and sculpture with help from Freud and his disciple, Melanie Klein.[21] His rich humanism predates any narcissistic notion of man as the meaning of all things, as the classic first part of his *Stones of Rimini,*[22] called 'Stone and Water', makes clear. In this early work, published when he was thirty-two, Stokes begins with Venice as the amazing, living emblem of how stone and water mean what they mean to men, to their livelihood, production and exchange, their sense of home and strangeness, their bonding of nature and culture. The city bespeaks the sea; its 'Istrian stone seems compact of salt's bright yet shaggy crystals' (p. 19) and he turns to register the barnacle-like encrustations on the bright white stone, the smooth polish worn by familiar human fondling. 'Again, if in fantasy the stones of Venice appear as the waves' petrification, then Venetian glass, compost of Venetian sand and water, expresses the taut curvature of the cold under-sea, the slow, oppressed yet brittle curves of dimly translucent water' (p. 20). Stokes images harbours, Wapping, Limehouse, Genoa, as well as Venice, to bring out the happiest, most significant conjunction of stone and water. The quayside is the loveliest and most emblematic of the unities of townscape: change and permanence hold their place peaceably beside each other, the mass of the wall defined by the heavy, massive stones, shaped and finished by the curved rim of the coping, completed and varied by the polished, black iron capstans, the tesselation of the smaller, rectangular paving and cobblestones. The solid stone is broken by the sun glinting on the grains of sand and quartz in its worked surface, the same sun which shimmers on the endless, restless, dazzling surface of the water. Counterposed one against the other, stone and water also penetrate each other; beneath the tide the stone staggers and wavers, is bent and elongated and compressed by the movement of the waves; on the tranquil blue day the level sea is as smooth and dark as obsidian.

The perfect interplay of movement and mass, perpendicular and horizontal, texture (smooth and rough) and composition (colour and form), is for Stokes the deep satisfaction which only art makes possible in life. Stokes, with all his reverence for art, makes light of exclusive definition. He understands that we see the world through the lenses ground by past experience. This is not to say that we simply see things the way our parents did; every age recuts the lens, and as Stokes himself is painfully aware, he writes at the edge of a cultural fracture.

Today, and not before, do we commence to emerge from the Stone Age: that is to say, for the first time on so vast a scale throughout Europe does hewn stone give place to plastic materials. An attitude to material, an attitude conceived in this book as being far more than the visual-aesthetic basis of Western civilization, can hardly survive long. The use in building of quarried stone must, we shall argue, increasingly diminish, and with it one nucleus of those dominant fantasies which have coloured the European perception of the visual world. In the work of men, manufacture, the process of fashioning or moulding, supersedes, wherever it is possible, the process of enhancing or carving material, the process that imitates those gradual natural forces that vivify and destroy Nature before our eyes. Hitherto there has always existed a ratio, full of cultural import, between carving and modelling, terms on which we thus bestow the widest application.

We emerge from the Stone Age: and perhaps the very perception of stone manifest in this book, rather than any argument adduced, proves this to be so. For what is dead or dying is more simply an object, and therefore easier to apprehend, than what is inextricably bound up with the very flow of life. Nothing in writing is easier than to raise the dead.[23]

Here, of course, Stokes does not have to give the name of industrial capitalism to the process he describes — mass construction, for profit and necessity, is in any case worldwide. But he identifies a source of splitting in cultural consciousness and social being which Marxism claims validly to be able to account for. On the waterfronts of old harbours, abundant, excessive nature is shaped but not tamed by provident and prudent culture. The blankness and blindness of modern townscape — whether in bye-law and high-rise municipal housing or in the enormous filing-cabinet offices of the city — sunder for ever the connections of nature and culture; as Orwell might say, they make totalitarianism more likely.

Stokes, at the end of the stone age, follows his insight to the meaning and love of stone itself. Time and again, in the 'Geological Medley' of *Stones of Rimini*, in the essay on houses in *Smooth and Rough*, in the 1945 essay *Venice*, in the essay on Turner in *Painting and the Inner World* (1963), he goes back to stone, above all to limestone and its metamorphosis, marble, as both fact and emblem of the origins and continuity of life inscribed in its grains by fossilized molluscs. Limestone sediments itself from water in delicate laminates, is readily shaped and smoothed by water, becomes fantastic, magnificent, serene, under the impact of water. Limestone, Stokes asserts, 'is the humanistic rock', carved by the hands of men it speaks of its own origins and composition — of the water it commingles, and of its inorganic immortality.

When Stokes places this sense of moral communion with stone in its historically original context, around the shores of the northern Mediterranean — Spain, France, Italy, Greece, Yugoslavia, then the relevance of Freud and Klein becomes clearer. The Mediterranean is the vast stage for a system of culture and exchange built on the slopes of its amphitheatre. Three thousand years of the slow accumulations of a stone-and-water technology found their best expressions below the clear blue sky and the silver olive groves in the careful limestone conduits and the fountains which irrigate the husbandry. The shapes of happiness which this economy makes possible are those which Stokes paraphrases from Melanie Klein as the essential formations of, at least, every European soul. Klein theorizes the bliss of suckling at 'a good breast' as that 'oceanic feeling' which is our later experience of communion, holy or secular. She theorizes the rage and depression of hatred as the recognition in the tiny infant of the 'otherness' of the longed-for object which may be withdrawn and which never finally yields up its unpossessable separation. The maturity to welcome completeness and to recognize its elusiveness, to withstand the pain of loss because it makes it possible to honour the facts of difference, is printed in the experience of the good and bad breast, and reprinted in the art with which we make our houses and cities homes fit to live in.

Perhaps this summary of what Stokes took from Klein will do to rebut the charge that aesthetics is badly distorted through a psycho-analytic microscope. Roger Scruton reproaches Stokes that 'such a general account of architectural experience cannot describe the crucial act of attention in which the aesthetic experience resides . . . it allows the object of architectural interest to drop out of consideration as irrelevant. The object has become a means to the production of feelings which do not require it.'[24] Scruton first simplifies and then mistakes Stokes's procedure. In the first place, Stokes doesn't give the subconscious pride of position in the human psyche: rather, he seeks a more total description of our experience of space and form. He creates as rich an account as possible of the body in the world. In a marvellous aside, for instance, he imaginatively fixes the special nature of the big cityscape like this:

What figure of today aesthetically best suits our streets, what figure aesthetically is best framed by our doorways? The answer is the man in a long overcoat with hand within pocket holding a revolver on which his fingers tighten. There is no gainsaying the aesthetic appropriateness of the thug in our streets and in our interiors. The idea of him saves our town environment from a suggestion of vacuum.[25]

He goes on, in his characteristically lapidary and speculative manner, to present the order and disorder of the built environment as prefiguring different historical metaphors for and organizing models of inner being. His lovely redescription of architectural experience is only psychologized in the sense that a city must be imagined before it is built, but he sees the building itself always as a way of thinking about order and disorder, and devising space so that neither destroys the other, discovering for both a proper meaning.

I shall exemplify the grace and sympathy with which Stokes recreates the tense, rich asymmetry of psyche and soma only by rapid reference to the essay 'Venice',[26] of which the first part is a brief guide to his special view of the 'blackness and whiteness' of the city, and the second a detailed analysis of Giorgione's masterpiece, *Tempesta,* which Stokes takes as concentrating, against a background of actual Venetian palaces, the virtues of the Venetian Renaissance, and therefore of the Mediterranean, and therefore of our civilization. Stokes's pertinence for us in this remarkable book is the eloquence and stateliness which he combined with a strong sense of his physical presence in order to bring home to us (in the good phrase) the meanings of the city. In a fine analysis of a photograph of the Torre dell' Orologio in the Piazza he moves naturally from the confident attribution of emotional quality called out by the buildings to a keen perception of the satisfying, shapely urban traffic the building enables.

There is poignancy in the tapering smooth shaft and the branching intricacy from its capital; in the separateness of the column from the pier to which capitals and columns join; in the base of the pier, part rectangular, part cylindrical: and now there is poignancy in the contrast between these steadfast, opaque faces of white stone and the watery reflections of the shop window beneath the arcade. This last would seem irrelevant were it not that it is characteristic of Quattro Cento building to afford a heightened awareness of approximations and of distinctness, and therefore of contrasts in which an approximatory element lingers to stimulate the unifying power of fantasy. The reflections in the mirror do not only contrast with the face of the stone in terms of their mobility and light and shade. I would say that they belonged to the architectural impression since they evince further the already existing parable of the stone. Such strong art collects surrounding phenomena within its own terms: the visual dogma becomes entirely satisfying. *When objects of the senses compel in the percipient the profoundest emotions of the contemplative state, the soul is at peace.* We then have the sense that what we are looking at has rolled up the long succession of the mind in spatial, instantaneous form: and then that the relationship between the objects seen, exemplify a perfect harmony of inner and outer things.

And so, though I cannot deny that this photograph is exceedingly lucky in its accidents, I do not consider it irrelevant to take advantage of them in view of the imaginative approximations that this piece of building stimulates. I attribute to the reflections of the piazza, to the street beneath the dark archway, to the stone building, the quality of a visual parable of unconscious, preconscious and conscious. For the Quattro Cento building by itself expresses the solution of manifold directions, manifold movements of the spirit as might a vigorous face. This philosophy comes to us entirely in aesthetic terms. (p. 111)

The italics make his point: it is Quattro Cento spirit which is here carried and relived by the unnoticing citizens.

Within the archway mills the life of the Merceria. The white clothes of the tourists and loiterers, the very hats of circular white, are resolved in a kind of geometrical sum by the panels and disks of white stone. What is moving here, what is less shapely, less defined, comes to possess a face as steadfast as a rose. The very distance of the alley rolls up to be this bright frontage. Correspondences occur rapidly to the mind under the pressure of such art.

The architectural members, not the accidents of the photograph in themselves, incline the mind to seize the connexions that these accidents afford. And again, such parables are not forthcoming from other architecture to the same degree, still less, from any building. Pattern of some sort is easy enough to come by, so too are stimulating collocations in photograph or cinema reel. But art of this calibre stimulates the profound visual contemplation to which I have no more than alluded. We can hardly define great visual art or visual art great or small, except in terms of this power.

The question arises in the end: why this satisfaction, this value, in one thing expressed in terms of another? Because it characterizes all human process, all thought and action and emotion. To live is to substitute. *Art is the symbol of human process.* (p. 112)

This is the rich theory which Stokes provides us with. For all the utter absence of politics from his pages, as he moves through Mussolini's Italy and with the Home Guard through Cornwall, he returns us from the book to the street; he makes possible a theory of value with which to interpret the street, and does so even when describing Giorgione's painting.

They are amiable and serene, yet like the other Giorgione figures, instruments of evocation. Their thoughts meet, their minds meet, not their eyes. There is a pause in living: there is an interchange between past, future and the present, between the figures, between themselves and each aspect of the landscape, between a deep-set wordless dream and an outward world. Although the hour is evening, he creates a situation of thunderous light where there is also dramatic change of tone to dramatize in turn the equal gaze of the protagonists. Moreover, despite this broad tonal range, despite this very first solicitude in art for the evanescent exaggerations of appearances due to the direction of their light, local colour is still intense, so that the calm evening value of each thing, though it be an architectural fragment or a building that crumbles − indeed, because of the cycles such qualities suggest − possesses added poignancy beneath the natural instruments of evanescence. In purging the whole of dominating drama, intensity of local colour dissociates the picture from the stress of a moment of time although that moment is vividly represented there; from a 'situation', and this without neglect of naturalistic appearance. Indeed, technically considered, Giorgione's revolution was a huge stride toward the representation of mere appearance in its broad and hitherto neglected features. Hence the divinity of the ease of his spiritual disclosure, hence, by the lack of any stylization, the full employment of a sense of affinities that has not been equalled. (p. 130)

You can hardly be more practical, indeed material, a cultural critic than that. The calm, easy, bodily lesson of Giorgione's figures is rendered in prose just as calm and plain. In his Envoi, Stokes draws the moral for today.

He uses psychoanalysis to restore the body to aesthetics, and to remove aesthetics from the museum and the auction room and set it down once more in an image of the good life as livable in a great city's public places. He makes 'home' a usable political concept, and 'homeland' a clean one.

PART III

Socialism, Action and Experience

7

Fabians in Arms: Tony Crosland and Richard Titmuss

To return at the end of the interval is to re-enter a drastically changed setting of the historical scenery. Of course it is clear that the work of the most powerful liberal theorists between the wars, Keynes, Collingwood and Leavis, persists up to the present day and beyond; it is furthermore a premise of this book that their presence in the tradition of which I write may be deduced not merely in the creation of their concepts and structures, but more impalpably and at the same time with even greater pressure in the whole climate and style of our modes of thought — in the cadence of mind itself. In any case Keynes was a main architect of the social machinery which shaped so much of social policy for the years after the Bretton Woods settlement in 1944, and as we have seen Leavis's thought altered and expanded enormously under the pressure of post-war history.

Notwithstanding these qualifications, the placing of the many revisions of English social theory in the period which begins with the triumphant Labour victory of 1945, must acknowledge as many historical fractures as it must the essential intellectual continuity without which we can none of us learn to think at all. This chapter takes the Fabian tradition which the power and genius of Keynes seized and transformed to such novel effect, and places it in the complex, intermittently generous and half-hearted reconstruction of the social order which Keynes' ideas and General Marshall's dollars made possible to Clement Attlee's victorious administration. To speak at this distance of the mood of a country is merely to announce allegiance to a favourite bit of mythology; however one generalizes, the class fractions in Britain in 1945 were divided in many ways about the immediate prospects. To go no further than the huge and heroic status of a single figure, the significance of Winston Churchill was much disputed. The famous appeal of his speeches — and many of the most famous were delivered to the modest audience of the House of Commons — was surely modified by a proper ribaldry when they got as far as the munitions factories and the coal mines. It is even likely that his most natural constituents were hardly in a position to grant him the idolatry which has grown among them as they have aged, and his historical achievement has receded and magnified into a television mirage. But given the impossibility of generalizing the mood or even the world view of a whole country nearly forty years ago, perhaps it can be alleged with sufficient plausibility that the election of the Labour Government with a majority of 145 in the House of Commons announced a national commitment to one half of a new social contract. The first half of that contract was to guarantee what has come in an ugly misappropriation to be called 'the social wage'. By this is meant that each citizen is partly paid for his labour in the tokens of welfare, health, education, social benefits and care. The transposition of these natural and necessary expressions of a proper regard for one's fellows into the cash metaphor 'wage' expresses, nastily enough, the other half of the contract. This was the guarantee implicit in the Marshall aid plan, that the restoration of economic activity would formally tie together the aspirations of individuals for happiness and fulfilment and the provision of material goods which would deliver those dizzy abstractions. That is to say, the abrupt and massive move from production for war to production for peace, was to be achieved by the restoration of the juggernaut of capital, powered by the state, and intended to provide sufficient national wealth to keep burning the home fires of the poor, the elderly, the sick and the small, as well as to provide a much wider range of all those easily wasted products neatly caught in the phrase 'consumer capitalism'.

Keynes both theorized and foresaw this development with few regrets. As I observed, he thought it would take a generation or two for people to learn how to use their new wealth in both rational and cultivated ways; in any case he had sensed from a respectful distance the grimness of a poverty which, as a later mythology has now almost denied, may still be found in the United Kingdom. It is not to stretch the limits of causality too far to say — as Russell put it — that Keynes abolished unemployment. If we let the slogan pass, we may turn to see what the new civil servants and their politicians sought to make of this historical opportunity. Naturally enough their most vigorous spokesmen were the British wholemeal socialists of Fabian reform who had read political economy as students at the London School of Economics and, classically, at Balliol College, Oxford. Their continuity, with our past great worthies T. H. Green, Keynes and others is clear; their spokesmen for this chapter are Tony Crosland and Richard Titmuss.

The two men sit easily enough together in the same sentence — more easily, indeed, than our eminences of *l'entre-deux-guerres* liberalism, Leavis, Collingwood and Keynes, who form the first circle of homegrown hermeneutics. Yet to choose them sweeps us suddenly forward to the present. Crosland was lost to a Labour Party which needed him most at that moment when, aged only fifty-eight and at the height of his parliamentary powers, he died suddenly of a cerebral haemorrhage in 1977; Richard Titmuss similarly died comparatively young and only, so to speak, the other day, aged sixty-five in 1973.

They are both, however, and supremely, social theorists and intellectuals of that Labour Party which for the first time to unshakeable power with Attlee, unanimously committed to steering the ship of state squarely into the centre of capitalism.[1] That party took its cabinet seats with its only experience drawn from the national coalition of wartime, with a vigorous programme of reform but entirely without the institutions, the bureaucracy, or the intellectual theory capable of seizing its historic opportunity and turning the confused but enthusiastic reformism of the active movement into the settled structure of a new society. It is now a familiar threnody uttered on the Left of British politics that that Labour government merely served the purposes of a temporarily rebuffed ruling class by justifying the introduction of a minimal welfare state, and by much more fundamentally restoring the energies of a debauched and exhausted capitalism without ever touching the deep structure of wealth, privilege, and ownership which was to benefit so directly from their innovations. Well, yes and no. The Marshall dollars could only be put to work in more or less approved-of ways; new international funding and world banking systems would permit so much and no more. And in any case, in a Britain drained by the war production effort, only survivor of a European industrial landscape laid waste by occupation and invasion, the Labour Party lacked the will, the vision, above all lacked the theory and the theoreticians to go beyond Keynes's generosity and libertarian individualism. What it had were the solid and doughty soldiers of the Left who had lived through the rout of the movement in the thirties, men (and about three women) of Parliament and Trade Union whose dominant political emotions were anger against the unemployment and the untended ill-health of the thirties together with a grim (rather than fierce) determination that the great goods of war — a decent ration book with some square meals in it, a proper doctor, a reliable fire and ambulance service, honest and worthy teachers, people you could count on to look after the children — should persist into the blue sunshine of this so-welcome peace. The men of this common experience and the modest projects to which it gave rise were not of a mind to theorize much beyond the Beveridge plan and the Butler Education Act of 1944, and if these references are too glancing for non-British social historians, perhaps it will do to say that the two documents sacralized the postwar codebook of English utilitarianism. The Beveridge plan[2] offered a model of a more or less accomplished social welfare and insurance scheme, thirty years after Lloyd George first sketched out in Parliament what the Fabians of the late nineteenth century thought up twenty years before him. The 1944 Education Act confirmed secondary education for all up to the age of fifteen, over twenty years after Tawney's stirring pamphlet of that name. Centrally important as these reforms were in British social history, nobody could say that they represented abrupt or unprepared-for transformations. Even after total war, the docile gentilities of British politics turned to reconstruction in a gradual, familiar vocabulary. The nationalization of railways and coal, of steel and gas, rewritten in the strident vacuities of latter-day ideological invective as doctrinaire adventures, were no more than the taking into care of bankrupt and shabby stock and assets. The major social achievement of the 1945—51 Government, the first, fully open, mutually supported National Health Service didn't even turn doctors into civil servants, but left them intact and independent, with their power, their mystery, and their fee-paying patients unimpaired.

It wasn't inevitable that things should have turned out this way; it was, however, very likely. The frames of English social theory held the practice of government pretty firmly in place. Keynes's flexibility and adroitness with the instruments of capital placed the state in the position of central banker and of investor; Leavis, we may say, confirmed in negation the utilitarian emphasis of public policy, simply because his sort of emphasis upon 'life' 'responsibility' 'maturity' is so firmly allocated by liberalism to personal and private things; Collingwood theorized the angel of history which, as in Benjamin's clumsy but impressive image, has brooded over England's twentieth century:

His face is turned towards the past. Where we perceive a chain of events, he sees one single catastrophe which keeps piling wreckage upon wreckage and hurls it in front of his feet. The angel would like to stay, awaken the dead, and make whole what has been smashed. But a storm is blowing from Paradise; it has got caught in his wings with such violence that the angel can no longer close them. This storm irresistibly propels him into the future to which his back is turned, while the pile of debris before him grows skyward. This storm is what we call progress.[3]

In my legend, Orwell kept his admirers going down England's mean streets, and Stokes sought a needful magic to turn those streets into Renaissance meadows.

By comparison, Crosland and Titmuss spin a much homelier idiom for theory. I shall take Crosland first because although ten years the younger he embodies very precisely the frame of mind which we may think of as characterizing the new Labour Party social theorist. I say Labour Party social theorist advisedly because, Orwell excepted, the names that we have taken in the second phase of English social theory have been decidedly those of men who align themselves with no particular party. Keynes of course, as we have seen, identified his interests largely as being those of the Liberal Party as it was until its final debacle in the 1929 and 1931 General Elections. Even after that point however he remained grandly an English liberal; his allegiance was to pre-war and post-war forms of liberalism, and, as I have emphasized, his ingenuity and genius lay precisely in that he could capture the post-war institutions of state intervention and turn them to new potentiality. His contribution as a statesman particularly in the delicate and massive negotiations which led to the Bretton Woods agreement cannot in any ready way be aligned in terms of party political preferences. In Crosland's case however we have somebody who, formed by many of the same institutions and frames of thought as those of Keynes and Keynes's own predecessors, identified from an early stage with the policy making and intellectual wing of the Labour Party which the Fabian society had long since become. Crosland was born in 1918, son of a civil servant and a university lecturer; he went to the modestly reputable London day and boarding school at Highgate where he would find the assumptions that characterized most of the gently progressive and no less gently traditional presuppositions of the English public school. In 1937 he took a scholarship to Trinity College Oxford, to read philosophy, politics and economics, or as it was by then known, 'Modern Greats'. His under-graduate career like those of so many of his generation and of the theorists to whom we now turn was abruptly broken into by the second war. He was conscripted in 1940 into the Royal Welch Fusiliers and eventually volunteered for service in the Parachute Regiment which he left on demobilization as a captain in 1945. He saw active service in four of the main theatres and returned to Oxford in 1946 to take a first class degree.

It is important to emphasize at this juncture the central nature of military experience for a number of the post-war heroes in this book. Edward Thompson who figures below as one of their intellectual leaders best summarizes the nature of this experience in its political reverberations.

I recall a resolute and ingenious civilian army, increasingly hostile to the conventional military virtues, which became — far more than any of my younger friends will begin to credit — an anti-fascist and consciously anti-imperialist army. Its members voted Labour in 1945: knowing why, as did the civilian workers at home. Many were infused with socialist ideas and expectations wildly in advance of the tepid rhetoric of today's Labour leaders.[4]

By the same token Crosland's military experience, fresh as he was from a traditional education in junior upper class liberal presuppositions led him through the ranks of that 'ingenious and civilian army' beyond anti-fascism to the English Labour Party. Many former soldiers have reported the active debate that took place in Italy, Europe, North Africa and the Far East during the last two of the war years on the social contract to which they were to return in Great Britain; the postal votes of the still armed forces in 1945 were ample testimony of the conclusion to which many of them came. The natural idealism which a man of Crosland's intellectual and domestic origins would have learned sorted well with the climate of this model army. He returned to Oxford where he became chairman of the University socialist club and, with so many of his like in both of the dominant political parties, became president of the Oxford union. Between 1947 and 1950 he held a lectureship at the University in economics, and it was during these years that he laid the foundations for the first of his most solid and durable statements about the prospects for labourism, *The Future of Socialism*.[5] In 1950 he entered Parliament as MP for South Gloucestershire and remained there until the Party was defeated in the 1955 General Election. At that time he completed the final draft of *The Future of Socialism* and after a brief interval as Secretary of an inquiry into the Co-operative Movement he returned to Parliament as the MP for Grimsby in 1959. He remained in that seat until his death in 1977 and during the intervening years took his most natural position as chairman of the Fabian Society, and published the sequel to his first book, *The Conservative Enemy*.[6] After the Labour Party's hairsbreadth victory in the General Election of 1964 he took his first seat on the Front Bench at the Department for Economic Affairs and went on via two important years as Secretary of State for Education to much more senior posts in the Cabinet, ending as Foreign Secretary, a post he had held for barely a year when he died at Oxford on 19 February 1977.

As a life it has many points of obvious comparison with that of T. H. Green. Like Green, Crosland was born into a family of some social standing and with settled egalitarian convictions. Like Green, he went to Oxford to study what had become the natural intellectual vehicle of the socially conscientious student; like Green also he turned to the practice of day-to-day politics in order to find means of translating his idealism into action. The critical difference, as we have noted, is the war service and here, for all Crosland's natural privacy of manner, it may be speculated that he underwent the major transformation which must take place in the sensibilities of all intellectually inclined members of the *haute bourgeoisie*, a transformation which is provided for the many twentieth-century political representatives of that resilient class either by revolution or by war. The hauteur and occasional glassiness of manner which may be detected in Green's social theory is absent from Crosland: the danger, exhilaration, boredom, terror and sheer ineptitude of an army at war provide a drastic solvent of any too over-academic an air in one's intellectual commitments. As an individual, Crosland himself was not without a certain haughtiness; he was an enormously big man, heavily built, powerful, and there was a decided comicality in listening to his irreproachably upper-class glottals and the alternation of heavy drawl and rapid speech with which he addressed a Labour Party conference. Such disjunctures are well known to the Labour Party. Once again however the man and the manner are inextricably part of the social theory. During Crosland's eighteen years as MP for Grimsby he saw a thriving, settled, and intensely local fishing town move from full employment and the prospects that the future of socialism in Britain would indeed bring them a brave new world — the world of freedom from want, of the proper provision of shelter, food and care to which Crosland gave his life — to the steady decline of the fishing industry, the slow, painful silencing of the busy throngs of the dockside, the joblessness, the shabbiness, the wretchedness. Crosland is the only parliamentarian represented in these pages, and at a time when to both its friends in this country and to interested observers abroad the Labour Party may be justly arraigned for its Philistinism, its incompetence, its broken promising and compromising, its raucous fraternal factionalism, it is perhaps timely to make a short detour into the texture of life as lived by a theorist who is also a member of Parliament.

The dedicated and conscientious constituency MP which Crosland undoubtedly was carries a quite extraordinary burden of responsibilities; his people have after all had their representatives at the centres of power for no longer than this century has lasted. A town such as Grimsby is, as I said, intensely local: it lies on the very edge of the river Humber where the mud of the estuary meets the hardly more than mud of the level land behind. Down the road is the wide seaside town of Cleethorpes, where the strip of hard, wide, yellow sand provides a site for another of the regular punctuation of working-class seaside towns that spot the eastern seaboard of the United Kingdom. A few miles inland stand the grim ironworks of Scunthorpe, and behind Grimsby the endless flat land, the small, by turns muddy and dusty farms of Lincolnshire. The long horizon and the grass speckled by wind define the land; everywhere the wide water invades it. The road stops at Grimsby: in front of you the Humber, the wharves, the harbourside, the last ships; to one side the black corrugated iron and high curved steel roofs of the warehouses, and beyond them the factories: at first jumbled, curiously neat, many of them small, with little cobbled courtyards to the side and down their back lanes, and then beyond, the new industrial estates, the long rather impressive brown brick or dark green rectangles bordered by clean, green, byelaw grass.

This brief elegy on an uncelebrated corner of the English landscape may serve to remind us that social theorists have the grain of their thought deeply altered if they move from the library to the constituency. Crosland wrote his main work in Oxford, in London or as MP in Gloucestershire; but the subject and object of his study is well prefigured by Grimsby. *The Future of Socialism* was written for such a place, and to those who twenty-five years on would speak dismissively of this book and its successor as old-fashioned I would retort on his behalf and as loyally as I could, that the book shaped, summarized and gave order to the whole project of the Attlee government, and went on to provide the most coherent and *feasible* programme that a British Labour government would be likely to undertake in the time available to it and with the intellectual materials to hand.

To patronize Crosland is almost as bad as to patronize his great mentor Keynes whose influence is apparent in so many of the pages of both the two major books. This is not to say that Keynes directly shaped Crosland's thinking on social questions: as I have emphasized Crosland was immediately preoccupied with the day-to-day praxis of politics (and the word praxis is advisable: for a man of Crosland's strength of mind and character allied to his decisiveness, thought was inseparable from action). There is every reason to think that he would have found the technical philosophy of pragmatism one which he would have endorsed, and the work of John Dewey whose name is most associated with that doctrine entirely congenial, but there is no need to cross the Atlantic for his tradition. All that we have seen of such men as Graham Wallas, of L. T. Hobhouse and above all of J. A. Hobson, provide us with more than enough of a list of his predecessors; when we ally them to the specifically political theorizing of such men so prominent in the Labour Party's hierarchy of thinkers as R. H. Tawney, G. D. H. Cole, Harold Laski and others then we have named the provenance of the man. Keynes of course dominates the list of those that I have named; and yet Keynes's is a name only glancingly invoked during the pages of *The Future of Socialism* and *The Conservative Enemy*. Important as the men and the books undoubtedly were, important as books must always be to members of an intelligentsia, Crosland like Green and like Keynes worked directly in and through the *experience* of which the books were only a part. Like any thinker on such subject matter, he sought to wring from the movement of contemporary history some sense which would enable that history to be more sensible about itself. He worked, that is, within the vocabulary and conceptual frames of the English Labour Party as those issued in action; the intractable material which he sought to order was the theory and practice of the Labour Party in power.

Those who speak of Crosland now as out of date and his social method as nerveless and enfeebled, are themselves historically anachronistic. In another striking metaphor, the firmer for being so familiar, Edward Thompson writes that many critics of English Labourism write as though history were an exceedingly long tunnel with a very small chink of light at the end, and that the point of being in history was to work towards that long distant light. But, as Thompson finally goes on, an awful lot of people live and die in the tunnel . . . and he continues 'the oppositional mentality of the British Left is certainly a limiting outlook; but it has grown up simply because our Left has had so bloody much to *oppose.*'[7] Crosland and Thompson would have disagreed on many issues;

indeed did so disagree. But whatever else Crosland was a great opponent. True, his opposition to conservatism and the settled privileges of the English ruling class is less ferocious and defiant than that of his predecessor in the mode, R. H. Tawney, but this is partly due to his having felt at first hand in the army the strength of a new, much more self-confident and assertive working class determined not to lose the victories won on the home front as well as in the other theatres of war, and partly to his having a programme of what to do in response to those caste arrogations of comfort and power, where Tawney had too often done little more than utter cadenced (and marvellously stirring) comminations over the enemy, and trusted to the moral strength of his case to win the day. But in politics goodness is not enough,[8] and good man as Crosland was, he had grasped this fact. Besides, he had a strong aversion to rhetoric, a commitment to dissolving the safe, friendly old enemies and demons of the Labour movement, their hardfaced bosses forever snatching the food from the bleeding lips of the starving poor. Accordingly, he gave his energies to what has come to be called 'revisionism', or elsewhere, 'Labourism',[9] and in both cases with a strong pejorative echo. Yet although Crosland's intellectual gifts were a good deal more modest, certainly, than those of Keynes, though not than those of, say, J. A. Hobson's, what he compiled was, first, an account of the changes wrought by history upon the British social structure, and secondly, a project for sustaining and immunizing this progress against whatever depredations the conservative enemy might think up in the future.

Those who animadvert upon Crosland for his revisionism, his datedness, his Fabianism, line him up with those 'many liberal-minded people, who were instinctively "socialist" in the 1930s as a humanitarian protest against poverty and unemployment, [and who] have now concluded that "Keynes-plus-modified-capitalism-plus-Welfare-State" works perfectly well . . .'.[10] But this amiable cartoon is Crosland's own, and he sketches it in order to reject it. These others would now 'be content to see the Labour Party become (if the Tories do not filch the role) essentially a Party for the defence of the present position, with occasional minor reforms thrown in to sweeten the temper of the local activists'. But that, in his own words again, is a mask for the attitude in 1962 of 'A dogged resistance to change [which] now blankets every segment of our national life. A middle-aged conservatism, parochial and complacent, has settled over the country . . .'[11]

It is surely the substantial fraction of the English middle class which

most embodied this complacency and conservatism when the broad
stream of centre politics used to flow tranquilly through the 10 Downing
Street leased at the time to Harolds Macmillan and Wilson with its light
flotsam of 3 per cent inflation and 4 per cent unemployment, and which
now rouses from the genteel round of fund-raising for the secular
charities to mobilize a social democratic party pledged to restore the lost
Eden of 1960. Crosland was no supporter of centrist politics, nor of
emergency coalition governments.[12] He was, however, vigorously
destructive of what he saw as defunct conceptual icons. Thus, his own
sense of history proclaimed him a revisionist; that is, he intended to
revise the field of concepts within which socialism defined as both body
of knowledge and theory of interpretation offers a heuristic for action.

His revisions were at times drastic, at times merely superstitious (or as
they say, ideological). In either case, his presence and influence have
turned out to be immense, and I say that aware enough of his
comparatively lightweight status as an original intelligence, of the
inevitably day-to-day nature of his thought, and of the way we may now
convict him of over-optimism, of simple-minded utilitarianism, of
impercipience about the durability and greed of property-owners and
capital itself. For what his two major books constitute are undoubtedly
the most solid and structurally consistent statements of what post-war
Labourism in power could actually achieve. Furthermore, they were
written out of a keen response to what a whole people, which was also at
regular intervals his electorate, really wanted. What they really wanted
— who would not is a question which now splits the nation into north
and south — were the two forms of life caught in the slogans, 'consumer
culture' and 'welfare state'. These phrases cover that mixed economy
which will provide sufficient public care — health, education, benefits
— and leave private life to look after itself. Public care, on this account,
will ensure the rescue of all those who are trampled over by the great
machines of capital reproduction; enough spare money will be left
behind in the rush to look after them. More importantly, as the machines
turn they will also leave enough other profits to make enjoyable the
spaces of private life, enjoyment of which is the justification for keeping
the monstrous show on the road.

Well, that is our life, and at least it looks a lot less full of care than pre-
war Britain. Crosland understood that, and put down the cause, rightly
enough, in part one of *The Future of Socialism,* to the transformation of
capital. He may be said to be *haut vulgarisateur* of the popular myth
that Britain's class system has become much more porous, that capital

and labour are much less divided than they were and needlessly at odds as they are, that the class struggle is no longer the motor of history, and that intelligent central planning and strong public expenditure can and should make for an equitable distribution of reward and welfare from the controlled accumulations of the mixed economy.

I use the phrase 'popular myth' in no disparaging sense. It connotes no more and no less than the essential narratives, compounded of knowledge, folklore, ideology, added to everyday aesthetics in order to smooth out the corrugations and lend a pseudo-scientific elegance and economy of outline, without which we none of us can interpret the world at all. Crosland's myth was in part self-evidently true, and it was progressive. It acknowledged the growth of the corporate trade unions as a great estate of the nation, it intended the equitable distribution of the social services, and it endorsed the use of Keynes's creations in economic control and energizing not just for the directionless accumulation of capital, but for the specific forms of expenditure — by free, happy consumers as well as by needy, but independent, informed users of social services. On the first part Crosland saw, as too few spokesmen of the Labour Movement all over the world saw with him, the candid delight with which people, the people, enjoyed their new leisure, their new comforts and domestic toys, washing machine, television and motor car. There used to be in circulation in the so tellingly named Home Counties and their newspapers a canting, mouthing threnody declaimed over the deplorable 'materialism' of the working class with their new pocket-money rushing to buy these playthings and 'status-symbols'. But these arrant snobberies could only mistake washing machines for status symbols if they had never done the washing themselves.

Crosland understood this, and welcomed early and openly the terrific extension of freedom brought by new machinery to the once poor, immobile and exhausted. In this, his allegiance to an essay such as Keynes's 'Economic Possibilities for our Grandchildren' of 1930 is direct, and so is his membership of the long tradition of social optimism initiated by John Mill and Green. It is sometimes thought chic to sniff at the proponents of optimism as both frivolously self-indulgent and unattuned to the necessary frugality of the human condition. Such supreme unction-spreaders have a long genealogy, from Jeremiah to *The Life of Brian*, and Crosland has a brisk way with Mr Michael Fogarty, one of their more sanctimonious admonitors, whom he quotes as writing:

'There is a surprisingly large amount of fat to be melted off the general mass of solid working- and lower middle-class families. The wastage here may well be far greater, in total, than in the small marginal "luxury" or "problem" groups which waste on a more conspicuous scale. The best-known surveys of recent years give the impression that the chief spending outlets of the British masses are pubs, pools, and prostitutes . . . A certain sparseness and asceticism . . . is part of the good life, and it would hardly be claimed that the British consumer has attained it.' Indeed it would not, and it is to be hoped that it never could be.[13]

It may seem heavyhanded at this date to spit in the eye of Mr. Fogarty; but the mixed members of my radically earnest band of hopefuls admittedly may sometimes wear a lean and hungry mien. Keynes, never, of course: he practised abundantly the leisure pursuits of twentieth-century cultivated man — collector of paintings and first editions, patron of opera and ballet, diner-out, host, and wit; Crosland, similarly, hugely enjoyed the social and sociable adjuncts to a hectically busy political life. There is every difference of quality and kind imaginable from, say, Leavis's commitment to art as the most serious form of thought and living to which a man may give his attention. Crosland, true to the Fabian and utilitarian values, saw the demands of production — the labour culture — as prior and all-directing; in this he paid brave tribute to the magnitude of Marx's achievement at a time when the Cold War was freezing hard, while also discarding Marx's grammar of motives and book of numbers. But work was for Crosland a necessity to create the conditions of freedom, and while the content of that freedom was the liberal individual's right to choose, he kept the faith that people would eventually come to choose the rather better in preference to the obviously awful, and in any case stood firm on the principle of equality as ensuring fair access, and as morally excellent in itself:

I regard a sustained rise in material standards as wholly desirable — probably because it will increase personal contentment, but certainly on grounds of personal freedom, since rising standards inevitably widen the area of choice and opportunity: on grounds of social justice, which surely requires that the masses, for so long deprived of luxuries which others have enjoyed, should now also be admitted to the world of material ease, if only to see whether they do in fact enjoy it: on strict egalitarian grounds, since rising consumption increases the fact and the consciousness of social equality, and so contributes to the fundamental aims of socialism: and on grounds of democratic anti-paternalism, since this is clearly what the workers want. Any anyone who tells them they are wrong, and that in fact they are simply becoming vulgarised, or Americanised, will be given rather short shrift, especially if he himself appears to have a good deal of material fat which might be melted off. (p. 222)

The husbanding of this market garden of the manifesto is organized according to the main headings of his two books. Crosland identifies the altered nature of monopoly capital, and builds a familiar-looking machine to trundle society along progress road. The state is placed in the distributor box, public expenditure mixed with venture capital fuel the machine from rapid growth, public welfare and personal consumption provide drive and torque, social equality a destination.

The automobile metaphor is bluff in both senses, no doubt. Its familiarity from managerialist utterances implies its proper condemnation, and Crosland would have dismissed it. Nonetheless, such a simple silhouette catches in outline the ineradicable and dominant model of labourist social thinking. The criticisms of it are severe, but who can doubt that this essential structure is the only plausible basis for governmental planning and public consent for at least our next generation? To that extent, Crosland remains spokesman of the times. Fred Hirsch has damagingly criticized the over-simplicity (and therefore unmanagability) of the model:

Underlying this approach is a view of consumption as a malleable aggregate. There is the product: its form can be fashioned to choice. Theoretical growth models can then be confined to a single consumption good. Practical consideration of growth prospects can be confined to the economy's supply capacity, possibly supplemented by some consideration of *aggregate* demand. Consumption comes into the picture only as a national income aggregate, and then as a determinant of the residual entity, savings.[14]

Real behaviour demands a subtler feeling for value and meaning than the machine responds to; time and cost, price and experience, more profoundly, altruism and expectations, are each more densely and chancily intertwined than may be allowed for in utilitarian political economies. Crosland was much too intelligent as well as sensitive to his Grimsby constituents not to have learned this in office; the essays in *Socialism Now*[15] bear witness to his revisions of himself. He saw that his own political economy had assembled a monster in statist bureaucracy; he never lost the cheerful, mature belief that the monster might be tamed to decent human purposes. His continuing strength is that he made available to a whole political movement the terms for commanding its own economy — as we see in the last chapter, Charles Taylor starts from very similar premises in proposing a new, but still recognizable economy for the zero-growth future. Crosland's failure was to leave his economy without a strong enough morality, and incapable of rebuffing new enemies from the Right. The weakness is most marked, as it is in all Fabian thought, at the very centre of the theory: in the great institutions of public welfare.

RICHARD TITMUSS AND THE POSSIBILITY OF ALTRUISM

Richard Titmuss (1908–1973), the second major representative of an always developing English tradition of thought supplies the omission. His life's meaning was the dedication of himself to understanding the institutional shape of central, necessary impulses of care and concern for others, and this of course is a much less programmatic occupation than that of the politician making ready for power. Criticizing Crosland for the limitations of his doctrine means identifying the moral, the conceptual, and the structural models and metaphors of that Fabian-derived utilitarianism as inadequate and dissatisfying. Utilitarianism as used in this book denotes computation of the social calculus which measures preferred policy in terms of aggregates of human happiness, defined as quantities of free choice expressed in quantities of material comfort and welfare. Now utilitarianism has been vigorously criticized of late,[16] but all its critics as well as its supporters agree that it relievingly purports to provide a neutral way of counting consequences by aligning them on a single scale as more or less leading to happiness (utility), and deciding what to do by weighing the results and going for the biggest.

The impossibility of trying for such a calculation over the whole range of social life is obvious. You just cannot follow Bentham's account of happiness as 'pleasure and the absence of pain', first because people's definitions of happiness are incommensurable, and second because some of them would in any case put other values above happiness, and therefore conflicts of moral goods are inevitable. In spite of the contradictions and blockages in utilitarianism, however, it is hard to see how to organize a mass society for which the shadowy idea of progress looms always as its teleology, without constantly going back to the attempt to make some form of utilitarianism work. This is partly so because the idea of progress and particularly progress to be planned for, to which liberal democracies are for our present season so overwhelmingly committed, is only thinkable in terms of the utilitarian calculus.

At this stage, notwithstanding Bernard Williams's irresistible criticism, it needs to be said that without the sort of revision performed upon Bentham by Mill, and upon Mill by the early Fabians, and so forth up to Crosland and Titmuss, we would not have the typical forms and institutions of the welfare state; we would not, that is, have had the brute data, let alone the principles of organization, information storage, client and clerical anonymity, which make our indispensable bureaucracies workable. This is not to say that Mill, before Max Weber, turned bureaucracy into actuality; after all, France and Russia ran enormous state bureaucracies of exemplary inefficiency for much of the nineteenth century, as Tolstoy and Balzac testify. But it is possible to claim that utilitarianism rationally expresses itself in efficient bureaucracy. For I take it that a characterizing feature of an ideology is that 'it is not merely believed by the members of a given social group but believed in such a way that it least partially defines for them their social existence. By this I mean that its concepts are embodied in, and its beliefs pre-supposed by, some of these actions and transactions, the performance of which is characteristic of the social life of that group'.[17]

State welfare economics and its associated planning mechanisms and concepts express utilitarianism. But welfare has deeper historical and moral origins and meanings than the blankness of the word carries, and these meanings take in such values as compassion, generosity, pity, loving-kindness, themselves sunk deep in the culture but not at all superannuated by either a changing history or morality. Crosland met this difficulty — the difficulty of incommensurable moral goods — by his insistence on equality as the socialist ideal; but in any case he never really pressed his planner's vocabulary much harder than a decent humanitarian could stand. Titmuss, as I said, provides a way of theorizing and understanding welfare which takes in a richer moral grammar and a more detailed human obligation than — in the tradition — either Tawney or Graham Wallas adduced.

It is satisfying and relevant that Titmuss is another individual theorist who signally resists the ready categories for classifying the intelligentsia. Of a deeply bookish and scholarly turn of mind, he never studied at a university until he became a professor; true to the rather grandly munificent customs of the London School of Economics, he was appointed to the Chair of Social Administration without a degree or university experience in 1950. At the age of eighteen, in 1926 he joined the clerical staff of the Prudential's county fire insurance office, and remained there (in Essex) until 1941. During these years, he became a member of the Fabian Society and the Labour Party, and learned from these institutions, as well as — harder and deeper — from the infinitely complicated business of fire insurance litigation, a proper respect for and sufficient assurance with the necessary handling of social statistics. Once war broke out, and the Thames became a main target of the Luftwaffe, Titmuss learned a lot more about fire and fire insurance at first hand, and learned a lot also about the social provision of first aid and nursing for war casualties of all kinds, the wounded from battle and air raid, as well as those less obviously conscripted by total war, who at the ages, say, of two or eighty-two were left homeless, untended, cold and ill, and were even more obviously deserving of medical attention than young soldiers, sailors, airmen. Yet more importantly, he learned, as so many of his generation learned, of the steadfast and greathearted human capacity to give, to give help, love, sympathy, possessions, money, when disaster breaks and when a natural enemy or the four horsemen are at the gate. It was the best of this generation, Crosland, Titmuss, Thompson, Williams, among them, who gave and give their bodies and souls to the effort to maintain that excellent and passionate mutuality when the last enemies had gone away, and the peace-time world was to be reconstructed.

In partnership with his wife Titmuss had written books on poverty and ill-health before the war. Immediately after the war in which he had become a treasured civil servant of the social services, and knew vividly how entirely possible it would be to refashion welfare in a short time and give decent health care to every Britisher, the official editor of the war histories, Keith Hancock, asked him to be the historian of wartime social policy. The result, written by a man neither an academic nor a policy maker, was *Problems of Social Policy,* published in 1950. With its success, and with the Labour Government lending its support to the institutionalization of social administration, as well as taking so much advice from the doyens of the party at the LSE, Titmuss went to found a new discipline at the School.

It is no light business founding a new subject in the deeply dug-in and clearly trenched divisions of intellectual labour in the snobbish universities of Great Britain. You need a discourse of membership, some sacred texts, a few heroic figures who set up the subject against resistance from the respectable, a recognizable research quarry and some notions of what kind of knowledge is producible from it. Titmuss, effectively, did the job alone: created the discourse, wrote the books, was the hero.

He began from Fabian sociology at a time when sociology itself was an unspeakable and an unspoken word in England, and by a series of brilliantly executed raids upon political theory, welfare economics, classical sociology, and civil service method, produced the subject which is now called social administration. In his hands and voice, the subject remained miles away from the assured emptinesses of today's managerialism and so-called policy sciences, instructively untainted by the tendency to unrequired and inaccurate predictions, and consistently kept clear and sharp by Titmuss's strong commitment to British democratic institutions and values.

This last, it is important to remind readers of such a book as this, is (I may say) not a nationalist point. If it must be, it is patriotic. Titmuss's patriotism transpires in his last and noblest book, *The Gift Relationship,* and his contention there, as throughout his work, is that the best values of a culture are always precarious, and may thrive or perish according to the extent to which the dominant institutions are enjoined to guard them. Thus, in a brave denunciation of lethal tendencies in the society, Titmuss generalizes readily about 'The Irresponsible Society'.[18] At just the time when more epicure theorists of western societies were announcing 'the end of ideology', the disappearance of class struggle, the advent of 'fine-tuning' in the political economy, and the final relegation of Karl Marx to the attic, Titmuss wrote in 1959,

When I was young what some of us argued about was the democratic process. We wanted to know in our academically illiterate way whether more dialogue, more democracy, was possible. We thought it a dreadful crime to prevent other people from speaking up. We realized that the poor (whether they numbered two million or ten million), the mentally ill, the disabled and other casualties or failures in our society were penalized, not only by their poverty, but because they were denied the social rights of protest and full membership of society. We believed in the possibility of an alternative government. We did not understand that government by the people could mean that power in government, the Cabinet and the City, could lie almost permanently in the hands of those educated at Eton and other public schools.[19]

Those impulses to radical earnestness have been kept alive in teaching social work studies, exactly because Titmuss forged a radical language for the subject. Himself a removed, austere, and intense man, of frugal life and deep, lambent feelings, he inspired in a small group of pupils much of that moral fervour about corrigible life-failures which a similar man, Leavis, fired in his pupils. Titmuss's first associates — Brian Abel-Smith, Peter Townsend, Peter Willmott, Robert Pinker, Roy Parker, David Donnison — have held close the connection between the scientific study of social action and the moral edge and heat that study must retain, most obviously when it attends to the subject matter of welfare — poverty, ill-health, misery, cruelty, want.

The key word is 'connection'. Moralizing is never enough in politics, any more than natural goodness is, least of all in the face of the 'several thousand statements . . . attacking the immense and corrupting burdens of 'The Welfare State' [a term Titmuss always resisted] by insurance companies, banks, investment and hire purchase firms, the *British Medical Journal,* the Institute of Chartered Accountants, the British Employers' Confederation, the Association of British Chambers of Commerce, the Institute of Directors, actuaries, judges, doctors, and other professional men'.[20] The list will do as Titmuss's demonology, and, unbowed before this tidal wave of effluent hypocrisy, he built the essentially political science of both welfare and counter-welfare institutions. (Anyone revolted by the most recent eddy of this tide loosed in the 1980s will find Titmuss's model still usable.)

In a famous paper, 'The Social Division of Welfare' Titmuss identified the administrative divisions of clerical labour between public social services, the fiscal system of welfare (income tax remissions and benefits, family allowances) which powerfully defines a subsistence minimum, and occupational welfare benefits (pensions, expenses, private medical insurance, flexible timetabling). These, Titmuss concluded, 'function as concealed multipliers of occupational success' (p. 52), and again and again he returned to the effort to document and theorize the movement of giant capital monopolies — of insurance and pension companies, of international corporations, of state institutions, which, biting upon each other in a massive interlocking of financial gears and their ratio, work to reproduce the structures of poverty and inequality supposedly dissolved by the new capitalism. The so-called 'rediscovery of poverty' by the Labour government of 1964—70 was made by Titmuss, but it was recently made clear with philistine callousness that this rediscovery was limited to a few explorers when the Secretary of State dismissed the classic new work of Titmuss's pupil Peter Townsend, *Poverty in the United Kingdom,*[21] in terms which vividly recalled Titmuss's own worst enemies named in the 1959 essay.

Titmuss imagined the concepts and metaphors necessary to understand the consequences of modern bureaucratic structures in both alleviating and creating suffering and wretchedness. But he never gave way to the tendency of both Durkheim's and Engels's sociology to suppose those structures to be determinate. His institutions are what they are in virtue of the meanings or meaninglessness which they enact and realize. This philosophical point is also a methodical one, and its strength and relevance are best brought out in his last book.[22]

The Gift Relationship, in a dazzling intellectual coup, selects the exact moment at which social fact and social value intersect, and makes this glowing intersection illuminate the hidden ideological structures of the many societies which surround it. As the full title announces it is a study of the way in which different societies organize the medical provision of their own lifeblood. Once more it is an assault mounted in Titmuss's long, unbroken battle against the market values of capital, the old enemy, which claim dominance for themselves in every arena of public life. As he constantly noted throughout his work, the comfortably-off are forever insisting that public services should be as answerable as any other market transaction to the laws of profit; those same killing voices are more strident and self-assured in Britain in the early 1980s than they have been at any time since the partial success which attended Aneurin Bevan as he first set up the National Health Service in 1948. *The Gift Relationship,* last of Titmuss's many essays on health care, is the final rebuttal of those mean-minded, tight-fisted, and entirely unimaginative custodians of their purse, defined as 'the taxpayer's money'.

For what the book establishes, in the teeth of cynicism and mere selfishness, is the formal and objective necessity of altruism, together with the incontestable evidence of its presence in the polity. By altruism, I follow Thomas Nagel[23] in meaning not extremity of self-denial, but the always potential human practice of putting aside vigorous self-interest, and acting strictly in consideration of the interests of others, without any ulterior or manipulative motives. It is worth noting that even the contemporary narcissist acknowledges the objective status of altruistic imperatives when he or she either confesses to a sense of guilt as motivating altruism, or locates the altruistic actions of others in a self-interest seeking to avoid the same guilt feelings. But guilt is not an original motive; it is a response. Guilt follows the recognition that the agent has failed to act altruistically. It embodies a recognition that there is an altruistic imperative. This imperative may of course be ignored, but that it stands as a formal or objective condition of action is brought out by anybody expressing resentment.[24] In order to express their sense of being wronged, even the moral cynic or sceptic has to invoke objective reasons, and perform the defining act of moral behaviour which is to imagine oneself in the situation of another person, or another person in one's own situation. Altruism, by definition, depends on an absolute human capacity to recognize other people as real, and really there; but of course this guarantees nothing, since we all of us more or less deny that reality in order to gain selfish ends. Maintaining altruism is therefore an effort; it requires forms and institutions of expression, and these may flourish or dwindle according to the moral rhythms of a culture.

Titmuss's book studies this lifegiving process at what is indeed its heart. Earliest among the social theorists in this book he takes to heart the lessons of the great European anthropologists, in his case Mauss and Malinowski, who have done so much to break open the complacent Europe-centricity of our thought. Starting from the many meanings of donation, of the gift, noting in passing ways in which giving gifts may exercise a variety of controls from pretty open coercion to the protection of both status and vanity, Titmuss identifies the essential altruism of the blood donor in his anonymity combined with his being an unpressed volunteer. *The Gift Relationship* documents in very absorbing empirics the variety of ways in which, particularly in the USA, blood may be bought and sold, may be all but required from certain classes of donor (for example, prisoners), may purchase medical insurance for the donor, and may carry clinically undetectable serum hepatitis, especially if sold by the very poor whose blood is one of their indispensable sources of a wage. Thus and thus Titmuss reaffirms the necessity and the possibility of public institutions, indispensably bureaucratic, which guard and foster a culture's generosity (gift-giving), compassion (care for those you don't know), loving-kindness, and even day-to-day efficiency.

What *The Economist* described in its 1969 survey of the American economy as the great 'efficiency gap' between that country and Britain clearly does not apply in the field of human blood. On the economic and technical criteria employed in this study in relation to blood distribution systems such a conclusion needs to be reversed; the voluntary socialized system in Britain is economically, professionally, administratively and qualitatively more efficient than the mixed, commercialized and individualistic American system.

Another myth, the Paretian myth of consumer sovereignty, has also to be shattered. In commercial blood markets the consumer is not king. He has less freedom to live unharmed; little choice in determining price; is more subject to shortages in supply; is less free from bureaucratization; has fewer opportunities to express altruism; and exercises fewer checks and controls in relation to consumption, quality and external costs. Far from being sovereign, he is often exploited. (p. 206)

In a moving chapter, 'Who is my stranger?' Titmuss quotes the varied reasons given anonymously by the very varied sample of British donors who were interviewed; not only were these all characterized by spontaneous and unaffected altruism — the kind of surprised and surprising readiness to give and not to count the cost which quickens and softens life itself in the most ordinary street — but also many donors appealed to the idea of a moral family or group of friends or workmates as a model for the larger society. And in this whole system, Titmuss saw the noble, essential, and above all mutual living of many values, and warned resonantly of the threat to these values and the life they permit, as the killing encroachment of the market and the bank continues.

There are other aspects of freedom raised in this study which are or can be the concern of social policy. Viewed negatively or positively they relate to the freedom of men not to be exploited in situations of ignorance, uncertainty, unpredictability and captivity; not to be excluded by market forces from society and from giving relationships, and not to be forced in all circumstances — and particularly the circumstances described in this study — to choose always their own freedom at the expense of other people's freedom.

There is more than one answer and there should be more than one choice in responding to the cry 'Why should I not live as I like?' The private market in blood, in profit-making hospitals, operating theatres, laboratories and in other sectors of social life limits the answers and narrows the choices for all men — whatever freedoms it may bestow, for a time, on some men to live as they like. It is the responsibility of the state, acting sometimes through the processes we have called 'social policy', to reduce or eliminate or control the forces of market coercions which place men in situations in which they have less freedom or little freedom to make moral choices and to behave altruistically if they so will.

The notion of social rights — a product of the twentieth century — should thus embrace the 'Right to Give' in non-material as well as material ways. 'Gift relationships', as we have described them, have to be seen in their totality and not just as moral elements in blood distribution systems; in modern societies they signify the notion of 'fellowship' which Tawney, in much that he wrote, conceived of as a matter of right relationships which are institutionally based. Voluntary blood donor systems, analysed in this book, represent one practical and concrete demonstration of fellowship relationships institutionally based in Britain in the National Health Service and the National Blood Transfusion Service. It is one example of how such relationships between free and equal individuals may be facilitated and encouraged by certain instruments of social policy. If it is accepted that man has a social and a biological need to help then to deny him opportunities to express this need is to deny him the freedom to enter into gift relationships. (pp. 242 – 3)

Policy has ends; ethics precedes economics. Titmuss indicates and enormously extends the Fabian framework, and puts down the customary argument of those further Left, to whom we now turn, that policy-making politics are done for. Whatever the power of their diagnoses and theory, they have to move towards what Titmuss and his pupils never fail to provide, modestly and in detail: the lived public experience of care and negligence, poverty and sufficiency, sickness and health, a bad life and a good one.

8

Culture and Politics: Richard Hoggart, the *New Left Review*, and Raymond Williams

The Fabians are and always have been intent on keeping the show on the road. Their strength is to start from where people really are, and ask what may be done with that. Crosland's two major books were written from the best moments of postwar reconstruction in which it was possible to start from where we are, to take the available instruments and set them to understand a present and think about a future which would give most of our people what they wanted, without too much upsetting those who might otherwise stop them. By the time his working papers from the haste, inaccuracy, honest effort and propagandizing of a government desk were published as *Socialism Now* in 1975, the gradualist programme was splitting down every seam.

Titmuss's Fabianism was of a more fighting kind, especially as the going got rough. His own experience, as clerk and as scholar, had told him that all socialist, indeed all democratic and human gains had to be defended and renewed: brutally profit-making medicine might suffocate the blood transfusion service as it has certainly made other gift systems such as bone-marrow donation very unlikely. He thought hard all his life about how to create and then how to protect welfare institutions which could only remain effective in so far as they retained their meaning: the Transfusion Service is the richest example of success in such maintenance. This dogged, earnest, and strongly re-creative labour on the part of the Fabians treads steadily on; we all owe much of everyday comfort and solace to it.

It commits the practitioner of the human sciences, however, to bitter and breakingly low settlements with the dominant way of things. However much it is always necessary, in Edward Thompson's metaphor, to make life bearable for all those living and dying in a dark tunnel, the manner in which you give such succour and the reasons you have for

158

offering it are critically conditioned by how far away you think the light at the end. The trouble with intellectual Fabianism and the policy it enjoined upon its political body, the Labour Party, is that it lost any comprehensive vision with which to pick up the light at the end. It made such hospitable accommodation to the present that it lost its powers of movement.

I speak in the tongue of the innocent idealist as though Fabianism, a subtle and longlived tradition of thought, were a single actor upon the stage of history. I have noted many men — David Donnison and Peter Townsend are two admirable examples — who keep the tradition and the action going, because somebody has to, and in any case the action alters, and the tradition with it. But even when its exponents stood closest to the centres of power, a new criticism began to declare itself against Fabianism, just because the necessary settlements were too low, and the light at the end of the tunnel was either an inordinately long way off, or nearly out.

For all those persuaded by total war that socialism was desirable and possible, the same light was dreadfully dimmed by Stalinism. If we take 1956 as the point of departure for what came to be called the New Left, then its significant moment was the moment of Suez and Budapest. All that was being gradually and painfully learned about Stalinist Russia by that date was thrown into hideous relief as the champions of socialist freedom shot the socialist insurrections of Hungary and Poland to pieces with tanks. At the same time Old Corruption at home had lied in its teeth to Parliament and Allies, and launched the ludicrous adventure of the Suez landings. Eden's and Macmillan's governments were bound tightly into the lies of the Cold War, the deadly race for ever more ruinous weaponry, the grudging extension of a capital-dependent independence to the colonial territories. These were the signs of the times, and signs were taken for wonders. It was time for new signs and images, if not for theories.

If Fabianism was the main discourse of political theory, and philosophy was preoccupied with the temporarily self-referring study of linguistic usage, the intellectual speech capable of sanity and affirmation was supremely at this date Leavis's English. But the men and women who wanted to speak it, would have it express the new picture of things they had learned from their own, new experience at home, at university, at war. I have suggested that the displacements of class and of authority, of the ideas of culture and community after the first world war, left the human sciences with no moral centre. Implicit in this suggestion is a genteel Hegelianism for which I would claim not so much truthfulness as usefulness, and according to its procedure would assert that in the intellectual competition which refracts the economic competition of capitalism, then at any one time a single discipline in the human sciences will dominate the others, and will frame and pervade the discourse of a generation. Leavis's and *Scrutiny*'s social theory routed the homegrown Marxism of the thirties, was strong in an anti-fascist liberalism, and was uttered in a vocabulary capable of combining both individual biography and the march of history, of speaking properly about life and death.

It sounded the natural language of any highminded young man or woman when they arrived at university after the second world war. Of course if they turned to politics there was plenty to do, and we have seen Crosland trying to do it. But the weakness of Fabianism is notoriously that it embodies no picture of the good life, and robust as Crosland is in endorsing his constituents' view of the good life as the possession of a comfortable home in a decent-looking town with easyish access to a day in pretty countryside, still, redeclaring solidarity with equality in health and education isn't really enough for a man to live for. Titmuss's noble exploration of the ways in which we may live for others emblematized in the blood donor system casts into stark silhouette the thinness of the Fabian world view.

At a theoretic level, we may say that the English lacked a means of imagining structure-with-culture. That is, they had devised — none better — new forms of industrial bureaucracy for the better treatment of men and women and their children; and they had to hand uniquely direct and vivid accounts of lived experience, the intellectualizing of the greatest national literature in Europe. But the second war typically prompted its most intelligent young men to revalue the latter in the terms of the former, especially when the unusual social fluidity of that war had promoted them from the English working class to the intelligentsia. The young heroes of Labour England, including our present subjects, Crosland, Titmuss, Hoggart, Williams, E. P. Thompson, were critically influenced by the curious social formation of a nation at war. In those circumstances new and impromptu forms of intellectual cooperation appeared overnight — you have only to read of the invention and deployment of radar to see how rapidly and thrillingly all the received barriers, of class, age, gender, subject and technology were dissolved and redistributed in a new community of common value and endeavour as a particular scientific goal was striven for in the name of victory. By the same token, warfare conditions gave rise to improvised forms of cultural inquiry, new subjects and objects of study, and when their authors and editors took off their uniforms and returned to civilian libraries, they could not find what they were looking for in the received classification.

In a single book, *The Uses of Literacy*,[1] Richard Hoggart (born in 1918) prefigures this complex process. The book itself advertises a new method — *the* new method, one might say, looking at the works of Williams, Thompson, Berger, alongside Hoggart, for each writer is forced by the exiguous nature of the theories to hand, to insist upon the paramount status of his own experience (or rather the experience he takes as his subject matter), and then to theorize that. We can see the working out with exceptional clarity in Hoggart's case.

Hoggart was born in Hunslet, a working-class area of Leeds characterized by the long terrace lines of small red brick houses, with outside lavatories, dark back alleys and narrow, flat cobbled streets which were the public living spaces for the local community, the whole ecology composing a townscape of which Hoggart is by now himself the worldfamous cartographer, draughtsman of 'Coronation Street' before the television programme sentimentalized history into mythology. Hoggart was orphaned when his already widowed mother died in 1926, and brought up by his widowed grandmother until her death, when he was about sixteen. He won, against all the odds, a scholarship to a local grammar school, a decade before that was made a more general (though never widespread) working class pattern by the 1944 Education Act, but throughout his boyhood until called up to what was indeed a new model Army in 1940, he had to understand his educated life in the terms of that other, informal education learned in the customs of sharp, almost demeaning and just about dignified poverty — in the language Hoggart himself uses, of 'mek shift and fadge' 'putting up with things' 'living and letting live'. Once in the Royal Artillery, on active service in North Africa and Italy, he joined in the pressure exerted by that 'ingenious and civilian army' towards the different definition of culture his generation was to produce, by acting first on its behalf as one of the new cultural bureaucrat-lecturers this new Army appointed, and then going on to follow Raymond Williams and Edward Thompson into university extra-mural departments, that margin of — in Williams's phrase — border country between educated and customary knowledge, between the theory of the leisure class and the leisure of the theory class.

It is a characterizing feature of so many of the figures in this book, and of all the immediately post-war heroes, that they worked in areas in which the deep divisions of intellectual labour which so organize and direct academic energies were in a state of confusion, or redefinition, or fluidity. Extra-mural departments in English and Welsh universities are unusually hospitable to teachers who live and work at the point where the lines cross between the absolute antinomies of industrial life: between work and leisure, theory and practice, reason and emotion, fact and value, them and us. Such hospitality is a consequence of the nature of their own guests, the students. The students in extra-mural departments are largely, as they say, mature; at their most pressing and convinced, that is, they come to their teachers and their studies with an experience prompting them to ask distinctly unacademic questions of what is in front of them, and looking for quite different theories to explain what has happened to them, from those on the usual circulation shelves. Just as Marshall's economics were not much help to the miners whose wages were cut in 1926, so English literary criticism, at least as doctored to suit undergraduates of the 1940s, would hardly serve ex-working-class ex-Army officers teaching evening classes in Hull and Hastings.

In its crudest version, that criticism had produced the contour line which Mrs. Leavis drew along the systematic production of popular printed fiction after 1800 or so, and continued it downwards. At the same time it drew in a negation of the same gradient, but marking up the co-ordinates of pre-industrial oral literature, which remain high in this diagram because 'organic', not 'mass' forms of culture, because expressive of a living language in a pious, time-sanctioned community, and not mass produced by commercial marketing for escapist fantasy removed from the pointlessness of industrial labour.

Leavis and Mrs. Leavis, it is important to state and restate, are at one and the same time responsible for the simplifying and sweeping power of this historiodicy, and far subtler and more qualified in the real use they make of it, especially as they come in their last years to treat Blake, Dickens, and Lawrence. But either way a strong, independent, tough intelligence such as Hoggart's could not take the theory as it stood. Resisting and revising it, he produced what the Fabians always lacked, a cultural theory of working-class life, and did so through what we may now call some of the most intelligent and moving fragments of hermeneutics written this century.

The power and meaning of his great book (as it is not at all too much to call it in this company) resides first in its plainness and truthtelling. Hoggart's own abjuring of the finesses of theory have led him to be on the one hand rebuked by latercomers of the Left for 'culturalism',[2] and on the other to be rearranged for their own purposes by grand theorists.[3] No doubt I shall here attempt something of both injuries, but my intention is to anatomize his method in order to bring out its daring, and to place his text in a structure of texts which have enabled subsequent social theorists to balance actuality against desire, scientific understanding against a vision of the good life, with so much greater plausibility.

To begin with, like Orwell and Stokes, he resolves the problems of text and the methodical dealing with the text by taking his own experience as his text. At the same time he splits open the familiar individualism of the belletriste for whom his 'response' to the texts is unproblematic because indisputable, by working not from his 'personal' but his class consciousness. Thirdly he avoids the mistakes to which Stokes may be liable in working conscientiously from psycho-analytic categories, by his disciplined use of the methods of practical criticism brought to the meanings of everyday life. Implicitly, many social theorists have cited details of everyday life as meaning this or that; we all do it; it is, in the strictest sense, our conventional, our *only* mode of being-in-the-world and finding it intelligible. Such practice is, supremely, the practice of poets, and Hoggart is on this count just another poet of the everyday. But at his historical juncture, he was able to change the conventional meanings, and to do so with command and tact of a rare order. We may say, that he was not the very first, but the first in the conversation of culture as carried on in English since 1945 or so, to treat social life as a literary text, and to revise the valuation of that life then in genteel circulation. He found a cultural theory which spoke only of the depredations of industrial life, the dehumanizing of personal encounters in urban surroundings, the final ruptures in the traditions and continuity which maintain value, identity, and a recognizable community of friends and neighbours. He set himself to construct a rich image of the partiality and partisanship of this decidedly party game. The threats to the big words — value, identity, and so forth — which only mean anything in quite small lives, he takes seriously, as any serious man must. But he can show, by the exceptional purity of his truthtelling, the winning for his own purposes of a plain, sober, tolerant style which leaves open its method for inspection in every plain turn of speech, that the working people of industrial England are far more their own people, far more unshakable, independent, vigorous, alive, than old theory had it, and that what they carry into battle with the new capitalism, particularly with its nastier weapons of mind-incarceration and feeling-corruption has a strength, humour, and resilience which will hold off the hordes of the hedonists for some time yet.

'A good table' is equally important, and this still means a fully-stocked table rather than one which presents a balanced diet. Thus, many families seem to buy less milk than they should and salads are not popular. Around this there clusters a whole group of attitudes, some of them plainly sensible, some founded on myth. 'Home-cooking' is always better than any other; café food is almost always adulterated. Small confectioners know they will fare better if they put 'Home-made Bread and Cakes' over their windows; in a sense the claim is still likely to be true, though huge electric ovens have probably replaced the original range in what was once the family kitchen behind the shop. The mistrust of cafés has been reinforced by the knowledge that they can hardly be afforded anyway, but much the same resistance often arises to the cheap works' canteens. A husband will complain that the food there 'has no body' and the wife has to 'pack something up', which usually means a pile of sandwiches with 'something tasty' in them, and she prepares a big hot meal for the evening.

'Something tasty' is the key-phrase in feeding: something solid, preferably meaty, and with a well-defined flavour. The tastiness is increased by a liberal use of sauces and pickles, notably tomato sauce and piccalilli. I used to notice that in the flusher early years of married life my relatives were often frying at tea-times — chops, steak, kidney, chips. By contrast, poor old-age pensioners used sometimes to simulate a tasty meal by dissolving a penny Oxo in warm water, and having it with bread. Meat has been much relied upon since it first became really cheap, and any working-class wife who has known thin times will have a fine knowledge of those cuts which are inexpensive and nourishing and also tasty. The emphasis on tastiness shows itself most clearly in the need to provide 'something for tea', at week-ends if not each day. There is a great range of favourite savouries, often by-products — black-puddings, pig's feet, liver, cowheel, tripe, polony, 'ducks', chitterlings (and for special occasions porkpies, which are extremely popular); and the fishmongers' savouries — shrimps, roe, kippers, and mussels. In our house we lived simply for most of the week; breakfast was usually bread and beef-dripping, dinner a good simple stew; something tasty was provided for the workers at tea-time, but nothing costing more than a few coppers. At the week-end we lived largely, like everyone else except the very poor, and Sunday tea was the peak. By six on that evening the middens up the back had a fine topcoat of empty salmon and fruit tins. Pineapple was the most popular because, in that period of what now seems extraordinarily cheap canned fruit, it could be bought for a few pence (there was a recurrent story that it was really flavoured turnip). Peaches and apricots were most expensive, and needed something approaching an occasion — a birthday or a sudden visit by relatives from a few miles away. The salmon was delicious, especially the red middle-cut; I still find it far 'tastier' than fresh salmon.[4]

Something of the best of Hoggart himself is in this passage, and that this is so is evidence about the method and the man. By his faithful recording of the details of the menu of the poor, he brings out what that menu means in more than material terms (but could not mean it without the material). It is worth noting how little food features as an index of civilization outside the pages of *The Good Food Guide,* but the relations of class and the kitchen go much further than waist sizes, and further too than generalizations either about good and bad taste or about that much-mentioned and vapid brilliance, the 'quality of life'.

For civilization, and its inevitable correlates, value, virtue, and the good life, are Hoggart's themes, and food is only one part of its baroque melody. That it is a part sufficiently indicates the realm in which he moves, and a later anthropology has taken issue with him for neglecting work itself, and the great edifice of power which it betokens and is. Say for now, however, prayers of thanks for so much richness. For Hoggart deals with domestic life — with food, with the furniture of working-class homes, with sexuality, communal life (clubs), popular songs, faces (particularly the faces of middle-aged mothers and fathers), religion (fate and luck) and — what the necessary recrudescence of Marxism has subsequently insisted upon — the narrow arc of human relations along the axis: power — exploitation: has little place here.

But power is famously hard to identify, as Hoggart's more ambitious and further-reaching contemporary, Raymond Williams, confesses, and understanding power itself cannot be achieved without this kind of analytic re-creation:

The manner of singing is traditional and has fixed characteristics. It is meant to embody intense personal feeling, but is much less egocentrically personal and soft-in-the-middle than the crooning styles; it aims to suggest a deeply-felt emotion (for the treachery of a loved one, for example), but the emotion has not the ingrown quality shown by the crooners. With the crooners, and particularly with the later exponents of special styles from America, one is in the world of the private nightmare; here, it is still assumed that deep emotions about personal experiences are something all experience and in a certain sense share. The manner of singing is therefore more open. On the other hand, it is not fully the public manner of the pantomime singer who has, at the end of Act 3, to 'give everything she's got' to 'Jealousy', with all the spotlights on her. Her manner is emotional, but the circumstances — the huge auditorium, the hundreds in tiers — call for a very broad brush, a simplification into boldly caricatured emotional strokes. Thus one arrives at the 'big-dipper' style of singing, the style used by working-class entertainers giving *individual* performances in the great public places. Here the voice takes enormous lifts and dips to fill out the lines of a lush emotional journey. Something of all this is in the club-and-pub style of singing, but reduced to scale and made more homely; the 'big dipper' adapted for use in a moderately sized room. Each emotional phrase is pulled out and stretched; it is the verbal equivalent of rock-making, where the sweet and sticky mass is pulled to surprising lengths and pounded; there is a pause as each emotional phrase is completed, before the great rise to the next and over the top. The whole effect is increased by a nasal quality, though one slighter than that used by crooners. The most immediately recognizable characteristic is the 'ēr' extension to emotionally important work, which I take to be the result partly of the need to draw every ounce of sentiment from the swing of the rhythm, and partly of the wish to underline the pattern of the emotional statement. The result is something like this

> You are-ēr the only one-ēr for me-ēr,
> No one else-ēr can share a dream-ēr with me-ēr,
> (pause with trills from the piano leading to
> the next great sweep)
> Some folks-ēr may say-ēr . . .

And when the choruses come along, because the singing is what I have called 'open', the company are likely to join in less self-consciously than in most other forms of community singing today. However quickly the feeling may be dissipated afterwards, they have for the present a feeling of warm and shared humanity.[5]

The power of sentimental music, of the experience of being in a crowd of like-feeling people,[6] and of such powerfully sympathetic writing, are alike in moving us, whether as listener or reader, and in ordinary speech, to speak of something as 'moving' is to confer approval upon it. Of course, as Hoggart himself implies, it is too rarely asked where and to what we are moved, especially if we are one of the crowd, but in this as so many other cases, he suggests a destination. For the story the songs tell is part of the ensemble of stories told by the many texts Hoggart scrutinizes which the working class of Northern industrial England possess, repeat, and endlessly deploy for their own manifold purposes and intentions. These texts can hardly be summarized; like any body of literature it is precisely their business to resist summary, and it is part of

Hoggart's impressive command that he insists by example and time and again, on the irreducible distinctiveness, substance, and defensive vitality of each of the many practices he describes. And this insistence partakes of a general principle of literary criticism, that a poem, and any other kind of text, 'is as it is, and not otherwise' (in Coleridge's words), because if it could be spoken differently, it would be a different thing, to be differently understood and interpreted.

So to generalize Hoggart's intensely practical criticism — what he called elsewhere[7] 'reading for value' — is to run the risk, in the eyes of more ideologically minded literary critics, of substituting abstraction for concreteness, theory for practice. Yet it is exactly Hoggart's significance at this point in the development of English social theory that he dissolves the distinction between theory and practice; his is the study of the material practices of a domestic culture — the relations of its expressive production, in a mouthfilling phrase; meeting his folks, in a folksier one. Either way of putting it is ideological, no doubt. On the one hand, Hoggart is early spokesman for the New Left, in cherishing and understanding the continuingly and reassuringly proletarian nature of Leeds life; on the other, right hand, he documents the assaults of mass-produced culture upon the basic decencies of the doggedly self-reliant, excellently bloodyminded, local and neighbourly Englishman.

Faults on both sides of the two readings, certainly, but truths also. The closeness, communality, tolerance and determination — these blandly general qualities Hoggart spends so much precious time in giving solid weight and actuality to — these transpire from his pages as warranting a North British version of the Socialist Realist worker, overalled, strong, spannered, muscular. At the same time, the same inanimate cartoon seen in the twilight of *Scrutiny*'s last contributors looks a beaten man, the springs of his action unbent (Hoggart's own metaphor), his sexuality reduced to the pinups of the Army storeroom, his healthy ribaldry to nerveless cynicism, his independent democratic voice to the shadow boxing editorial of the *Daily Mirror*.

These outlines are visible in the pages of *The Uses of Literacy.* Hoggart has taken up and revised the *Scrutiny* theory of industrial culture, sticking to the view that the old pieties and sanctions, carried and expressed in a trenchant, proverbial and vigorously traditional idiom, *do* sustain a living and knowable community, and that these values have survived against all the odds the worst darknesses of industrial society. In the second part of the book, 'Yielding Place to the New', he draws on the same metahistory in order to document the further decline of the

West, its 'indifferentism', its 'candy-floss world' of the newer mass art, its 'sex in shiny packets' and its 'scepticism without revision'.

It is a familiar outline, especially when its paraphrases appear as threnody in the mouths of such characteristic oddities of the times as, among the elderly, Malcolm Muggeridge (in the USA, William Buckley) and, among the juvenile middle-aged, Auberon Waugh (in the USA, Tom Wolfe). If this is Hoggart's dominant melody, then, full and swelling as it is, it is only another Labour Party tune, singable in a major key as long as the big majorities lasted, usefully transposable to the minor as the working class and its political institutions drifted apart.

The real book is, on my reckoning, a much bigger thing than a lament. In the first place, written and thought about as it was in the border country which is neither everyday life nor academic study, along the high tension which keeps us all taut and humming between public and private lives, work and home, tradition and novelty, custom and education, Hoggart has *renamed* the ordinary so that it becomes once again the fabulous. Academic distributions of labour generate their own hierarchies, systems of prestige, privilege, payment; they uncompromisingly reproduce their own society's class structure. Hoggart's book changed that class structure, and wonderfully moving as it is, moves thoughtful students back into their own historical experience. This is his second contribution. In its materiality, its daring, its rich recreation of the human meanings of unreflexive action, his conceptual discovery is very similar to Titmuss's in *The Gift Relationship*: for he replaces experience at the centre of the human sciences. Inevitably what counts for him as experience is selectively identified, in history and in geography, but in forcing the practice of literary criticism through the limits of the received tradition and into the texts of a differently felt life, he reforms both the method and the subject-matter of a whole intellectual generation. The methodical transformation, however technical this sounds, is his greatest achievement. As a later, American anthropologist observes,

To put the matter this way is to engage in a bit of metaphorical refocusing of one's own, for it shifts the analysis of cultural forms from an endeavor in general parallel to dissecting an organism, diagnosing a symptom, deciphering a code, or ordering a system — the dominant analogies in contemporary anthropology — to one in general parallel with penetrating a literary text. If one takes the cockfight, or any other collectively sustained symbolic structure, as a means of "saying something of something" (to invoke a famous

Aristotelian tag), then one is faced with a problem not in social mechanics but social semantics. For the anthropologist, whose concern is with formulating sociological principles, the question is, what does one learn about such principles from examining culture as an assemblage of texts?[8]

The quotation brings out the theoretic form of such very practical criticism. For Hoggart's last innovation is situated in the context of his method: to revalue experience in this way *is* to bring to mind new theory. For a generation, across class and geography, his book enabled an entirely new recognition of what the experience of that generation had meant. Far from the rather distasteful fingering of popular culture by the Jewish Marxists of the Frankfurt Institute of Social Research,[9] and far from the raucous relativism of some latterday popular culturalists,[10] Hoggart gave back to itself a generation shaped and nourished by the BBC's light music (Vera Lynn, who else?), standup comics (Al Read and Tommy Handley, Blackpool and Watford), succulently sweet or savoury awful food (condensed milk and HP sauce) and their cinematic equivalents (*Passport to Pimlico* and *Whisky Galore*).

When these fragments, scraps, bits and greasy relics of the culture arrived in academic life, a different theory of universals arrived with them. Hoggart's single book coincided with the start of a much grander intellectual project, still under construction, which brings together the dimensions of theory and experience in what is far and away the most ambitious piece of postwar architecture reviewed in these pages.

RAYMOND WILLIAMS: LETTERS AND POLITICS

It may be objected that this book is too much a work of hagiology. It may be rejoined that the making of many books involves at least probably a sufficient number of good men and fine women, and that to admire their work is no less to admire those best parts of the authors which declare themselves in those works. Yet beyond this apt, pat point, it has been and remains my critical hermeneutic that the exigencies of twentieth-century English thought placed in its necessarily peculiar history require for interpretation the reconstruction of the heuristics, purposes, and intentions of particular theories out of the battle to make sense of a lived experience, both personal and impersonal. On this account a theory in or out of a book, is no more and no less than the agent's intellectual model with which to make sense of, grapple with, overcome and turn to his own the endless, otherwise omnipotently meaningless assault of events in all their inanity. And in a book devoted to the sufficiently heroic endeavours of these individuals both to refuse the easy purchase of chainstore theory, *and* to insist intransigently on making theory as best they could out of the chancey mixture of history and autobiography they had to hand, then not only is a little decorous hero-worship a proper part of the method, but Raymond Williams is a plausible candidate, with Edward Thompson, for leading hero of the years in which the forward march of consumer individualist values halted itself at the cliff edge, and the call for different, new, vastly more mutual, altruistic, and less destructive values-with-practices became paramount.

Williams (born in 1921), as the prologue notes, is more than a suitable case for treatment on the model of this book, he is the foremost exponent of the method. While it is both true and important that he, Titmuss, Hoggart, Thompson, and Berger — together with well-known peers in other cultural disciplines, Peter Worsley in anthropology, Doris Lessing in novels, David Holbrook in education, Basil Bernstein in sociology, R. D. Laing and Aaron Esterson in psycho-analysis — had to make their subject matter out of the intersections of career and history, of biography and eventuality, Williams has always been much more self-conscious and intellectually reflexive about the whole business, and has indeed made that very condition his business. In his case, and in a powerful and insistent manner, he has made his biography a type for all biographies, and to study him, we must study it.

In the most direct and unignorable way, therefore, his work pushes what we habitually call the writer's background not merely into the middle of the stage, but into the middle of the auditorium. What we are listening to, in other words, becomes the locus of our own action. In part, of course, this is true of every thinker-actor in this book: that is why I have chosen them, and that, precisely, is the intellectual method they signify and teach. But such an account is largely made possible by Williams's own work; however much, in some celestial examination order, he might prove to rate less than Collingwood, say, or Leavis, he stands with Thompson as the most influential because most exemplary intellectual of the thirty years in which English consumer culture was the dominant frame of mind (hegemony as Williams might say), inside which the people of England, Wales, Scotland and Northern Ireland made their very different settlements.

Williams was born in 1921 in the village of Pandy, near Abergavenny, a solid market town at the heart of the recently renamed Welsh county of Gwent. His father, sturdily recreated as Harry Price in Williams's first novel,[11] was a signalman with the Great Western Railway, a private company until the railways were taken, bankrupt and unreplenished as I noted earlier, into state ownership in 1947. Williams's father was also an active trade unionist and officer of the branch Labour Party, and Williams himself was at an early stage in his life active and articulate in the politics always woven much more thickly into the texture of a deeply resistant and individual national Welsh culture than was ever so explicitly possible in working-class England. Williams is a Welshman, he learned his politics as the trains carried coal from the Welsh valleys northwards past his father's signal box, and he learned it as he left the Welsh village, colonized and depleted by 900 years of English occupation and the successive depopulations of farm and traffic, left it alongside so many of his countrymen for new work and opportunity in England, emigrating across the border and carrying their hopes and his own ambitions.

He came to Cambridge, as a friend and associate points out,[12] with an unusually complete and coherent experience behind him, and a consequently shaped, focused, and self-confident identity capable of bringing that experience to grip on the future with singular energy and purchase. He carried and carries everywhere the history of his own life, of his family, and of his class. His father, as *Border Country* makes richly present to us,[13] was a man of notable strength, bodily and spiritual, and his commitment to the settling of his life and family in the fullest and most historical sense of 'settling', together with his long, taciturn, and passionate labouring to hold together all parts of his life — beekeeping, the signal box, the Labour Party, market gardening, his son's prowess, his marriage and home — in unity and commonwealth, these provide Williams with absolute and enduring material and model for his own life's work.

And yet, as he writes so finely in *Modern Tragedy,*

We come to tragedy by many roads. It is an immediate experience, a body of literature, a conflict of theory, an academic problem. This book is written from the point where the roads cross, in a particular life.

In an ordinary life, spanning the middle years of the twentieth century, I have known what I believe to be tragedy, in several forms. It has not been the death of princes; it has been at once more personal and more general. I have been driven to try to understand this experience, and I have drawn back, baffled, at the distance between my own sense of tragedy and the conventions of the time. Thus I have known tragedy in the life of a man driven back to silence, in an unregarded working life. In his ordinary and private death, I saw a terrifying loss of connection between men, and even between father and son: a loss of connection which was, however, a particular social and historical fact: a measurable distance between his desire and his endurance, and between both the purposes and meanings which the general life offered him. I have known this tragedy more widely since. I have seen the loss of connection built into a works and a city, and men and women broken by the pressure to accept this as normal, and by the deferment and corrosion of hope and desire. I have known also, as a whole culture has known, a tragic action framing these worlds, yet also, paradoxically and bitterly, breaking into them: an action of war and social revolution on so great a scale that it is continually and understandably reduced to the abstractions of political history, yet an action that cannot finally be held at this level and distance, by those who have known it as the history of real men and women, or by those who know, as a quite personal fact, that the action is not yet ended.[14]

We cannot doubt, paradoxically private and reticent as Williams often is, that the man driven into silence, and unregarded by the many passengers for whose safety he was along several miles of railway responsible, is Williams's father. And in any case, this passage, tainted a little by too many first person pronouns, couched perhaps in a rounder rhetoric than the unsympathetic would find convincing, brings out movingly many of his main themes in his most characteristic style. 'Themes': 'style': this is the terminology of the literary-practical critic, for whom anatomical analysis is, first, the sensitive description of elements of composition — tone, imagery, rhythm, organization — followed by a further description of an individual 'response' (sometimes promoted to the status of *the* individual response), a description which mingles in an unexamined way with appraisal.

Leavis made clear the immense superiority of his later thought to this version of the testing of judgement. As a technique, much may be said of it in defence of its practice as the dominant form of literary discourse in England, from sixth-form 'A' level syllabuses on and up. But it failed Leavis at the key moment at which he wanted to begin to write about the novel, and for the reason that the forms of novels themselves resisted such treatment. In finding a way to write about the novel Leavis developed a prose capable not so much of critical comment upon, as direct encounter with and entry into the experience of the novel. It is hard to speak of the rarity of this achievement. Adrian Stokes's presence in this book is largely upheld by his gift to bring off the same quick, ready representation of his own experiencing of the experience (paintings or streetscapes) of others. So, too, Hoggart writes in such a way as to make the reader feel a strong bond holding him into the circle of experience which is both Hoggart's and the people's of whom he writes.

Such writing is the good novelist's gift, we may say, and it is much to the point that Williams has published four novels,[15] as much part of his body of work as his more conventional theorizing. Indeed, in his *Marxism and Literature,*[16] he writes of the need to dissolve absolutely the category of 'imaginative literature' which all too often seems to mystify the ideas literature expresses, and to remove their resonance and applicability by confining them to a sound-proof sitting-room marked 'aesthetics'. The aesthetic is the domain of private feeling, and although Williams doesn't say so, the academic study of literature — the dominant subjects in which are rightly enough classed as the humanities at university — is largely performed at undergraduate level by women; the teachers are mostly men of course. Confining novels and poems to private life, the ideal definition of that private life largely being lived by women, is a social mechanism for cutting letters off from politics, and it is this unnatural, time-serving severance that Williams works to heal. A good world is a world in which there is difference only in degree and not in kind between the many linguistic practices of men and women; I may anticipate an argument proposed in the last chapter, and say on Williams's behalf (though not in his words) that all theory takes the form of narrative, and that political science, novels, and factory-floor mythology and anecdote, are all alike in the narrative form they take for the representation and the interpretation of the experience they render intelligible in virtue of that form.

This is to jump ahead. But it is also to congratulate Williams, as unimpudently as possible, on having started his great project from the social theories of men and women deeply preoccupied with — in the conventional sense — English literature. In *Culture and Society,* writing about D. H. Lawrence, Williams says,

Lawrence started, then, from the criticism of industrial society which made sense of his own social experience, and which gave title to his refusal to be 'basely forced'. But alongside this ratifying principle of denial he had the rich experience of childhood in a working-class family, in which most of his positives lay. What such a childhood gave was certainly not tranquillity or security; it did not even, in the ordinary sense, give happiness. But it gave what to Lawrence was more important than these things: the sense of close quick relationship, which came to matter more than anything else. This was the positive result of the life of the family in a small house, where there were no such devices of separation of children and parents as the sending-away to school, or the handing-over to servants, or the relegation to nursery or playroom. Comment on this life (usually by those who have not experienced it) tends to emphasize the noisier factors: the fact that rows are always in the open; that there is no privacy in crisis; that want breaks through the small margin of material security and leads to mutual blame and anger. It is not that Lawrence, like any child, did not suffer from these things. It is rather that, in such a life, the suffering and the giving of comfort, the common want and the common remedy, the open row and the open making-up, are all part of a continuous life which, in good and bad, makes for a whole attachment. Lawrence learned from this experience that sense of the continuous flow and recoil of sympathy which was always, in his writing, the essential process of living. His idea of close spontaneous living rests on this foundation, and he had no temptation to idealize it into the pursuit of happiness: things were too close to him for anything so abstract. Further, there is an important sense in which the working-class family is an evident and mutual economic unit, within which both rights and responsibilities are immediately contained. The material processes of satisfying human needs are not separated from personal relationships; and Lawrence knew from this, not only that the processes must be accepted (he was firm on this through all his subsequent life, to the surprise of friends for whom these things had normally been the function of servants), but also that a common life has to be made on the basis of a correspondence between work relationships and personal relationships: something, again, which was only available, if at all, as an abstraction, to those whose first model of society, in the family, had been hierarchical, separative and inclusive of the element of paid substitute labour — Carlyle's 'cashnexus'.[17]

That long quotation could serve as a basic text for the study not only of Williams's thought, but of the practice of hermeneutics and the necessity of imagining the good life which together are the ground of this book. The passage was written twenty-five years or more ago, certainly; Williams has thought himself much further along a difficult road since then, and it has long been a merely literary exercise to detect in a writer's early work many of the matters which he developed later on. Well, there is much he has grown beyond in *Culture and Society,* as he acknowledges in *Politics and Letters,* but here we find in summary Williams's determination to hold in close, tense, difficult relation the diffuse material of politics and letters, of power and privilege and reward (Max Weber's trinity of political indices) in their invasion and pervasion of the stuff of the sensibility — feelings, ideas, kinship, needs, fantasy.

It is much contended by social theorists of the Left[18] that the deployment of quotation is a disagreeably redundant legacy from the bad old days of practical, that is, non-theoretical criticism. But such declarative repudiation of the incorrectness attached by definition to the positions of other intellectual alliances has a general as well as a particular arrogance and self-righteousness attached to it which characterize the enclave social methods of many Leavisites and Marxists alike in the past decade. Such blank hauteur, the opposite of real intellectual method, will not look to left or right from right or left in proceeding along the narrow way towards the strait gate which alone leads to intellectual redemption. Refusing to dirty one's hands with the murky methods of materialism or idealism (depending on your camp-following) is to prove your fideism by your works. Thus, to protest theory above practice, or principles above theory, or one subject over another, the pure waters of one bibliography over the dangerous pollutions of another, keeps competition going in the genteelly vociferous market-place of English intellectual life, but does little for the advancement of learning or the disinterested practice of culture.

In all his best work Williams has calmly and resolutely kept up his kind of English, which is to say as he did once himself, that Leavis and Marx have been the two main influences upon his thought. He has taken Leavis's lead in identifying the critical experiences of industrial society as being the fractures of many kinds of continuity, in belief, language, community, and identity, and for the first time since William Morris, has transcribed Marx's concepts and diagnosis back into the stuff of the English experience.

English? And Williams so much a Welshman? Let us say, that with Richard Hoggart, and their earliest associates in the periodicals *Politics and Letters* and the *New Reasoner,*[19] Williams prised successful and intelligent social theory out of the hands of English liberalism and placed it for a quarter century firmly in the care of native socialists, of Celts, and of working-class nonconformists. It is not a polemical assertion to say that, some highly idiosyncratic economics apart,[20] there has been no really impressive social theorizing by English conservatives since Michael Oakeshott's best work in *Experience and Its Modes* and *Rationalism in Politics,*[21] for all the ungainsayable fact that there are plenty of intelligent conservatives congratulating themselves on ruling what remain very comfortable roosts at Oxford and Cambridge. Yet if social theory at its best since 1950 or so has favoured different versions of socialism with which to interpret the world, it is surely safe to say that Raymond Williams has most enabled that theory to speak sanely and affirmatively and in the real language of men. Inasmuch as Marxism in its latest attire is an absolute prerequisite in the armoury of the social theorist, then Williams is the man who has retranslated Marxist concepts into a spoken idiom.

In *Culture and Society* he disclaims membership of the broad Marxist church. In *Marxism and Literature* he acknowledges publicly, by deeds and faith, his return. It is in both senses a hard thing to say about a man and thinker of such unusual integrity and completeness, a person clearly capable of determined and rational thought, and with the necessary virtues to carry through the decisions he comes to, that on occasions he seems to flinch from acknowledging the deadly and disgusting things done in the names of both Marxism and communism, the hateful guilt borne by some socialist intellectuals, including heroes such as Liebknecht and Rosa Luxemburg, Benjamin and Brecht, for their lying and distortions wittingly performed in the names of freedom and the masses, and that elsewhere Williams accepts with surely far too little scepticism the routine demonology of Marxism. In the teeth of the USSR, of Poland and Czechoslovakia, Cambodia Year Zero, to say nothing of the transparent dottiness of minor Marxist sects in the West or the obdurate stupidity of the French Communist party, it is very difficult to keep tranquil faith with actually existing socialism,[22] and to see it as having the faintest chance of making something come of something. In holding the old enemy, capitalism, and its various new guises from Mrs. Thatcher via the multinational corporation and the White House to the insane arsenals of Armageddon, squarely in his sights, Williams lets himself off the essential precision and attention to the possible which is needed to keep belief in socialism alive.

Of course he's right to do so; but not always so very right.[23] On the one hand, if a man or woman cannot make a decent home with honour and probity on the Left, where may he or she live? On the other, to live in the honest puzzlement and self-righteous independence of exile is to sentence oneself both to homelessness and ineffectuality. Williams, in contrast to Leavis, chose and chooses membership, affiliation, allegiance. All his working life, he has sought to recover, in his own fine phrase from *The Country and the City*, a 'knowable community', a community of a sort he had known deeply and right through himself, in Pandy, and which he and others sought to renew in intellectual terms later on.

One such renewal was his part in founding *New Left Review,* a journal now central to the making of English social theory. It is a deservedly celebrated history on the further pinions of the left how, from the deeply unpromising days of the Suez invasion, in the lowering climate of the Macmillan administration, before the earliest stirrings of CND in the bosoms of draft-dodgers from the Cold War, out of the dead sea of the Labour Party's abysmal deeps in 1956 and 1957 there came a troop of ex-communists and revolutionary socialists to start the *New Reasoner,* then *Universities and Left Review,* and finally *New Left Review.*

The group of intellectuals and academics who set out from the stepping stones laid in the periodicals contained great names, unknown then and now, it is satisfying to say, standing on the library shelves in highly heterodox but solid achievement: Peter Worsley, Alisdair MacIntyre, Charles Taylor, Stuart Hall, Doris Lessing, John Berger, Michael Barratt Brown, and half a dozen others. Above them, the two men towards whom I suppose intellectuals on the Left have most turned for strength, refreshment and courage when feeling more depleted and broken-spirited than ever in the lone and level sands of dissident British politics since Budapest: Edward Thompson and Raymond Williams.

The first twelve issues of the *New Left Review* gave intellectual heart and a rallying rhetoric to the New Left movement which flourished in the espresso coffee wake of CND. The tabloid format, the grainy social realist photography, the instantly intelligent commentary on the world of the times — on the unilateralist victory at Scarborough, on Algeria, on Cuba — the reviews of a recrudescent class-conscious culture of films (Reisz and Richardson), of novels (Lessing, Sillitoe), of drama (Arden, Osborne) — the pace and immediacy of those signs of the times were easy to take for wonders. It is no wonder that so many students took new bearings from *NLR.* A way of putting it would be to say that these were the students for whom becoming teachers was the natural way to give their moral and political commitment context and action.

The break came after the twelfth number. The magazine characterized itself by its large-hearted left eclecticism; it reviewed eagerly and critically the relevant books (Thompson's review of *The Long Revolution* is a classic of English socialist thinking aloud) but it had in no sense taken up a theoretic stance — after a couple of years had had neither time nor inclination to do so.

CND was the first mass political activity outside Parliament which the country had seen for more than a generation; there was much to do on the road from Aldermaston. But the extra-Labour Left in Britain has latterly put a very high premium upon the clarification and definition of theory as a precondition of mass political action. The customs of the old country of the Left had been less exacting and the sometimes bitter dispute between old and new Left, Romantic socialists and Marxists, was joined.

Williams has worked all his life to hold together theory and experience, both for ecumenical purposes in the socialist movement, and for the larger purpose of imagining the unity of a life, and of all lives. But at this point in the magazine's development a certain faltering in the stride of the old new Left left a gap in editorial organization which a new, vastly self-assured and fluent figure was ready to fill. Perry Anderson was and remains the new leader; he has now edited well over a hundred numbers of the magazine with unflagging energy, a powerful and often florid vocabulary, and a dauntless commitment to the great traditions of western Marxism.

Centrally, Anderson defined an ambitious, clear and comprehensive policy for an academic Marxist journal. *New Left Review* became a vehicle of policy in a way which gives that dead metaphor new life: it was fast, exclusive, and it ate up the historical and geographical miles. Its passengers were strictly vetted not, indeed, for their orthodoxy in any narrow sense, for *New Left Review* has been admirable for its ecumenical range and resourcefulness. But the nature of the journey and − in a favourite word − the proposed trajectory of the vehicle, demanded a tight ship and a close crew. Apart from the abiding respect it shared with an astonishing variety of otherwise contesting left-wing groups for Raymond Williams, his personal magnetism and unrivalled intellectual stature, and apart from one or two other spiky exchanges with Edward Thompson and Michael Barratt Brown, the old new Left disappeared overnight from the journal.

They were a loss. The crackle and sparkle the early numbers showed, their immediacy and rapid polemics, would have done much to temper the relentless severity of the praxiology which followed. Editorials of the sort Stuart Hall was so good at would have eased the strain of the extreme and jargon-clotted abstraction. For *New Left Review* is quite unirrigated by the waters of Babylon. The aridity comes out in what was the new editors' first and boldest venture, one which makes the relevant numbers now unobtainable. Scattered across the first eight years of the new provenance were Anderson's and Nairn's bold rewriting of the structure of British hisjtory in an effort to uncover 'the origins of the present crisis'.

In this bid at retotalizing the meaning and direction of the nation's development, they identified as its problematic structure of unresolved contradiction, three crucial determinants. First, the fact of its partial and premature bourgeois revolution, which left the landowning classes solidly in charge after 1688; second, the anti-metropolitan and centrifugal tendency of its highly local industrialization; and third, the coagulation of a proletariat, once the most insurgent in the world but rendered, alas, powerless by its antedating the Marxian concepts which would have given it leverage on its situation.

The strength and attractiveness of such roomy historical accommodations are obvious. In this father's house are very many mansions. It makes possible the intermittent comminations spoken over the death of social democracy and labourism; it permits, in a pyrotechnic show of metaphorical virtuosity, the French experience of revolution to be used as the stick with which to beat British and other forms of social oblivion back to life. In Anderson's single most influential paper, 'Components of the National Culture', this history is implicitly used to allege the anti-theoretic and hopelessly empirical cast of British academic mindlessness; in a glittering *tour de force,* Anderson rounds up and indicts for its lack of historical and political sense every subject in the brochures.

The obverse of this systematic rebuke to the specific forms of British capitalism is the *Review*'s hospitable Europeaness. At a time when the Frankfurt Marxists from Adorno to Habermas were largely the names of comic foreigners, *New Left Review* has kept the names in small circulation and consistently sought to resituate the German theories in British and transcontinental soils; the same with the French Marxists of the *Ecole Normale Superieure*: *New Left Review* was first on the scene with Levi-Strauss, has been the only jounal to keep up with Sartre, and decisively introduced the hardest faced and most clenched-jawed of the French Marxists, Louis Althusser, to Britain, as well as a cosmopolitan reach which has brought in a fine haul, the biggest catch of which has been *New Left Review*'s single-handed resurrection of Gramsci as the greatest revolutionary Marxist in the West.

It is an incontestably magnificent achievement. At the merest level of practical politics, a Cabinet which had read the *Review* on falling profits, on nationalism and the break-up of Britain, on the Middle East or on Latin America, would be better educated and better served than by the Treasury or the Foreign Office.[24] Yet for all that it is such a bright, dry air that *New Left Review* breathes, its terrific bracingness doesn't have too much taste or heart. The magazine has undoubtedly rekindled its great tradition in novel and usable forms; it has led the recrudescence of serious Marxist theory across the human sciences; the really serious criticism that I may make of it is, however, that even in its liberal entertainment of very various Marxisms, it tends towards a humourless fixity of theory miles away from the life really lived by those for whom it most seeks to theorize. And so, while it is hard, in spite of its jargon-laden and leaden abstractions, to overstate the gratitude owed to *New Left Review* by all serious English intellectuals, it is exactly what John Dunn has called[25] its 'poised General Staff perspective' 'sustaining [its] views as an elaborate and comprehensive system [and] professionally concerned . . . to establish . . . its coherence and to extend its scope' which so contrasts in my potted history with the rugged outlines of the Williams landscape, green valley and mountain alike.

Rugged and uneven that landscape often is. It is also shrouded at times in thick fog. It is bound to be so. Any original thinker, grappling with deeply recalcitrant material the concepts for re-ordering which have to be continuously revised and at times created from scratch, will have frequent difficulty bringing his subject into focus. And as I noted in relation to Leavis, the effort to shape the prose of your times so that it will carry the best of those times — the finest life it can imagine — and match up to the best wisdom you possess, is the very heart of understanding human action, and its proper and justified epistemology. The formulation makes it clear how hard the task is. In Williams's case, his prose (and therefore his thought) falters by this standard either when its essential vocabulary becomes too cumbrous, as well as too portentous and foggy, or when his polemics single out the enemy in a way which too simple-mindedly trusts to their sameness and substance across the decades. In the first case, he overreaches his theory and, faced by the magnitude of his own ambition to write a Marxism (in his useful phrase, a 'cultural materialism')[26] capable of reconnecting economic base to cultural superstructure in a modern state, falls on occasion into the empty space left by an ingenuously disregarded absence of understanding. In the second case, trusting as he so directly does to the truths of his own experience, the experience fails him either by delivering banality or by serving up the wrong or the too crudely named enemies for commination.

The very best of this process, along with the veeringness of judgement, comes out in *The Country and the City,* which is a large, uneven, total attempt to revise, to rebut, and to replace the English ideology most of all as it shapes and reshapes the key notion of community.

The modality of the book is resistance, perhaps the best, certainly the most characteristic stance of all my chosen thinkers. He gathers up the grand historical themes of *Culture and Society* and *The Long Revolution,* in which books first he summarizes the English tradition of thought about industrial-capitalist society, its personal liberations and its intense, failing battle to re-establish a non-exploitative community, and then, in *The Long Revolution*, goes on to seek to dissolve the dominantly ideological symbols of the bourgeoisie — the individual and his or her liberal fulfilments, high culture and the spiritual grace it confirms. He replaces the master-legends of old liberalism with what is always, now and in England, a minority, resistant account of lived experience as social, of tragedy as general and historical, of change as guaranteed though never for better or worse, of men and women at once collaboratively and antagonistically making their own world, though never in circumstances of their own choosing.

In *The Country and the City* he brings together his long meditation on letters and politics, imagination and power, in a sustained effort at an historical revaluation which, taking Marx's model of city-dependency in any rural or any country's production, challenges and reinterprets the whole reading Leavis provides of the map of English literature. It is much more, of course, than an argument with one man (even the English Marx against the English Hegel). It is an argument about the material meanings of an exceedingly material landscape, and that landscape as redefined and repossessed by writers about it.

The meditation, absorbed and absorbing as it is, has its longueurs, and has its wilful subjectivities: the arrogance of class declared by the English country house, its casual cruelties and neglect, are not all there is to read either in the less assertive examples of the picturesque tradition — John Soane and Norman Shaw, say, as architects, rather than John Vanbrugh or Waterhouse — or in the mild-mannered gentilities of the English market town.[27] But even where Williams's literary or political judgements seem too brisk (Ben Jonson), too angry ('hired mouths') or just too generous (Grassic Gibbon), the open and irresistible appeal to common standards of justice and mercy, gentleness and generosity in his reading of (say) Crabbe, Dickens, Hardy, and the new novelists of the once imperial territories, goes along with a novel (and novelist's) way of seeing, the structure of which impels Williams's method: the depth, permanence, and pervasiveness of what he calls 'the structure of feeling'; the historical forces which go to shape and reproduce entire 'social formations'; the profound alterations effected upon our conception of our own experience by the relations of production which hold us together and apart — most tellingly seen by Dickens in his manifold images of London life; the ideological distortions wrought upon writers by those who want them to say congenial things — Hardy as the key example. All this composes at once a theory and a method. The theory pictures the relations of our imaginary narratives to our real centres of power; the method insists on pressing these relations upon the actualities of experience, whether in novels or our everyday conversation, informally dramatising[28] the disconnections and contradictions we find natural.

To put it so is to share a little in Williams's inclination to ellipticality. Perhaps the best way to focus upon the factification of his work, still so much in progress, is to turn to his most recent novel, *The Fight for Manod* — not published until 1979, but in composition for most of the previous decade.

The novel is the third in his trilogy of Welsh novels and brings together the characters of the first two books. It also completes a study of the social relations (both manual and mental) rooted in the three curves of capital investment of the past 140 years, as accumulated in three modes of communication production: railways, cars, electronics. *Border Country* was dominated by trains; in *Second Generation,* the University of Oxford worked in bland disharmony with the Cowley carworks; in *The Fight for Manod,* the mature demographic historian who left Brynmawr station for Cambridge in 1938 or so and the fiery young radical who threw over his Oxford PhD in about 1960 to work on the car lines come together to advise the Labour Government on the prospects for building a new town in the mid-Wales valleys, a post-Milton Keynes kind of new town intended to manufacture and to test in its normal working a complex, novel system of communication technologies. The human needs are plain, as the older hero of *Border Country* declares in a fine statement at the final big meeting before the Minister of the Environment, the interested investors, the EEC functionaries, and the two Welsh consultants.

the crucial factor — you must really appreciate this — is who the people are to be. For this is a country bled dry by prolonged depopulation. Not far away, in the valleys, there is a ravaged and depressed old industrial area. If it can be clearly seen that in these new ways, bringing the two needs together, a different future becomes possible, a future that settles people, that gives them work and brings them home, then through all the dislocation, through all the understandable losses and pains of change, there could still be approval, significant approval: not just the design of a city but the will of its citizens.'

'You are eloquent, Dr. Price, but I don't quite clearly follow. Are you saying that this city should be confined to Welsh?'

'I don't mean nationality. I mean that the storms that have blown through that country — storms with their origin elsewhere — should now be carefully and slowly brought under control. In one place at a time, one move at a time, we should act wholly and consistently in the interests of that country, and those interests, primarily, are the actual people now there, caught between rural depopulation and industrial decline, the end of two separated orders, and there in Manod, if we could see it, is a real way beyond them. But only a real way if it belongs to the people on whose land it is being made.' (*Fight for Manod*, pp. 193—4)

It's a very good novel, much sparer than the other two, the dialogue constantly stirring the reader to a vivid realization of how hard it is, as they say, to communicate. But Williams takes this difficulty far beyond the chronic banality of 'communication problems' to the thick, obscure obstructions in the veins of people's bodies and feelings as they struggle to get clear what they know and how they can act upon that knowledge. And at the end, if we reduce a rich and immediately recognizable wide world to a diagram, the action possible is shared by Matthew Price and Robert Lane: the one historian, spokesman with a rare probity and incorruptibility of his people's intelligentsia, and the other scholar-bureaucrat, sometime Fabian and Oxford social theorist, now a planner-managerialist of the middle echelons in the power elite. Peter Owen, the hot, sharp, angular radical is left to patrol the margins of actual social organization, driven out of community by his own passionate uncompromisingness, rehired by a different system of communication for what Lane calls 'the long complacencies of denunciation' after he has hunted down profiteering in land deals based on illegal breaches of confidential documents.

Lane and Price conveniently foreshorten the long, continuing arc of Williams's thought into a still tense and difficult praxis. Lane compellingly summarizes what is surely, for all Williams's obvious dislike and suspicion of Lane's kind of man, Williams's own judgement upon England, upon Britain, now.

'The whole of public policy, is an attempt to reconstitute a culture, a social system, an economic order, that have in fact reached their end, reached their limits of viability. And then I sit here and look at this double inevitability: that this imperial, exporting, divided order is ending, and that all its residual social forces, all its political formations, will fight to the end to reconstruct it, to re-establish it, moving deeper all the time through crisis after crisis in an impossible attempt to regain a familiar world. So then a double inevitability:

that they will fail, and that they will try nothing else.' (*Fight for Manod*, p. 181)

But then, as an American friend says to Price a little later,

'Come on, Matt, you want it to happen. You want that city to be built.'
'Well, I want that country replenished.'
'That country? you mean Wales, or that valley?'
'Well, I could even say Britain, if you pushed me. I want the pattern to break, to some new possibility.'
'But that's what's wearing you out. You can't push a whole system.'
'Neither push it nor settle inside it.' (p. 187)

Williams's deep commitment and lived allegiance is to working *for*, always, and working against only when he has to; well, like Price, like Williams. Theory into practice.

9

History and Biography: John Berger and E. P. Thompson

Titmuss and Williams may stand as counterposed statues in a bare landscape, marking the parallel paths taken by a dissenting intelligentsia during the past generation. Titmuss's prose, in its strength and direct truth-telling, is a measure of his intentions in theory: he spoke the facts in the name of necessary and feasible action. He and his followers set out a programme of what to do. Williams's prose, as the last pages of *The Fight for Manod* bring out, registers the deep difficulty of knowing what to do: of keeping your being and your culture, your feelings and your history in a sufficient union, for you to be able to shake off sheer fatigue and bitter frustration, and know what your purposes are. Williams's power is to bring out the real meanings of that experience without glossing its obscurity, indeed at times insisting with a rare and moving honesty that it is the obscurity of experience which has to be lived with, in your body and soul, and sorted out, a bit at a time and as best you can, in terms of everyday life and work and encounter. The grappling with obscurity in his work is always brave and sustained, even if what he takes for granted as the clarities and certainties look a lot less convincing to others than he takes them to be. But it is far more than expressing the self-importance of the over-theoretic and powerless intellectual in the still comfortable West to say that Williams is one of the trio of men whose attention to the possibilities of understanding and action made imaginable by Marxist Socialism, with its tense claims to the status of science and redemptive doctrine, allied to their living a real, visible life in the polity, who mark the spot at which thought becomes valid and valuable action — that sequence of moments Marxists themselves call praxis.

JOHN BERGER: MEMBERSHIP, MANNERISM, EXILE

John Berger (born 1926) is the most enigmatic of the last three of my theoreticians, and also the most singleminded. He was old enough to feel intensely — and like Williams and Thompson, he is plainly a man of very intense feelings — about the second war, but unlike the other two just too young to fight in it. Now a military unit is notoriously weird, and in parts, notoriously horrible; but if its strong bonding and fixed structures are allied by historical chance to believable ideals and given competent expression, then its versions of manliness and friendship prefigure an image of knowable community which a socialist may certainly cherish. The war against Fascism offered Williams and Thompson brief glimpses of such a form of life; they could put it beside their other, happy examples of community — Williams's life in Brynmawr, Thompson's (as we shall see) in the socialist Methodist circles of his father. Berger has always seemed to live a more solitary life, to think in a spikier, more oblique and harder idiom.

On the family cart to the nearest bus station there is not much left to say. They pass many people walking, riding, grazing cattle. The road itself is a passing of stories, with its listeners in the grass on either side.[1]

There is one girl who is a little taller than most of the others and among the nearest to us. She has an aquiline nose and large, dark eyes. Her veil is so crisp that it looks like a linen napkin. Her family are perhaps richer than those of the others. She is proud and self-possessed — as though, if she were sleeping, she would sleep in exactly the position she had decided upon. For her the religious experience which she is now undergoing is part of her private plan for her own development. It is no seduction. It is a long-arranged engagement. But none the less intense. All that will be done unto her will be done in the way that she selects. Always provided that no disaster occurs so that her wishes and decisions become incidental, her life no more than a movement which catches a sniper's eye.

By the West door the man who sells tracts sits behind his table and reads a newspaper.

The girls as they answer sound like doves.[2]

Towards the south one can also see the plain, intensely cultivated, the colour of greengages. Such a view is archetypal. It is the antithesis of a view of the grave.

Across the plain moves the shadow of one white cloud. Where the shadow is, the green is the green of laurel leaves.

The crowd, which is made up of hundreds of dispersed groups, is easy and at home. It is as if the mountain were their common ancestor.[3]

Before, she lived in her body as though it were a cave, exactly her size. The rock and earth around the cave were the rest of the world. Imagine putting your hand into a glove whose exterior surface is continuous with all other substance.

Now her body was no longer a cave in which she lived. It was solid. And everything around, which was not her, was movable. Now what was given to her stopped at the surfaces of her body.[4]

She shivered. He pulled up the sheet to cover her. As he did so, he saw her body stretched almost straight, save that one hip was slightly raised. There are women — often they are wide-hipped and plump — whose bodies become unforeseeably beautiful when recumbent. Their natural formation, like a landscape's, seems to be horizontal. And just as landscapes are for ever continuous, the horizon receding as the eye of the traveller advances, so, to the sense of touch, these bodies seem borderless and infinitely extended, quite regardless of their actual size. His hand set out.[5]

Berger's most characteristic images have about them the painter's, sculptor's attempt to reorder the dialectical traffic of percept and concept so that the familiar is seen along an entirely new plane. The struggle for originality is not merely that, of course; it is the reach of the mind's eye to all the unseen aspects of a subject and the subsequent rage to order the look of things so that what hasn't been seen before can be brought to light, a particular light too, the light of a thinker holding his lamp up in the easy darkness we are used to.

Berger was an art student in the 1940s at the Chelsea and the Central Schools of Art, and exhibited at some of the most genteel and plush-upholstered of the avant-garde galleries off Bond Street. In a phrase he has made his own, his way of seeing is often and strongly reminiscent of Adrian Stokes's. The quotation describing the Italian girls at their confirmation has the suddenness and rightness of Stokes's view of the city street as given point and meaning by the Bogart figure with a gun in his mackintosh pocket. The mannered, deliberate, slow-paced paradox by which the woman, naked and alone in her bedroom, is described in the novel *G,* about Don Juan, is marked like Stokes's redescriptions by the strenuous effort to stop too rapid reading, to insist on the obstacles of language so that a clearer, stronger and, always, more totalizing and kinaesthetic image results.

The studied, effortful nature of Berger's thought as rendered in his prose is like a careful drawing; a drawing with none of the lambent brilliance and swift sinuousness of line commanded by Picasso or Tiepolo, but by a draughtsman at work determined to teach, to make his audience see the familiar in a conceptually different way. It sounds banal to put it so. The post-Romantic conventions which define art as necessarily 'original', distinctively individual, convention-breaking, and so forth, have turned into advertising slogans, as cultural competition has become more open, and cultural authority more completely diffused. Berger, deeply affected by what he understood as the Cubist painters' making possible an image of an unprecedentedly hopeful relation between man and nature, is intent upon using the syntax of his social theory in the same manner as a painter pulling the conventions awry in order to ensure the novel interpretation of the world which has become necessary.

A Cubist painting like Picasso's *Bottle and Glasses* of 1911 is two-dimensional insofar as one's eye comes back again and again to the surface of the picture. We start from the surface, we follow a sequence of forms which leads into the picture, and then suddenly we arrive back at the surface again and deposit our newly acquired knowledge upon it, before making another foray. This is why I called the Cubist picture-surface the origin and sum of all that we can see in the picture. There is nothing decorative about such two-dimensionality, nor is it merely an area offering possibilities of juxtaposition for dissociated images — as in the case of much recent Dadaist or Pop art. We begin with the surface, but since everything in the picture refers back to the surface we begin with the conclusion. We then search — not for an explanation, as we do if presented with an image with a single, predominant meaning (a man laughing, a mountain, a reclining nude), but for some understanding of the configuration of events whose interaction is the conclusion from which we began. When we 'deposit our newly acquired knowledge upon the picture surface', what we in fact do is to find the sign for what we have just discovered: a sign which was always there but which previously we could not read.

To make the point clearer it is worth comparing a Cubist picture with any work in the Renaissance tradition. Let us say Pollaiuolo's *Martyrdom of St. Sebastian.* In front of the Pollaiuolo the spectator completes the picture. It is the spectator who draws the conclusions and infers all except the aesthetic relations between the pieces of evidence offered — the archers, the martyr, the plain laid out behind, etc. It is he who through his reading of what is portrayed seals its unity of meaning. The work is presented to him. One has the feeling almost that St. Sebastian was martyred so that he should be able to explain this picture. The complexity of the forms and the scale of the space depicted enhance the sense of achievement, of grasp.

In a Cubist picture, the conclusion and the connections are given. They are what the picture is made of. They are its content. The spectator has to find his place *within* this content whilst the complexity of the forms and the 'discontinuity' of the space remind him that his view from that place is bound to be only partial.

Such content and its functioning was prophetic because it coincided with the new scientific view of nature which rejected simple causality and the single permanent all-seeing viewpoint.[6]

This is Berger as plain expositor, seeking to recreate in the present tense the rapid dialectical traffic of our quest for interpretation and understanding, when we look seriously at a painting — or any other image. 'What does it mean' is the first, natural question to put to the picture or the percept; how long you take to answer it depends on what will satisfy you.

In his prose Berger strives to express the process whereby the Cubists set down the complex sign (prefiguring a theory) which ordered in a single frame the many planes of their way of seeing. 'The Cubists were the first artists to attempt to paint totalities rather than agglomerations.' Berger's method, as the moving images of the townsfolk on the mountain or the migrants on the road signify, constantly re-presents his individual actors moving tinily but bravely across the great span of a historical geography.

This can lead him to vertiginous foreshortening in his historical explanation. At these moments he seems in something of the predicament Wallace Stevens describes:

> He stood at last by God's help and the police;
> But he remembered the time when he stood alone.
> He yielded himself to that single majesty;
>
> But he remembered the time when he stood alone,
> When to be and delight to be seemed to be one,
> Before the colors deepened and grew small.[7]

Berger stands upright at the end of his grand political avenue only with the help of a simple, global Marxism whose sentimentality, as in this passage, masks itself theatrically by praising the realism of soldiers and scoffing at philosophers:

The majority of the world is now engaged in struggling for a freedom which was inconceivable before the nineteenth century: freedom from exploitation: the freedom for all to live as the equal beneficiaries of the world's material and spiritual production. The struggle must go through many phases. It begins as a struggle for a single national, racial or class freedom from imperialist exploitation. But this new freedom has already outdated and destroyed the older notion of freedom as an individual privilege — and hence also the notion of the privilege of individual heroics.

Events force us now to admit the courage of a people or a class: not the courage of a people as represented by their professional armies, but made manifest in the actions of the entire population, men and women, young and old. The truth of this is realized by military strategists if not by moral philosophers. The strategy of total war recognizes that it is necessary to try to break the courage and resistance of a whole people.[8]

Maybe such tootings of the soul arise from an uneasy, suppressed recognition that in this particular book his heroic example, the Russian sculptor Neizvestny, an extraordinarily brave man and (judging from the photographs) a powerful artist, can't bear the political weight Berger heaps upon him. But such intellectual largesse is scattered through his work so prodigally that it is hard not to feel the emptiness of the bank upon which his natural generosity, itself naturally expressed in anger and hatred at all the dreadfulness and cruelty which resists and breaks generosity, draws so large a moral overdraft.

This is evident at times in the structure of his novels as much as in the manners of his prose. In his novel *G,* he reincarnates a Don Juan whose nearest semblable was Mozart's hero, and uses him as the bass narrative of a long, gripping essay on modern sexuality. This structure brings out with equal force Berger's singular genius (a term he detests and never uses except to derogate it) and his mannerist, methodical liability to intone structural and political crassnesses and simplifications. On the first plane of his intelligence, he thinks himself into G's killing judgement on the sexuality of, in Henry James's phrase, 'the absolute bourgeois . . . without poetic ironies' who subjugate their women by the accuracy with which they select a woman for her publicly acknowledgeable attractiveness, for her not-too-open, suitable sensuality, and for her status as property, a quality as tangible as a hand, a rich head of hair, a soft mouth.

This terse analysis gives rise to one of Berger's most brilliant meditations, upon the nature of bourgeois women, especially married or betrothed women between, say, twenty and forty-five, and their deepest sense of themselves and their sexuality as these are defined by the secret agencies of capital.

> Men surveyed women before treating them. Consequently how a woman appeared to a man might determine how she would be treated. To acquire some control over this process, women had to contain it, and so they interiorized it. That part of a woman's self which was the surveyor treated the part which was the surveyed, so as to demonstrate to others how her whole self should be treated. And this exemplary treatment of herself by herself constituted her presence. Every one of her actions, whatever its direct purpose, was also simultaneously an indication of how she should be treated. . . .
>
> It was with a woman's presence that men fell in love. That part of a man which was submissive was mesmerized by the attention which she bestowed upon herself, and he dreamt of her bestowing the same attention upon himself. He imagined his own body, within her realm, being substituted for hers. This was a theme which occurred constantly in romantic poems about unrequited love. That part of a man which was masterful dreamt of possessing, not her body − this he called lust − but the variable mystery of her presence.
>
> The presence of a woman in love could be very eloquent. The way she glanced or ran or spoke or turned to greet her lover might contain the quintessential quality of poetry. This would be obvious not only to the man she loved, but to any disinterested spectator. Why? Because the surveyor and the surveyed within herself were momentarily unified, and this unusual unity produced in her an absolute single-mindedness. The surveyor no longer surveyed. Her attitude to herself became as abandoned as she hoped her lover's attitude to her would be. Her example was at last one of abandoning example. Only at such moments might a woman feel whole.[9]

The strain in these passages is as apparent as it always is in the best of Berger where he is so unforgettably successful, as he puts it himself in *A Seventh Man,* in 'dismantling the world as seen from one's own place within it, and [reassembling] it as seen from his'. He goes on:

> For example to understand a given choice another makes, one must face in imagination the lack of choices which may confront and deny him. The well-fed are incapable of understanding the choices of the under-fed. . . To talk of entering the other's subjectivity is misleading. The subjectivity of another does not simply constitute a different interior attitude to the same exterior facts. The constellation of facts, of which he is the centre, is different. (p.55)

This is his constant endeavour, as it is of any hermeneutician, any moral human being. It goes wrong when Berger's marvellous powers of reperceiving the grains on the surface of individual life are dotted upon too huge and empty a historical map. Thus in *G* he cuts abruptly from Beatrice, alone and naked in her bedroom looking at a wasp sting on her foot, out to the victory of British imperial forces over the Boers in 1901; and in his astonishing and beautiful account of his own doctor in the Forest of Dean, he moves with quite regardless incongruence from the account of the meaning of a man's life — a fine man, whose manliness is coterminous with the excellence of his doctoring — among poor, dependent, but tough, uncomplaining and also independent people, to theatrical because quite unlocatable gestures: 'I do not claim to know what a human life is worth — the question cannot be answered by word but only by action, by the creation of a more human society.'[10]

The ambition of traditional and contemporary Marxism to be both science and gospel is a stirring one; no serious intellectual can be but profoundly marked by it. Berger is exemplary both because he has refined its broad instruments until they may be inserted into the intimate details of everyday lives — the doctor's, the migrant workers', the Russian sculptor's as he quarrelled with Kruschev, and most recently, the peasants of the Haute-Savoie where Berger now farms and writes — *and* because he gives himself away to the Messianic loosenesses of Marxism-as-redemption.

His lesson in my context is threefold. First, he shows us with greater reach and insight than Williams that the social theorist must be a novelist; must, that is, reorder the constituents of everyday syntax in which we all tell our necessary, interminable stories, so that we can understand hitherto untold tales situated in the subjectivities, so to speak, of speechless men and women: Hungarian painters,[11] amiably randy office boys,[12] peasant crones.[13] Secondly, he brings the diagnostics of Marxism to a point capable of revealing the identities of historical change in the details of the self; theory interprets experience with a vengeance. Thirdly, however, experience revenges itself on him. For in stretching this strong compelling Marxism to the limits of the world, in trying, rightly, to write each personal history as though it were the history of the world, he loses his grip upon the real lives as lived and felt in his best writing, and therefore breaks the essential links between thought and action, being and culture, will and compassion.

EDWARD THOMPSON: THE INTELLECTUAL AS HERO

E. P. Thompson (born in 1924), with Raymond Williams and John Berger, is the third and by now the most nationally and internationally celebrated of a trio of British theoretical socialists who between them have provided the idiomatic and the conceptual links between political theory and social practice, and between — as I have just put it — compassion and will. In the grim face of Socialist Marxism's last fifty years, that visage so hideously calm and resolute in pursuit of terror, murder, mass callousness and negligence, they have reasserted the rich humanism, the vision of love and the promise of happiness implicit in the great tradition of their church. More than that, they have reconnected the link which Stalin broke and which Western Marxists have ignored, between science and faith, between the understanding of how the world is and how it *ought* to be.

In the two or three years since 1979 however, Edward Thompson has made a different move in praxis, though it is one adumbrated by my own earlier subject and the eponymous hero of his first long book, *William Morris*, as well in their different ways by Keynes and Crosland. In becoming the best-known of the public spokesmen in Europe on behalf of the Campaign for Nuclear Disarmament he has, first, and inevitably in terms of the incessant spectacularity of our political culture, become a star; secondly, and by dint of his own prodigious energy in the cause of CND, he illuminates all his academic labour in the light of that giant but by definition temporary undertaking (temporary because in 1982 no one knows what the outcome will be; success or failure will then throw different shadows over the great pile of his writings). In striking similarity to Morris, Thompson has become the best-known and best-loved of the post-war intellectuals. It is invidious, perhaps, to distinguish him from Williams in this way, when Williams has taken the chair or the platform at so many political meetings, but Thompson's celebrity now requires me to treat his work in a rather different way, certainly as having in some parts a vaster audience than the political intellectuals who buy, in still large numbers, Williams's books as soon as they come out. By contrast, Berger's inaccessibility and exile throws into relief Thompson's always craggy, individualist, but vividly *public* mode of thought and modality of address.

There is another, more technical but large and unignorable influence upon any informed discussion of Edward Thompson's work. In 1980,[14] Perry Anderson, who usurped the throne of *New Left Review* in 1962, published a magisterial assessment of all Thompson's work, paying magnanimous and graceful homage to his achievement (honoured, though fraternally, in faintly posthumous sonorities) as the supreme socialist historian now writing in English, but remaining to fight a heavy-weight and bone-crunching contest, going the full distance with Thompson himself. His criticisms of Thompson's voluntarism (in the chapter on 'Agency'), of his relative casualness with non-British history and British imperialism, of the distortions of Thompson's hagiography (for instance, in his treatment of Dean Swift), his sallies into the theory of ideology at the end of *Whigs and Hunters,* all constitute a masterpiece of polemics, and cannot be either parrotted or paraphrased here.

But although historiography has been asserted in these pages to be the heart of the matter of the human sciences, Anderson's argument does not focus quite what it is I seek to identify in Thompson's continuing life and work; or when it does, it does not understand nor explain them. And at this moment, as earlier, I turn to Thompson's biography not — to press the disciplinary point home again — to 'explain' in the manner of bad literary criticism the public works from the private life, but to show how theory is wrung from one man's experience lived in the idiom of his membership of other men's history.

Thompson was born in 1924, son of a Methodist minister and missionary to India. His father, Edward John, was a fierce, gentle and lifelong supporter of the movement for Indian independence, associate of Gandhi and close personal friend of Nehru.[15] He came close, according to his son, to conversion to Buddhism; he was a Methodist, a novelist, and a man of great warmth, loyalty, and ready friendship. Frank, Edward's brother, parachuted into Bulgaria during the war, fought along-side the partisans as a British liaison officer, was tortured and executed by the Nazis in 1944, and given the title of National Hero by the Bulgarians, with a railway station named after him. (Compare the naming of recent colleges in the ancient universities of England: Wolfson, Wolfson, Robinson). Both father and brother remain heroes to Edward, son and brother,[16] as embodying the best of English Methodism and Romantic Socialism — that powerful, life-driving tradition of dissent and idealism which informs so much of the books reported here. Frank's poems, Edward the father's novels, the lives of both, and in their wake, the life and work of Edward Palmer are all given over by the noblest lights of English middle-class Methodism to an exceptional high-mindedness. They shared a bold libertarianism, an absolute commitment to equality, but also, not in spite of, but because of Methodism's sedate gaiety, its decent respectability and subfusc domesticity — a good table, a homely house — they also cherished brotherhood, a strong sense of family, family merrymaking and kindnesses; they easily retained the love which politics always seeks to exclude from its conduct, and present political theory cannot even name.

And this last is Thompson's signal contribution to human theory. Not only was he his father's son, himself an officer at the age of twenty in the 6th Armoured Division in Italy and France fighting against Fascism, but also he read English literature for the first part of his degree under Leavis at Cambridge before turning, like Leavis, to History for the second part. It makes sense of such an experience that, working extra-murally in both institutional as well as intellectual senses, he forges a moral-scientific language capable of connecting love and politics, fraternity and power, murder and mercy.

He shares his endeavour with Williams, of course; the one revaluing literature, the other history in terms of a native socialism. And of course he is hardly alone in the notable reconstruction of postwar British historiography signalled by Christopher Hill's[17] Marxisant revision of the English Civil War and Eric Hobsbawm's[18] chronicles of vagrants, bandits, and footpads, as well as by the founding of the journal *Past and Present*. What Thompson has taken the lion's share of has been, however, the public debate among the intellectuals of the Left about Marxism, Communism, and Socialism, and in one way and another his own presence, both intellectual and moral, his fervour (and his sometimes fervent intemperance and sentimentality) and his capacious, generous and impulsive nature, have dominated to his advantage the interminable debates about theory and practice, revolution and reform, and in his onetime avatar's phrase, responsibility and history.[19]

In 1956 when Russia put down the Hungarian uprising in Budapest with tanks, the British Communist Party was torn asunder between the Stalinists, dully and obdurately faithful to Moscow, and, as we may call them, the Morris men. The Morris men, E. P. Thompson and John Saville their best writers, left the party in thousands — without, as Thompson gratefully remembers, breast-beating or well-audienced apostasy. They just left; and 1956, as I began this book by noting, became one of the emblematic dates in the little red diaries of the post-war Left. In any case, that schism was one necessary, painful move in the ceaseless battle for Thompson and his fellows to stand and to be seen to stand against the deadly clichés of the cold warriors and their remorseless self-advancement. Thompson wishes to name the time-servers for what they were and are, and wished also to stand visibly in the great might of the socialist tradition against those who had been sincerely and intelligibly dismayed by the horrible depredations of the socialist godhead who failed so completely in one country that spectators thought that was the best he could do.

So it was natural for Thompson to be one of the first founders of the journal which became a bestseller as *New Left Review*, at the same time as the first and merely British CND took to the road from the Atomic Weapons Research Establishment at Aldermaston in Berkshire, and walked to Trafalgar Square. I have potted that history in the previous chapter, and it is important in understanding Thompson's giant contribution to the practice of the human sciences in English, to understand even at the (dire) risk of lapsing into individualistic and bourgeois psychologism, that he gave himself greatheartedly to the CND and the brand-new *New Left Review* at the same time as he was working on his classic *The Making of the English Working Class*.[20] When the putsch came at the magazine, and the old Etonian (*sic*) bought it out, Thompson both as historical authority and as contributor was shunted anonymously into the sidings. When his work was noticed, it was at his most vulnerable, and Anderson arraigned him contemptuously for his political misjudgements and serious rhetorical lapses as he editorialized about CND. Thompson was deeply hurt in his most open, generous, and public heart. It is clear to see: indeed not only does he make no attempt to hide the hurt; it is both motive and subject matter of his great essay, 'The Peculiarities of the English' and present in the allusions of his 'Open Letter to Leszek Kolakowski' as well as the long title essay[21] on the then leader of French intellectual Marxists, Louis Althusser. But it is the condition, in Thompson's practice, of what it is to do history at all that the historian extends the full range of his moral sympathies to those classes, causes, and individuals who may naturally be said to merit it. He enormously extends R. G. Collingwood's injunctions to understand the author's intentions with regard to his text, into the whole field of human action, and particularly the feelings which systematically form and inform it. In this also Thompson parallels Williams — indeed they may both be said to have taken such a lead from Leavis, but to have particularized his theory of intuitions by insisting on the social and relational nature of both intuitions and feelings. (After all, where else do they come from?) After Collingwood and with Berger (who quotes

Collingwood's *Idea of History* at length in *G*), Thompson commits himself as a feature of his own large-heartedness to extending moral sympathy and imaginative understanding as far as he can.

The dangers of partisanship are obvious, most of all to a historian. But it it part of the method — and the method must be the man, another way of creating the congruence of role and identity — that the methodist keep as open as possible to the intuitive promptings of his sympathy; without this he cannot practise the kind of history he wants, for he simply cannot recover the intentions of his preferred actors from the linguistic conventions surrounding them.[22] In a book such as *The Making of the English Working Class*, he has to work from the quick, delicate taking of hints made possible by an extraordinarily sensitive and educated imagination. The attention is to the words on the page, certainly, but in this remarkable book the pages of his primary sources were scarcely ever consecutive: they were taken from Cobbett's single-handed newspaper of the early nineteenth century, the *Political Register*, from such goldmines as Samuel Bamford's famous autobiography, *Passages in the Life of a Radical* (1841), which includes his eyewitness account of Peterloo; far more, however, Thompson worked from the archives, such as they are, of dozens of unknown, long defunct newspapers as well as the impounded papers of, for example, the Framework-Knitters committee and similar illicit organizations of early working or radical movements, added to chapbooks, hymnals, placards, fragments and bits of threatening letters or the hardly literate or legible reports of coppers' narks.

How do you tell a story from such bits and pieces? You ask the great heaps of material questions: questions about what these men intended by what they wrote and how they behaved. Questions of any kind however are themselves speech-acts. Collingwood neglected to go beyond the phrase 'absolute presuppositions' with which he covered the ideological tendency of metaphysics only asking himself, as well he might, where his own questions came from, whether he was to put them, in his own example, to '*Hamlet* or a rotten little Roman fort'. Thompson has indeed absolute presuppositions and these shape his question-and-answer logic as he pieces together stories into history, life-in-earnest into a theory of what was going on. To do this, he must start *intentionally*:

I am seeking to rescue the poor stockinger, the Luddite cropper, the 'obsolete' hand-loom weaver, the 'utopian' artisan, and even the deluded follower of Joanna Southcott, from the enormous condescensions of posterity. . . . (*Preface*, p. 13)

It is by now a justly famous opening, and if like most prefaces it was written after the book was finished, it is more a statement of how the author hoped it would be received, than about what he was setting himself to do. Nonetheless, both at start and finish it is plain that Thompson has a story he wants to tell, and it cannot but be the case that shaping the story to the rhythms and reflexivities of that 'want' commits him to subjecting it to his own way of seeing the world, until at last the story he can tell is one that he understands.

So much is a gesture towards a phenomenology of storytelling. We identify the events, actions, motives, as events only inasmuch as we can recognize them according to our validated criteria of recognition. Then we find a shape to fit them. Such a shape is the product of a system of categories with a complex hierarchy of judgement and allocation, endlessly shuttling within it. The allocations are made according to our sense of consistency; conflicts of judgement are resolved by appeal to principles of domination; the whole narrative (or theory) is ordered by other, supreme considerations whose supremacy is only challenged and disordered by the advent of uncategorizable events or actions, or by new facts of the matter.[23]

Hidden in this synopsis of a theory of narrative repeated through this volume is the deliberately general, even loose idea that theories, metaphors, models, and fictions are alike 'ideological' in the human sciences as providing templates for the theorist (whether novelist, historian, or common man) to fit over the indistinguishable chaos of ordinary and extraordinary life, and make it stand still to be recognized. Thompson has his theory: it is that the English working class 'made' itself; that is, created by struggle and self-education a collective or class consciousness with which to oppose and even push back the power of its masters, and that this self-making took place, more or less, between the beginning of the French Revolution in 1789 and the first Reform Bill in 1832.

Thompson's book has been extensively criticized in its detail and its concepts: he meets his critics in a postscript to the 1968 edition. They have challenged him about the deferential side of the labouring poor, and argued that even if class consciousness can be said to be a causal entity in historical change, which is itself very dubious, the English working class cannot be said to have been capable of self-knowledge (and therefore conscious) until later in the century; and that anyway the Methodism which looms so large in the history as revised by Thompson was too ambiguous, schismatic and irregular to act so largely as a force for conservatism or anything else.

Some of these criticisms Thompson concedes, others he rebuts. It is not of importance here to determine the historical accuracy of these matters. I am concerned to establish two things: the relations of theory and experience in Thompson's method; and the significance of representing such a new past as the history of today. In the first it may help to think of Thompson as a latter-day voice of that most English idiom, the three-decker novel. George Eliot, Charles Dickens, Thomas Hardy, Mark Rutherford, Mrs. Oliphant, even Trollope and Mrs. Humphrey Ward, all engaged with the great surges and dwindlings of a whole society; they looked out for those signs and wonders which could be taken as somehow metonymizing vast and immaterial movements, however matter-of-factly they might be lived in the systems of production. Dickens, greatest of them all, caught up and created a debtor's prison to contain Frederick Dorrit, John Chivery, Miss Fanny, Mrs. General, Mr. Merdle, Arthur Clennam, Maggy the halfwit, and Little Dorrit herself in order to figure out the dominant meanings of Victorian life. The Marshalsea prison is his metaphor for the financial society Marx grounded in *Capital*.

By this token, Thompson's majestic books, *William Morris: Romantic to Revolutionary, The Making of the English Working Class,* and *Whigs and Hunters: the Origin of the Black Act,*[24] are large historical novels written for the present. In the first place, he orders theory by experience, and vice versa; any theory is underdetermined by the facts, but the facts must read believably within the frame of the theory. In the second, the enterprise to rescue his historical subjects from 'the enormous condescension of posterity' is politically situated in the present. A working-class history gives the present working-class a new past to live from; it changes the social memory so that, differently understanding how the present came about, the agent thinks forward to a new set of possibilities. The heroes of *The Making of the English Working Class*, like Morris and the poachers of Windsor Forest charged under the Black Act, tower over the blanker politics of our puny age, just as Captain Cuttle and Fagin, Uncle Pumblechook and Mrs. Wilfer seem to the bookish so much larger than the life lived by Dad's army or Grandma Giles. Robert Owen, Henry Hunt, Samuel Bamford, John Binns, Colonel Despard, William Pitt, are giants of the rich, echoing green of England in 1825.

They live and act in public. They pass rapidly and confidently before us like the figures in the streets of Dickens's London, strongly typified, decisive in character, clearly motivated. The pace and sweep of Thompson's *theory* is dazzlingly silhouetted in such moments as this, when a popular hero is hanged for his part in drunkenly attacking a gunsmith's shop after a demonstration.

Cashman himself was chiefly indignant at the injustice of his case, at being drawn in a cart through the streets and 'exposed like a common robber'. 'This is not for cowardice,' he exclaimed.

'I am not brought to this for any robbery. . . . If I was at my quarters, I would not be killed in the smoke: I'd be in the fire. I have done nothing against my King and country; but fought for them.'

The execution assumed the character of a great popular demonstration, and the scaffold had to be defended by barricades and an 'immense force' of constables:

As the Sheriffs advanced, the mob expressed the strongest feelings of indignation: groans and hisses burst from all quarters, and attempts were made to rush forward. . . . Cashman . . . seemed to enter into the spirit of the spectators, and joined in their exclamations with a terrific shout. . . . 'Hurra, my hearties in the cause! success! cheer up!'

On the scaffold Cashman rejected the ghastly solicitations to confession and repentance of two Anglican clergymen: 'Don't bother me − it's no use − I want no mercy but from God.' Then, addressing the crowd, 'Now, you buggers, give me three cheers when I trip'; and, after telling the executioner to 'let go the jib-boom', Cashman 'was cheering at the instant the fatal board fell from beneath his feet'. After a few minutes dead silence, the crowd 'renewed the expressions of disgust and indignation towards every person who had taken a part in the dreadful exhibition', with cries of 'Murder!' and 'Shame!' It was several hours before the people dispersed.[25]

Thompson's history gives back to a class which had never had its history fully told an epic trajectory and a pantheon of heroes. Its figures are not riven or even reflective, as Berger's are. They march in large and statuesque formation over forty years. It is as though Thompson sees politics as perpetually the battle of upright men and women simply and honestly seeking to throw off the subjugations and oppressions of their masters and to do so as members one of another, impelled not only by material conditions but also by the mobilities and loyalties of that clear membership. He says as much in the title essay of *The Poverty of Theory*, when he admonishes the new model Left for its ignorant and immature repudiation of 'moralism'. But he says in addition, in the same essay:

That facts are *there*, inscribed in the historical record, with determinate properties, does not, of course, entail some notion that these facts disclose their meanings and relationships (historical knowledge) of themselves, and independently of theoretical procedures. . . . The historical evidence is there, in its primary form, not to disclose its own meaning, but to be interrogated by minds trained in a discipline of attentive disbelief.

'Attentive disbelief.' His theoretic and his personal commitments to the history of his own people, and their rulers' monstrous disregard of the real foundations of the lives of those people — shelter, food, necessity — lead Thompson back to history and forward to politics. In *Whigs and Hunters* he cuts the historical evidence through a different plane, not, in his phrase, as 'links in a linear series of occurrences' (*Poverty,* p. 221) but as 'links in a lateral series of institutional relations', in this case the law. Yet this narrative also has a radical and a conservative tale to tell. In *The Making,* the freeborn Englishman reclaimed what was his own; in *Whigs and Hunters* the same Englishmen went to law and dodged the law to take (or poach, depending on which side you are on) the game of Windsor Forest. Thompson recaptures for the Left both poacher and highwayman, revising their simple novelettish stereotypes through the dry rasp of legal reports, until they stand again as freeborn men subverting the enclosures of their own true ground by the carpetbaggers of Walpole's early eighteenth-century political settlement.

The point, as always with Thompson, is as much political as historical. Like Morris, like Titmuss, he is profoundly patriotic, and no less scornful of the bragging or the mean patriot. Thompson's Englishness is a deep allegiance in him, a strong chord which sounds at the very bass of his crowded and majestic music. At the same time, he is in his political vision dedicated to internationalism — to India, to fellow socialists in Eastern Europe, to the feasibility of human brotherhood. The inquiry into law is a case in point. He ends *Whigs and Hunters* with a fine disquisition against those Marxists who entrap the very concept of justice in ideological toils. Thompson insists not only on the objective possibility of justice, but also on England herself as having, historically, given that concept substance and durability at a time when it was elsewhere in thrall to monarchs. This great pride aligns him with the long tradition — that whole mode of deeply national thought and feeling which this book celebrates and amplifies. As much as anything, it is at the root of his long malediction spoken over Louis Althusser. In his 'Open Letter' to the lapsed Polish Marxist, Kolakowski, collected in *The Poverty of Theory,* Thompson writes,

I belong to an emaciated political tradition, encapsulated within a hostile national culture which is itself both smug and resistant to intellectuality and failing in self-confidence; and yet I share the same idiom as that of the culture which is my reluctant host; and I share it not only through the habits of a writer but out of preference. This, if I am honest, is my self, my sensibility. Take Marx and Vico and a few European novelists away, and my most intimate pantheon would be a provincial tea-party: a gathering of the English and the Anglo-Irish. Talk of free-will and determinism, and I think first of Milton. Talk of man's inhumanity, I think of Swift. Talk of morality and revolution, and my mind is off with Wordsworth's Solitary. Talk of the problems of self-activity and creative labour in socialist society, and I am in an instant back with William Morris. (p. 109)

This Englishness, along with the dangers of vanity and prosy self-indulgence, which he acknowledges and to which he is liable, is indeed his very self, and as I have noted, a thinker *is* his best self in his best method of performance. So when Thompson turns tremendously on the new Marxist mouths who have learned their only vocabulary from Paris, he speaks directly in the English idiom of what it is to be both empiricist and socialist, moralist and historian.

A cloud no bigger than a man's hand crosses the English Channel from Paris, and then, in an instant, the trees, the orchard, the hedgerows, the field of wheat, are black with locusts. When at length they rise to fly on to the next parish, the boughs are bared of all culture, the fields have been stripped of every green blade of human aspiration: and in those skeletal forms and that blackened landscape, theoretical practice announces its 'discovery': the mode of production. Not only substantive knowledge, but also the very vocabularies of the human project — compassion, greed, love, pride, self-sacrifice, loyalty, treason, calumny — have been eaten down to the circuits of capital. These locusts are very learned platonists: if they settled on *The Republic* they would leave it picked clean of all but the idea of a contradiction between a philosopher and a slave. However elaborated the inner mechanisms, torsions, and autonomies, theoretical practice constitutes the ultimate in reductionism: a reduction, not of 'religion' or 'politics' to 'economics', but of the disciplines of knowledge to one kind of 'basic' Theory only. Theory is for ever collapsing back into ulterior theory. In disallowing empirical enquiry, the mind is confined for ever within the compound of the mind. It cannot walk abroad. It is struck down with theoretical cramp, and the pain is tolerable on condition that it does not move its limbs. (pp. 358 − 9)

And this is his great theoretical contribution, and his Englishness: that insisting always on the power of radical thought and the necessity of socialism, he also speaks in an idiom which can conserve the moral ideas capable of stirring men and women to acts of courage, ardour, faithfulness — of love, joy, peace, longsuffering, gentleness, truth. The history he has written backwards is the ground for political moves forwards.

So this is a man whose ephemeral journalism, like Berger's and Williams's, is seamlessly part of his thought. It is spoken in accents adjusted to his platform — the weekly journals, *New Society, New Statesman,* or the national dailies *Times* and *Guardian* — but it is spoken by the same public voice and man who is author of the history. What is striking about this public prose is its resonance and seriousness, its capacity to address itself surely to the historical fact of cultural identity (in my example, Scottish and Welsh political civilization — the miners), and the pride and loyalty in membership which that entails, and at the same time to deploy this eloquence in the cause of the best of Romantic socialism.

It is a characteristic of slackly incantatory idealism that it nominates this or that writer as the only one to maintain certain strains in the language. Obviously nobody knows for certain what language is used elsewhere, nor what kills off a certain linguistic strain. What we *can* say is that Thompson keeps up a public political language which pumps the blood of radicalism through arteries become sclerotic with consumer living. He speaks *for* many people, that is plain; these cadences still move their blood, but it is a precious faint heartbeat. Only at moments such as the going out of the lights in the miners' work-to-rule in 1972 could he make it tremble:

One tends to think of history as a reserve of the conservative and the 'traditional'. But there is still today an enormous reserve of radicalism stored within our culture. Nor is this hyperbole. It was evident in the past fortnight that there was one possible way for Heath to defeat the NUM, a way which would have warmed young Churchill's heart. The *Daily Telegraph* (15 February) explicitly evoked this course of action: 'the use of troops to break the picket lines around the power stations, and to requisition stocks of coal at the pit-head, will become unavoidable'.

And why was this not done? Not (one may be certain) because the government was squeamish about such intervention. It would surely have considered this if the strikers had been 'unofficial' or less formidable. Not even because Mr. Maudling has other uses for the troops in Londonderry and Newry. It was because that energy, glowing in the alternate culture of an alternate 'nation', would have been ignited in a flash. And that ignition would have burned on towards a General Strike more potent of decisive change than that of 1926, a more special and perhaps more implacable case.

The pits of Ballingry and of much of West Fife have now closed down. And we had supposed, poor fools that we are, that all that heroic and intelligent history, all that 200 years of inconceivable stubborness and courage, was quite dead. But out of that history has come this moment of illumination; we stir uneasily as, once again, there are men in our streets shouting 'One and All'. It is a moment of cultural transmission, as the pent-up energies of the dead flow back into the living. We shall burn that history for many years, as we have burned the black forests which for generations they have raised. For the future historian it will seem that this week of darkness in February 1972 was an incandescence.[26]

The metaphor could be transformed into theory. By the same token, Thompson singlehandedly rebuts the old belletriste case that the day of successful pamphleteering passed in the nineteenth century. His CND pamphlet *Protest and Survive*[27] has sold hundreds of thousands of copies, and is the best-known single document of a European and North American movement with a cast of millions.

On Thompson's part, I plead an innocent voluntarism of agency. In conclusion, however, it is enough to say that he criticizes, openly and by example, a theory and a practice in the human sciences which reduces all human exchange to the narrow axis marked by the points 'power' and 'exploitation'. He requires both human science and human socialism to use a far richer and more accurate assembly of antinomies, and in both his theory and his practice, caustic, mocking, good- and bad-tempered, stirring and eloquent as it is, he carries history forcefully forward from past understanding to future action. That there is an innocence in this, as there was in the project of his hero Blake, is undeniable; but without innocence, experience, his crucial category, stops dead.

Thompson, Williams, Berger, Hoggart; Crosland, Titmuss; Orwell, Stokes; they still are listened to, by different, smallish groups of men and women for their sane, affirmative speech. They remark whatsoever things they see which are pure, lovely and of good report. They rouse their listeners to just and common action.

10

Life and Death in English Academic Theory: Isaiah Berlin, the New Provisionals, and the Left

The spokesmen for a native socialism who have filled the platform of the last two chapters remain at the very height of their powers. Any attempt to conclude by considering the contemporary stage of social theory in England, or even to risk proposing an agenda, can only do so with the recognition that Thompson, Berger, Williams, at the very least, will all publish stage-shifting and scene-changing books in the immediate future. I have spoken in their praise, and it will take a great deal more than the weight of these pages to bury them.

And yet a book such as this claims to be can hardly stop there. These honourable men have been praised; their lessons learned. Sharp, unaccommodating, distinctive, and contentious as all their voices are, the claim that those mixed voices speak polyphonically but in the same musical tradition as the predecessors I have named stands more securely now that each has been given due space. That is to say, the list of these men, at once historical thinkers and actors as they all are, is much more than a bibliography. There are many terms, cognates which seek to catch in a single net the elusive, heart-warming familiarities which draw us back to a particular group of writers: Thompson's 'the English idiom', George Steiner's 'the inward cadence', the customary application in intellectual history of 'tradition', my own conventional uses of 'temper' and 'temperament', or of 'bearings' 'climate', and 'configuration'. In any case, I choose to identify certain key elective affinities in this body of texts and this association of men: in certain similarities of experience and social formation; in a community of ideas and values; in the working away at common themes; above all in the effort to find a way of living well in intellectual life, and of making their conclusions carry weight in the polity.

I realize that this is to write of Green and Morris, of the Fabians and

Keynes, of Leavis and Collingwood, as well as of all the postwar socialists, with an innocent-sounding individualism, a marked tendency towards the heresies of liberal idealism, and a mildly goofy and adolescent fondness for hero-worship. To do so at a time when Parisian structuralists license the deturpation of the author, and his substitution by the structures of literary production which write down the author as a function of the text, is to profess a reckless philistinism on behalf of old Anglo-Saxonry. Well, I would certainly vanish beneath Thompson's mantle; and in any case, the Parisians have done much of a necessary kind to prevent the continued, empty assumption of liberal descent that a book is the unimpeded utterance of a living man. The dissolution of a substantial part of the bulk and outline of 'author' into structures of production, into the revisions and refashioning by the reader working upon the writer's text,[1] into the ideological systems of social formation and convention which is the only ground anybody has from which to make sense of intention and identity, all this busy discipline has drastically relativized and contextualized the old notion that thought and action, the study of the great texts and the living of the good life, stand in a simply linear and consecutive relation one to another.

We are all structuralists now. And yet an unregenerate humanism stirs to the moving and the motive power of these authors and their texts, their speech and their writing. Listening to Morris as he stumped the working men's halls of Hammersmith and Putney talking about art and socialism, to Keynes as he damned Churchill's cruel budget, to Orwell home from Spain, to Richard Titmuss reckoning up the pains of illness amongst the English poor, to Edward Thompson naming for what they are the lies and hypocrisies of the weaponry barons, is like returning to the company of your friends and your home. Heaven knows what each would have made of the other; but turning from each of these books to another is an analogy (no more: a book is not a man) for turning to honoured, trusted friends for their wisdom, for strength and guidance, for the keen pleasures of intellection, or for the old excitement which is like terror, as new ideas rise to the rim of the mind and become potential of action.

> You that would judge me, do not judge alone
> This book or that, come to this hallowed place
> Where my friends' portraits hang and look thereon;
> Ireland's history in their lineaments trace;
> Think where man's glory most begins and ends
> And say my glory was I had such friends.[2]

So ultimately, the community in which these writers move is best brought out in the image of friendship, a common and equal fraternity of the wise and the brave. It isn't easy to write in such terms and escape charges of sentimentality; better perhaps to meet them on the way. But in any case the deep confusions and conflicts of morality and politics in a country and a culture which has made so much of what it commends to itself as pluralism, but whose genuine tolerance and freedoms have been softened and remoulded to the deadly-sweet structures of consumer capitalism (in a phrase) have left the noble ideas of friendship, of moral and intellectual kinship and brotherhood, severely attenuated. Inasmuch as adherence to the value of friendship commits the holder to loyalty to an institution as well as to a man or woman, then at a time when the hold of institutions is looser and their walls more porous than for many years, friendship itself is harder to find and live in.

Friendship; kinship; affinity; brotherhood; descent. The nature of the tradition of which these men are members is held somewhere in the field of force of these words. But this is an intentional community; such men would come together in the first place because of their purposes. The complex preoccupations and impulses of their thought compel them to a theory of praxis, and praxis, to mean something, is shared and social. The social theory of this book as I began by putting it intends to vindicate the ringing claim that you cannot separate scientific under-standing from moral experience, and that to designate experience as moral in the first place, presupposes that it is identifiable as such, that is, as bearing upon the historical criteria of badness and goodness, meaning and emptiness, membership and identity.

The natural question to ask of these men and their tradition is, what must we do to be saved? Or in Lenin's secular version of the same frightening question, 'What is to be done?' But it is plain that the use we presently make of a magus is not of the customary kind in which the supplicant asked the oracle for counsel, and then tried to follow the enigma; just as it is also plain from the interplay of theory and experience summarized here that none of these magi would give such counsel anyway. Nonetheless in their solid English way they propose a theory of practice (as we may as well say), and it has been a premise of this book that should it suggest in a modest way a mode of thought and of action. This is, after all, a heritage we may enter into without, as is said in another connection, being afraid with any amazement.

The clear implication of this third section is that any such entrance will need to be paid for, now and in England, in a broadly socialist coin.

To say so intends no supreme unction-spreading: there will be a time to notice the special awfulness of those who even at this late date suppose themselves to be guaranteed historical privileges of both understanding and precedence by the mere accident of their conversion to Marxism. What is more, to retain an account of an intellectual life which practises the human sciences as shaped in the conceptual structures made possible by generations of socialism, requires the English practitioner, as this book insists, to start from the earlier precedent of Idealist earnestness and the Radical movement. Those strong doses of English politicization were drunk down by Keynes, Leavis and Collingwood. As Raymond Williams remembers,[3] Leavis didn't indict 'technologico-Benthamite civilization' because he didn't know the word 'capitalism', and Leavis supremely criticized the militarily successful version of socialism precisely for its base surrender to narrowly material and mechanical forms of life and dreams of hope. That grand liberal inheritance cannot be wasted, and now may transpire in the best of British romantic socialism, which if such a large phrase can suffice to cover so much, includes *both* the great tradition of practical care and welfare for the wretched of the British earth, *and* a vital sense of the distinctive and creative responsibility of individuals to a destiny larger than their merely private interests.

That is my ecumenical point. It will not do to dismiss the admirable Fabian project as incapable of bringing about the just society; Fabianism as the doctrine which upholds a practice of constant remediation of frightful and avoidable misery and want is perfectly indispensable. Its representatives bequeath to its present practitioners the essential, laborious instruments of numerical organization, of empirical inquiry, of human organization in the relief of poverty and the provision of rights. For a human science to *be* human, there are the obligations of generosity, tenderness, loving-kindness, mutual help, which Titmuss so beautifully catches in the institution of giving blood. The assorted disciplines — economics, sociology, administration — should have as part of the definition of their project the moralization of theory such that it is always checked by the relevant historical meanings.[4] Thus, as Keynes said straightly, an economics which ignored the deepening immiseration of the miners in the name of its theoretically satisfying roundedness is a lousy economics. An administrative science which confines itself to the form and not the content of institutions fails because it has no meaning; means become ends, and therefore meaningless. This, as Weber saw, is the deep danger of bureaucratization, however necessary that Fabianized system is to mass industrial society.

The so-called policy sciences are those most in need of a theory of meaning; the voice of an emancipated Fabianism still has plenty to say to them. The cultural-political sciences, however, badly need a policy. In either situation, the contention of this book is that these English (and Welsh) voices, working in the deep, lived contexts of the British experience, have much to say to the manifold different contexts of our brave new world, so long as they are reworked to suit a different ground — the new African States, say, or India, among the ex-imperial territories; Norway, Finland, Yugoslavia, Hungary, as well as France and Germany among the European states.

Transplantation is a tricky process, however much the new imperialisms of knowledge and of bureaucracy may make the attempt inevitable. The significance of English social theory resides in its exemplary battle with a dense, intractable and historical experience. Understanding it is, indeed, like learning a language, and only when you think in that language, its idiom and locutions, and no longer translate, can you interpret properly what its people mean. The proper way to halt the revaluation of this version of its tradition is to offer a short history of the present; to acknowledge, that is, what the old and the not-so-old masters have to teach us, and then to see who is carrying on and going forward in something like the same terms.

It is a conspicuously difficult thing to do. On one hand, there is something useful but dismal in offering a short trot round the current roadworks, pausing to bestow a tick or a cross at each construction site. On the other hand, to generalize about the present practice of English social theory as the country's uncertainty about its nationhood and its preferred values deepens and becomes more tattered and torn, is to pretend to discern tendencies where there are only the books the commentator happens to remember. But it will not do to gesture with complacent largeness at the waste land, and collect a cheque from the television producer. I have reaffirmed that the old English social theory of practice is still in vigorous business at the old stand. Who is it recruiting, and what will *they* produce?

ISAIAH BERLIN AND THE NEW SCIENCE

Any response to these questions must be, in the present subdued babel of intellectual disputation on the direction of the future and how to think about it, distinctly provincial, maybe personal. Besides, I have just used the buttery word 'ecumenical', with an eye to insisting on an absolute lack of sufficient theory with which to map out the present, however powerful the descendants of both Marxism and Liberalism have proved to be. To insist on the contextual, provisional nature of the radical tradition and its idioms, to praise it for its very wary and everyday meyaphysics as well as for its gingerly treading a thin line between materialism and idealism, to dispraise it also for its ruminative philistinism, is at the present warmly to commend a non-academic licentiousness in reading around, in finding plausible ways of pinning theory on experience which regard neither doctrinal nor departmental boundaries. At their best the human sciences are joined in the mutual effort to theorize practice (which is only a fancy way of saying, to imagine the good life) but without leaving a dizzy gap between actuality and desire. If the suggestion mooted earlier about Leavis and Collingwood is at all valid, that the centre of intellectual energy naturally seeks out and informs the disciplinary practice which best combines innovation with procedure, culture with being, energy with structure, then the present centre and its lambent flame is to be found where many disciplines cross, and where political issues most become visible, at the intersection of belief and action.

To be ecumenical, to look for help wherever you can find it, is then to exalt an eclectic, common-sensible intellectuality to the status of a discipline. Very well. Accepting this modestly exigent programme is not so docile a move that the blandishments of the absolute bourgeois sound in our bien-pensant ears. Rather we may be in a position first of all to demand, however difficult the definition, intelligence of our theorists, and then truthfulness, historicity of experience, practical reason and usable theory, and only last of all, ideological soundness.

By these lights the most heartening sign of the times is Isaiah Berlin's study, *Vico and Herder.*[5] Berlin himself (born in 1909) seen from a distance, is a purely Establishmentarian figure; seen through Perry Anderson's ungenerous astigma of 1968,[6] he is 'a fluent ideologue'. Either way, he is the son of Jewish—Russian expatriates, was born in 1909, educated at an English school of the grand *haut bourgeois* style (St. Paul's), and became a tutor in philosophy at Oxford in the 1930s, friend, colleague, and intellectual swordsman with the formidable J. L. Austin. During the war his charm, his eloquence and the great breadth of his cosmopolitan humanism were conscripted by the Foreign Office for service in the Washington Embassy. There having written a critical biography of Marx[7] before the war, he wrote — out of his Jewishness, his Russian forebears and his deeply Anglicized spirit, and in the bitter frosts of the Cold War, his first versions of his essays on liberty, and his classic rebuttal of Marx's more cast-iron versions of determinism, 'Historical Inevitability'.[8]

It is not my business to weave these thirty-year-old essays into the texture of this book. For whatever their provenance, and passionate, florid, and dauntless as was and is Berlin's liberalism, he is far more than a routine Cold Warrior or henchman of those lapsed American socialists who declared the advent of 'the end of ideology' just because their intellectual middle age coincided with the zenith of the postwar arrival of the state and its mental hirelings in the heart of capitalism. Berlin, deeply a product of All Souls' College and Oxford philosophy, latterly winner of the rare Order of Merit, Master of a new college, honoured on all sides at his seventieth birthday, is a marvellously sensitive thermometer of an intellectual moment, and serves here as first guide and spokesman to latter-day English hermeneutics. The essay on inevitability caught the best in those moments of the Cold War in which English liberalism, horrified by the disclosures about Stalinism, its mass murders, brutal disregard of common justice, cruelty and waste, reaffirmed its most active elements. In the combined essays on Vico and Herder, Berlin draws upon his effortless, polyglot elegance of exposition and commentary to restate the premises of a human science first outlined by Vico between 1725 and 1744, and counterposed to the triumphant advance of Cartesian rationalism.

As a work of scholarly reinterpretation, Berlin's rehearsal of the Neopolitan Vico (a nice example of an *un*predictable flowering of genius in utterly inhospitable soil) and the Romantic Herder is no doubt beyond reproach. But of course Berlin surely intended a timely restatement for the present day of a practice in the human sciences which resisted 'technologico-Benthamism' in its evaluative framework, and reductive positivism in its methods.

It is always easy to call the enemy bad names. It is harder to know what to do instead. Berlin presents Vico as first modern theorist of human activity (his great work, as is well known, was called *The New Science*) whose central concepts define a triple spiral of thought in which human nature is not timeless and changeless but situated in the motions of history, particularly of men's and women's historical self-understanding, in which we all by living in our own activity understand it more inwardly than we can ever understand external nature, and in which each singular language is the defining ground, the pervasive and mind-informing atmosphere in which thought breathes and recognition lives. These profound and profoundly non-Cartesian, humanistic ideas led

Vico to coming near to the definition of the idea of a culture without which identity cannot take shape, and the outline and substance of which must be sought in the many linguistic institutions of a society, its art, religion, laws, morality, music and fable.

Berlin brings out the innately teleological striving of Vico's vision of men and, seeing it as an anticipation of the great nineteenth-century progressivists Hegel and Marx, is quick to notice in Vico as later in Herder a pessimism and realism which, whatever the crassnesses of cyclical models of history and whatnot to which they inclined, remain salutary warnings against simpleminded views that correct theories inoculate action against evil, and history against failure. Berlin represents Vico as making crucial philosophic moves for human science, distinguishing mind-definable truth (*verum*) from observable factuality (*factum*), principles from propositions, 'categories of cognition from those of the will', and asking always that descriptions of experience be made 'as concretely as possible, emphasiz[ing] variety, differences, change, motives and goals, individuality rather than uniformity or indifference to time or unaltering repetitive patterns'.[9] It is not hard to hear his firm endorsement of these preferences, and Berlin goes on to place at the centre of Vico's whole method the indispensable motion of the empathic imagination, the faculty in which moral necessity (altruism being impossible unless one can begin to imagine oneself in someone else's position) is coterminous with scientific understanding (such science being literally unthinkable without a grip of sorts on the purposes and intentions of others).

Presented like this, Berlin's Vico is a hero for times in which mutual understanding and tolerance as well as a strong sense of what is really worth living for are much needed; it is easy to see why Collingwood read and admired Vico, why E. P. Thompson does so as well, how congenial such thought would be to Leavis or to Stokes. This is Vico through Berlin's eyes, and in an incomparably graceful and forthright encomium, Bernard Williams sets out why Berlin's liberalism constitutes an indispensable *gain* to the practice of the human sciences, and a dimension of reference which these sciences cannot systematize or abjure without falling into induration, rigidity, and vices of practice which lead only to the Gulag.

What truth is it that is known to someone who recognises the ultimate plurality of values? In philosophical abstraction, it will be *that there are such values*, and, put in that blank way, it can be taken to speak for an objective order of values which some forms of consciousness (notably the liberal form) are better than others at recognising. But that way of putting it is very blank indeed. It is more characteristic of Berlin's outlook, and more illuminating in itself, to say that one who properly recognises the plurality of values is one who understands the deep and creative role that these various values can play in human life. In that perspective, the correctness of the liberal consciousness is better expressed, not so much in terms of truth — that it recognises the values which indeed there are — but in terms of truthfulness. It is prepared to try to build a life round the recognition that these different values do each have a real and intelligible human significance, and are not just errors, misdirections or poor expressions of human nature. To try to build life in any other way would now be an evasion, of something which by now we understand to be true. What we understand is a truth about human nature as it has been revealed — revealed in the only way in which it could be revealed, historically. The truthfulness that is required is a truthfulness to that historical experience of human nature.[10]

That splendid statement may serve to explain the strains in those present social theorists who, recognizing as the best are bound to do the strictly political issues more and more intractably present and neglected in their country's circumstance, work to restore a socialism capable of both impelling understanding and creating a better life.

MARXISM AND UNCERTAINTY: THE HISTORY OF IDEAS AND IDEAS OF HISTORY

Such work goes forward in an intellectual climate deeply inimical to truth-telling or truth-hearing. The special stridencies of those who have taken tents in the camps of the hard left are no worse for thought than the more dulcet susurrations of the older guardians of Faculty standards. The strong pull towards declaring your membership with your ideas is qualified on one hand by dismay at discovering where the applause is coming from, and on the other by reluctance to lose your friends.

Presumably it was always so. At a time of the breaking of nations, when rough beasts slouch along and hearts are fed on fantasies, then the temptation to lapse into cliché and slogan, on the side of world-weary passivity or of the kind of action called activism, is bound to be strong. But it has been an intention of this book that it determine so far as possible what common ground may be stood upon with reasonable confidence, which is to ask, what intellectual men and women ultimately may be said to live for, just now, and also that in summoning these writers for help, for understanding, for review, it makes positive use of the theories they propound.

This is not a cue for writing a manifesto. I have spoken, as I noticed, with deliberate looseness of theories, models, metaphors, narratives, as though they were, if not synonymous, then very much of a family. The network of thinkers identified in these pages connects, so to say, in a system of paths, hidden tracks, beacons and bearings to form a secret map of the culture. The map is historical; it is the cartography of the past hundred years in which the dissident theorists have sought from different positions of power to corral and redirect the four headlong horses of the new apocalypse, capital, technology, communications, godlessness, to more comely and careful ends. The way to read the map is to look back and see which lights now illuminate the road we have travelled; and then look forward to see who makes any offer with a lamp to the immediate future.

Three groups step forward: the Marxists, the action theorists, and the plain, blunt men. In the first case, we have heard in the last two chapters from their strongest spokesmen, still vigorously at work. And on every side there are dire examples of what it is to deploy those ideas without rooting them in a vernacular. The Centre for Contemporary Cultural Studies founded at the University of Birmingham by Richard Hoggart in 1963 became after his departure to UNESCO the main, indeed the only though unofficial institute of Marxicology in the Kingdom. Stuart Hall, a name much and rightly honoured on the Left, became its director then in the face of considerable if covert resistance by the Alma Mater, and subsequently the Centre swung into extraordinary productivity with its *Working Papers* and the long list of authologized collections published from those periodicals. Some have been footnoted here; Hall's own work and that of his successor Richard Johnson are such as one can only be grateful for. It has irrigated the hitherto dry and fissured waste land in which organizational Marxism has been living since 1956. But quite without claiming that these remarks constitute a sufficient estimate, the Centre's work may be taken as an example of that narrow, mean, bushwhacking and bible-bashing dugout life which is the reverse side of the well-upholstered academic complacency which still characterizes the assured bookmaking of the many. The Birmingham Centre's Marxism cuts itself off from most of the most active intellectual life of the Anglophone present, spiting its nose and our face as a result. Perry Anderson's increasingly authoritative work, and such a book as Cohen's

Karl Marx's Theory of History[11] stand as models of how to secure present Marxism's place in the polity of ideas.

Cohen is a philosopher, and it is worth observing here that, in my much-used metaphor, the intersections of action and belief, cognition and will, value and meaning, have been most busily investigated by the philosophers this past decade while historians and anthropologists have worked alongside them with the tools of linguistic analysis in order to resituate the claims of relativism and constancy, of intention and structure.

Two men, starting from different disciplines serve to emphasize the present dissolution of subject distinctions in the human sciences in the common effort to map the historical relations of theory and practice. For the sake of diagrammatic clarity, the first, Anthony Giddens, we may take as the new English scientist of structure; the second, Quentin Skinner, as the historian of intentionality.

Giddens (born in 1938) is a theorist of quite astonishingly prolific production at the present time. I may say, with an irony quite at my own expense, that he is the most un-English of the assortment of contemporary contributors who compose the galaxy of this chapter. He has drawn largely and powerfully upon the founders of classical sociology, Marx, Weber, and Durkheim, and like Skinner, Taylor, and MacIntyre, all still to come, has brought the accomplishments of modern philosophy to bear directly upon the understanding of social action. His enterprise may be characterized by comparing it to that of Jurgen Habermas in Frankfurt, who appears as a frequent reference — and the breadth and deployment of Giddens's reading is strikingly catholic and eclectic. Like Habermas, Giddens intends the large ambition of taking from the founding fathers the various theories of social structure which confounded Liberalism, but transcribing these according to his notion of 'the duality of structure' in order to accommodate both a theory of voluntarist action and a theory of structure not (as often in Durkheim and always in Marx) constraining or even determining, but as the medium of action itself and 'at the same time . . . its outcome in the reproduction of social forms'.[12]

He began to move towards making this exceedingly abstract formulation operational by reviewing the advent of the new and continental hermeneutics. He has not drawn upon native versions of agency and meaning as provided by the literary—critical paradigms and discourses which both Thompson and Williams work from, but his rejection of positivism in social science, his review of Apel, Habermas and Gadamer,[13] and his subtle, fluent blending of hermeneutic and interpretative method with the hard truths which all social agents collide with when they meet the structures of order, power, and conflict, bring Giddens to a very similar position. His social theory has at times a tendency to almost playful over-mechanization. It is a playfulness entirely lacking from the top-heavily inclusive model-building of Habermas, and it comes in part from that tradition in classical sociology which insists, with Talcott Parsons or even with Sartre, in getting absolutely everything of social reality in, and in part from Giddens's own unquenchable prodigality of invention in the field of his discourse. Either way, there are times when he seems to assume that explanation is the ready result of putting the social action in at the top of the analytic machine, cranking the handle, and printing out the results. But much more impressively, the main push of his recent work is away from the smallminded and often bumbling dealings with epistemology which characterize the busy bees of sub-Marxist sociology, and towards what the American Richard Rorty, classes as 'edifying philosophy'.[14] Rorty notes that philosophy, academically defined, has preoccupied itself since Descartes and via Kant only with the status of knowledge claims; 'edifying' philosophers, practising on the periphery of the subject, furnish us not with epistemology but with creative and useful redescriptions of ourselves.

Giddens shares none of the American's genial irresponsibility towards relativism. But in his newest book[15] he seeks to ally one of Rorty's heroes, Heidegger, with one of his own, Marx, in the gallant and convincing effort to bring the lived experience of time, geography, and being, within a credible and non-sectarian historical materialism. The ambition, and the achievement, has its polemical edge in the present world, of course; and so it should have, although at the same time Giddens declares that he does not accept the label of Marxist. But at this early stage of his impressive project, a project to which he calls the entire bibliography of the anthropologists in order to place it in a world geography, he is the likeliest of his generation to produce a believable account of how, in an endlessly changeful history, world social structures may hinder or enable any transition from capitalism to socialism.

Quentin Skinner (born in 1940) is by now the chief architect of the intentionalists' new conceptual framework. He has taken Collingwood's instructions further to heart than anyone else by insisting not on historicism but on the historicity of political concepts, and on the paramount requirement that to understand (and therefore to be in any kind of position to learn from) the great texts, a reader must return them to the contexts of convention within which alone the intentions and purposes of the author may be released for inspection. In a brilliant series of papers[16] he assembled and cleared away the methodological problems created by taking Collingwood to heart. He then counted himself in a position to explain[17] the formation of the central, dominant concept of the state in modern political ideas, in terms of its gradual definition in a varied series of texts arising from the disparate contexts of Renaissance dispute on the nature of thrones, dominations, and powers. Skinner's own slogan for his enterprise is, 'Max Weber meets the Speech-Act',[18] by which he means that in taking John Austin's theory of performative utterances he may explain the arrival of the protestant ethic in the spirit of capitalism by appeal to its legitimating force at a time when money-making was held in slightly less general esteem than it is today.

Broadly, Skinner may be said to be working in the field of ideology or discourse theory. His importance here is however that he syncretizes the gains of literary and linguistic analysis by returning texts to the density of historical experience, and forces even the most structuralist of hermeneuticians to study the details of agency in every movement of ideas in action.

Skinner is one of the best and latest representatives of the men and women contributing to the debate initiated by Peter Laslett[19] in, coincidentally, 1956, when he asked whether political theory was dead of inanition. Of course as this book declares, the answer was roundly, no, particularly in 1956. But Skinner, with Alisdair MacIntyre and Charles Taylor, has returned political theory squarely to its academic home. MacIntyre (born in 1929) is, like Skinner, a chapter subject in himself. Lapsed Catholic, lapsed Marxist, collaborator with E. P. Thompson on the *New Reasoner*, he has been a most resounding though occasional moral—political commentator for the past quarter-century. I nominate him in this company, however, only for the theoretic moves in his newest book,[20] *After Virtue*. There he turns upon that most grisly, misleading, and omnipresent hero of technologico-Benthamism, the expert managerialist, and shows why his confident predictions can only be empty, his narcissistic techniques arrogantly manipulative, his self-congratulatory solutions merely irrational, entirely unsuited to ordinary human purposes, and guaranteeing failure. In opposition to this dummy of the good man, MacIntyre proposes a new Aristotelian whose moral meaning is contained by the narrative of his life, a narrative given form and direction by the effort to live a life he can be proud of. The model of an autobiography, the individual's justifiable pride in which is a function of his place in social life, depends on the heroic or the implausible restatement of common, mutual and beneficent ends in that social life. Charles Taylor (born in 1931) serves to join philosophers to honest men and women seeking in deeply uncongenial conditions for that common end.[21]

Taylor himself is perhaps out of place in this limitedly English line. He is a Canadian who has alternated many years in Oxford with many in McGill, and has stood for the Canadian parliament. But he speaks the English idiom like a native, as they used to say, was a founder member of *New Left Review*, and it is a pleasant congruence with his place at the end of this book that he followed (as next but one) Isaiah Berlin into the Chichele Chair of Political Theory at Oxford and All Souls' College. From the long, solid, and serpentine range of his work, I select only two, terse arguments. In the first, he brings his lifelong study of Hegel[22] to bear upon the practice of the human sciences, acknowledging the human scientist's incorrigibly relative and historical position, but taxing him to practise his evaluation of human endeavour past or present according to three criteria, whose realization in an imaginably better future can only be premissed on their finest versions alive today. The three criteria of his hermeneutical trigonometry are freedom, fulfilment, and self-awareness (or self-criticism) and these may suffice to furnish him and us with sufficiently flexible and optimistic measures of action and practice, as well as remaining faithful to the astoundingly different chances the world provides for living a decent life and telling a good story about it.

Taylor attaches these ideas to specific attempts to detail a world future in which a gentle and compassionate socialism might actually work. It is a note to end on. There are still plenty of men and women working for that difficult but not doomed plausibility. But as has been much pointed out,[23] any such endeavour on the part of that fraction of the intelligentsia designated here as social theorists will need to avoid both the fashionable taste for the rancorously subversive, and the more enticing banality which lies beneath a combination of earnest edification with cleverness, and hardly exorcized from these pages. Adequate social theory needs a rich alliance of generosity with a strong sense of comic irony. A request for a political theory of the Left which deals mercifully with suffering and rejoices in laughter is quite substantial enough as an agenda for the rest of the century.

Notes

PROLOGUE: TEXT AND METHOD

1. For a short history of 1956 see Francois Fejto, *A History of the People's Democracies*, Penguin, revised edition 1974.

CHAPTER 1: TRADITION AND ENGLISHNESS: POLITICS AND BELIEF

1. See World Bank, *Annual Report 1979*; also G. Barraclough, 'The End of an Era', *New York Review of Books*, 27 June 1974, 'The Great World Crisis', *NYR* 23 January 1975, 'Wealth and Power: the Politics of Food and Oil', *NYR* 7 August 1975.
2. I depend much in these summary remarks on John Dunn, *Western Political Theory in the Face of the Future*, Cambridge University Press 1979.
3. 'Little Gidding', *Complete Poems and Plays* Faber & Faber 1969, p. 195.
4. ibid., p. 196.
5. Isaiah Berlin, *Concepts and Categories*, Hogarth Press 1978, pp. 159–60. For the view that, even so, much of the *structure* of Hegel's thought remains important see Charles Taylor, *Hegel and Modern Society*, Cambridge 1979.
6. In Isaiah Berlin, *Vico and Herder: Two Studies in the History of Ideas*, Hogarth Press 1976.
7. e.g. Perry Anderson's reference to Green's 'aqueous Hegelianism' in 'Components of the National Culture', *New Left Review*, 50, 1968.
8. e.g. Jacques Derrida, *Of Grammatology*, trans. G. C. Spivak, Johns Hopkins University Press 1976.
9. I am not innocently supposing, according to de Tocqueville's thesis, that the *philosophe* caused the French Revolution. Such a belief, if it is still to be found, could not survive a reading of Robert Daunton, *The Business of Enlightenment: A Publishing History of the 'Encyclopédie' 1775–1800,* Harvard University Press 1980. My point is that, as I put it before, the new ideas were called to legitimate the Revolution.
10. Alasdair Macintyre 'A Mistake about Causality in Social Science' *in Philosophy, Politics, and Society,* 2nd series, ed. Peter Laslett and W. G.

Runciman, Basil Blackwell 1962. Alasdair Macintyre did not reprint this admirable paper in his volume of essays, *Against the Self Images of the Age,* Duckworth 1971, apparently because he believes it is mistaken in essential ways. I cannot agree, but whatever mistakes it may contain are not to be found in this quotation.

11. See particularly John Searle, *Speech-Acts,* Cambridge 1969.

12. A point I take as it stands from Andrew Harrison, *Making and Thinking,* Harvester Press 1978. We return to it more broadly in the chapter on Collingwood.

13. A title and an argument now made well-known by Peter Berger and Thomas Luckmann, *The Social Construction of Reality,* Penguin 1971.

14. Alan Macfarlane, *The Origins of English Individualism,* Basil Blackwell 1979.

15. The progress of individualism as a political doctrine in e.g. the Caribbean and Central Africa is mordantly followed in V. S. Naipaul's two novels, *Guerrillas,* Penguin 1977, and *A Bend in the River,* André Deutsch 1979.

16. *'England, Your England' and other Essays,* Secker & Warburg 1953, p. 206.

17. An inheritance long antedating the Revolution, and the sort of experience written deep into our culture by the Cold Wars I and II, and beautifully rendered in Nadezhda Mandelstam's *Hope Against Hope,* trans. M. Hayward, Collins 1971. None of Mandelstam's story would have seemed strange to Turgenev.

18. The real history is documented by Noel Annan, 'The Intellectual Aristocracy' in *Studies in Social History: A tribute to G. M. Trevelyan,* ed. J. H. Plumb, London 1955.

19. First, brilliantly, and tendentiously announced in Perry Anderson's paper, as cited. Then documented in an exceedingly selective form in various essays in *New Left Review,* collected as *Ideology in Social Science,* ed. R. Blackburn, Fontana 1974.

20. I am grateful here to conversations with Nicholas Garnham and to his valuable paper 'Revolution and reformism: twin cul-de-sacs?' in *New Universities Quarterly* 32, 2, Spring 1978, special issue 'Morality and the Left', ed. Colin Crouch and Fred Inglis.

21. A point I take from Ioan Davies, 'The Management of Knowledge', *Sociology,* January 1970.

22. For a study of seventeenth-century constitutionalism, see John Wallace, *Destiny His Choice: the Loyalism of Andrew Marvell,* Cambridge 1968. For a literary study of the divines, see Christopher Hill, *Puritanism and Revolution,* Secker & Warburg 1958. For Milton's prose see William Haller, *The Rise of Puritanism,* Columbia University Press 1938. For a decidedly polemical view of the political meaning of puritanism, see

Michael Walzer, *The Revolution of the Saints: a Study in the Origins of Radical Politics,* Weidenfeld & Nicolson 1966.

23. By T. W. Adorno and Max Horkheimer, *The Dialectic of the Enlightenment,* New Left Books 1974.

CHAPTER 2: THE LONG SUMMER: IDEALIST RADICALS
AND THE OXFORD AND CAMBRIDGE INTELLIGENTSIA
– T. H. GREEN AND WILLIAM MORRIS

1. Now known as the Taunton Commission (1868); for official reference see J. S. MacLure, *Educational Documents: England and Wales 1816 – 1968,* Methuen 1965.

2. Accurately criticized by Green in the section on Education in the *Works.*

3. A view which Green criticizes in the first pages of *Prolegomena to Ethics.* References here are to the version edited by Green's famous pupil, A. C. Bradley, republished with an introduction by R. M. Lemos, Thomas Crowell, New York, 1969. All references to Green's writings, not including Bradley's edition of the *Prolegomena to Ethics* are to the *Works* edited by Green's close friend and admirer R. L. Nettleship, Longmans Green 1911.

4. Classically defended and attacked (in my view, victoriously) by J. J. C. Smart and Bernard Williams, *Utilitarianism: For and Against,* Cambridge University Press, 1973.

5. *Works,* III, p. 367.

6. D. G. Ritchie *The Principles of State Interference* (1891) quoted by Peter Clarke, *Liberals and Social Democrats,* Cambridge University Press 1978, p. 26.

7. In Melvin Richter, *The Politics of Conscience: T. H. Green and His Age,* Weidenfeld & Nicolson 1964.

8. Stefan Collini, *Liberalism and Sociology: L. T. Hobhouse and Political Argument in England 1880 – 1914,* Cambridge University Press 1979, p. 253.

9. Richter, p. 376.

10. Richter, p. 346.

11. e.g. Geoffrey Hawthorn, at least in the slightly embarrassing title *Enlightenment and Despair* to his very good *A History of Sociology,* Cambridge University Press 1976. His satisfactory point is that sociology in the 1920s and 1930s was not at all desperate, exactly because Green and Hobhouse had won the day. See pp. 104 – 11, 164 – 70.

12. *Prolegomena to Ethics,* pp. 179 – 80.

13. Quoted by R. L. Nettleship in his classic *Memoir of Thomas Hill Green,* Longmans Green 1906, p. 112.
14. *Memoir,* p. 114. See also *Works,* vol. I, pp. 127–8, 281–2.
15. I take points here from Alasdair MacIntyre, *A Short History of Ethics,* Routledge & Kegan Paul 1967, and his excellent brief summary of the *Prolegomena* at pp. 247–8.
16. *Works,* II, p. 144.
17. Isaiah Berlin, *Four Essays in Liberty,* Oxford 1954.
18. Nettleship, *Memoir,* p. 117.
19. Implausibly discovering it in the Prussian State. See Taylor, *Hegel,* chapter XVI, 'The Realized State'.
20. Nettleship, *Memoir,* pp. 170–1.
21. 'Lecture on the Work to be done by the New Oxford High School for Boys', *Works* III, pp. 458ff.
22. *Works* III, pp. 475–6.
23. I cannot unpack all the difficulties implied by my own formulation at this point. The question of what equality *can* mean is taken up later. Here the interested reader might turn first to W. G. Runciman, *Relative Deprivation and Social Justice,* Routledge 1966 in order to consider how such commensurability might actually work; see pp. 262–3.
24. See on Green's economic naivety, C. B. Macpherson 'Post–Liberal Democracy', in his *Democratic Theory,* Oxford University Press, 1973, pp. 175–6.
25. E. P. Thompson: *William Morris: Romantic to Revolutionary,* Merlin Press 1955, reissued with new postscript by the author, 1977.
26. Charles Tomlinson 'Descartes and the Stove', *The Way of a World,* Oxford 1969, p. 15.
27. See J. W. Burrow, *Evolution and Society,* Cambridge 1966.
28. These remarks go over ground already lightly turned in the prologue. It is exhaustively filled by Quentin Skinner in the list of his papers cited in the bibliography. The main primer to his ideas is his 'Meaning and understanding in the history of ideas', *History and Theory* VIII, 1969.
29. Collini, p. 9.
30. 'Tradition and the individual talent', *The Sacred Wood,* Methuen 1920.
31. T. W. Adorno, *Minima Moralia,* New Left Books 1974; H. Marcuse, *One-Dimensional Man,* Boston Beacon Books 1964.
32. Summarized in Marx's earliest works (which Morris did not know: he read *Capital* for his marxism); see Thompson, pp. 236–8. In Marx, see (with Engels) *The German Ideology* (1848), ed. T. J. Arthur, Lawrence & Wishart 1970.

33. cf. Leon Edel (ed.), *The Letters of Henry James*, Macmillan 1966, vol. I, p. 18.

34. See F. Inglis 'Nation and Community', *Sociological Review*, 25. 3, 1977, and W. L. Creese, *The Search for Environment*, Yale 1966.

35. As set out e.g. in R. G. Collingwood, *The Principles of Art*, Oxford 1938, Book I, 'Art and Not-Art'.

36. In Nikolaus Pevsner, *Pioneers of Modern Design: from William Morris to Walter Gropius*, rev. edn, Penguin 1960; see especially pp. 20 – 26, and 40 – 54.

37. May Morris, *William Morris, Artist, Writer, Socialist*, 2 vols. Basil Blackwell 1936.

38. *Works XXII*, p. 233, quoted in Thompson, p. 236.

39. 'Socialists and the Jubilee' (Socialist League Handbill) quoted in Thompson p. 481.

40. For the summary and for further reading see David McLellan, *Marxism After Marx*, Macmillan 1979.

41. From 'The Society of the Future', *The Political Writings of William Morris*, ed. A. L. Morton, Lawrence & Wishart 1973, pp. 201 – 2.

42. *Commonweal*, 18 February 1888.

43. *Commonweal*, 18 February 1888.

44. 'What we have to look for', *Commonweal*, 30 March 1895, quoted by Thompson, p. 503.

45. See Peter Clarke's useful book of that title as a contrast from the time to Morris's situation. Also Collini, and below, pp. 56 – 60.

46. All three collected as *Three Works by William Morris*, ed. A. L. Morton Lawrence & Wishart and International Publishers 1968. For critical study, see John Goode, 'William Morris and the Dream of Revolution' in John Lucas, *Literature and Politics in the Nineteenth Century*, Methuen 1971, and a brilliant few pages in Perry Anderson, *Arguments Within English Marxism*, New Left Books 1980, pp. 157 – 75, 'Utopias'.

47. See Inglis, *Nation and Community* and Creese, *Search for Environment*.

48. Anderson, p. 182.

49. Matters we return to below, with Adrian Stokes.

CHAPTER 3: POWER AND POLICY: THE FABIANS
AND JOHN MAYNARD KEYNES

1. First published, MacGibbon and Kee 1935, reissued 1966, this edition, Paladin 1970, p. 195.

2. Of those already cited see Collini, *Liberalism and Sociology*; Clarke, *Liberals and Social Democrats;* Hawthorn, *Enlightenment and Despair*; and Dunn, *Western Political Theory*. See also Martin Hollis, *Models of*

Man, Cambridge 1977, and Anthony Giddens, *Capitalism and Modern Social Theory*, Hutchinson 1974.

3. For its detailed history, see Norman and Jeanne MacKenzie, *The Early Fabians*, Weidenfeld & Nicolson 1977, and Margaret Cole, *The Story of Fabian Socialism*, Heinemann 1961.

4. Quoted in Thompson, p. 687.

5. Clarke, pp. 82–90.

6. Graham Wallas, *The Great Society*, Macmillan 1911.

7. Macmillan 1908.

8. First published 1902; here referred to in the 3rd revised edition, Allen & Unwin 1938. (See Clarke, *Liberals and Social Democrats* for a bibliography of Hobson's writings.)

9. V. I. Lenin, 'On Imperialism' in *Selected Writings*, Foreign Languages Publishing House, Moscow 1970.

10. First published by Unwin in 1904, edited with an introduction by P. F. Clarke, Harvester Press 1972.

11. See, variously: *The Labour Movement*, 1897, edited with an introduction by Philip Poirier, Harvester 1974; *Liberalism*, edited with an introduction by Alan Grimes, New York 1964; and Workman's Insurance, *Nation*, IX, 1911.

12. As may be seen by reading the standard and absorbing biography, Roy Harrod, *The Life of John Maynard Keynes*, Macmillan 1951.

13. As beautifully and movingly as Keynes himself does it in his *Treatise on Probability*, 1921. However I could not have understood even the brief passages in this book that I did without the help of G. L. S. Shackle, *Epistemics and Economics*, Cambridge University Press, 1972. See also Shackle's Keynes Lecture, 'Time and Choice', in *Proceedings of the British Academy*, LXII, 1976, pp. 309–30.

14. In *Essays in Biography*, 1933, otherwise vol. X of *The Collected Writings of John Maynard Keynes*, Macmillan 1951 (henceforward *JMK*).

15. In 'My Early Beliefs'.

16. In 'Keynes, Lawrence, and Cambridge', *The Common Pursuit*, Chatto & Windus 1952.

17. See also Keynes's unusually reverent treatment of Marshall in the *Essays in Biography* (*JMK* vol. X).

18. D. E. Moggridge, *Keynes*, Fontana 1976, p. 100.

19. Harry G. Johnson, 'The Keynesian Revolution, for Good or Ill', in *On Economics and Society*, University of Chicago Press 1975, p. 90. On the monetarists, see his chapter 7.

20. 1st edition 1936. Here quoted from *JMK* vol. VII, pp. 372ff.

21. *New Statesman*, February 14, 1939, p. 216.

22. 'The Economic Consequences of Mr. Churchill' reprinted in *Essays in Persuasion*, Macmillan 1931, pp. 259–61 (*JMK* vol. IX).

23. *Essays in Persuasion,* pp. 5 – 6.
24. *Essays in Persuasion,* pp. 14 – 18.
25. *JMK* vol. VIII.
26. *JMK* vols V and VI.
27. John Rawls, in *A Theory of Justice,* 1971, has recently and classically theorized this view of justice by means of a so-called 'thought experiment' in which people judge what is just for them in a new, ideal republic without knowing what their position in it is going to be. Fair, but abstract. Keynes, however, had to make his fairness work in the most deeply entrenched class system in the world.
28. Quoted by Moggridge, p. 26.
29. A point made by his pupil, Joan Robinson, in *Economic Philosophy,* Penguin 1964, p. 73.
30. See Robinson, pp. 91 – 2.

CHAPTER 4: RESITUATING IDEALISM: R. G. COLLINGWOOD

1. R. G. Collingwood, *An Autobiography,* Oxford 1939, reissued with an introduction by Stephen Toulmin, 1979, p. 87.
2. *An Autobiography,* pp. 48 – 9.
3. 'Preface' to *Lyrical Ballads* (1802), Oxford 1911, p. 238.
4. Consider this selection of Collingwood's Oxford contemporaries as students of 'Greats': A. D. Lindsay, William Temple, Arnold Toynbee, G. D. H. Cole, J. B. S. Haldane, Gilbert Ryle.
5. It is not just a private anecdote to say that I was told to read it as an undergraduate at Cambridge in 1959 by F. R. Leavis.
6. Collingwood translated Croce's autobiography and his book on Vico, as well as the entry 'Aesthetic' in the famous 14th edition of the *Encyclopaedia Britannica* (1929); see W. M. Johnson, *The Formative Years of R. G. Collingwood,* Martinus Nijhoff 1967.
7. My metaphor was real enough for Collingwood. He published an early paper on 'The Devil' in L. Dougall (ed.), *Concerning Prayer: its Nature, its Difficulties and its Value,* London 1916.
8. Letter to Roy Gardiner, 16th July 1926.
9. When critically ill in 1939 he joined, at their invitation, a group of his students on a long and arduous journey under sail to Greece. See *The First Mate's Log of the 'Fleur de Lys'* (1940).
10. See *The Autobiography of Arthur Ransome,* Cape, London 1976.
11. *The Idea of History,* ed. T. M. Knox, Clarendon Press 1946, p. 115.
12. It is the way fully explored by Louis Mink in his very good book, *Mind, History and Dialectic: the Philosophy of R. G. Collingwood,* Indiana University Press 1969. Mink however is formidably abstract,

and doesn't take the line proposed here for understanding Collingwood in his and our world.

13. Mink, p. 18.

14. I put it like this advisedly, in the opinion that Collingwood would have much approved David Wiggins's justification of such a phrase in 'Truth, Invention, and the Meaning of Life', *Proceedings of the British Academy,* LXII, 1976, pp. 331–78.

15. Clarendon Press 1924, 5th impression 1970.

16. His ideal is clear however, as witness this quotation from his lecture 'Ruskin's Philosophy' (1919) privately printed as a pamphlet in Kendal in 1922. 'When I speak of a man's philosophy, I mean something of this sort. I see a man living a long and busy life; I see him doing a large number of different things, or writing a large number of different books. And I ask myself, do these actions, or these books, hang together? Is there any central thread on which they are all strung? Is there any reason why the man who wrote this book should have gone on to write that one, or is it pure chance? Is there anything like a constant purpose, or a consistent point of view, running through all the man's work?'

17. An instructive comparison with *Speculum Mentis* is John Dewey's essay, *Art and Experience.*

18. *Speculum Mentis,* p. 90.

19. Clarendon Press 1938.

20. Which is where Ernest Gellner rather surprisingly, leaves him — though with a blessing on his head; see his 'Thought and time, or the reluctant relativist' in *The Devil in Modern Philosophy,* Routledge 1974, pp. 151–65.

21. *The Principles of Art,* Oxford: The Clarendon Press 1938: 'Art as Theory and Art as Practice', p. 290.

22. Clarendon Press 1942.

23. With J. N. L. Myers, he was co-author of *Roman Britain and the English Settlements* vol. I of *The Oxford History of England,* Clarendon Press 1936. Collingwood wrote pp. 1–324, 462–478.

24. See Gellner, 'Thought and time'.

25. Telling rebutted by J. W. N. Watkins in 'Historical Explanation in the Social Sciences', *Theories of History,* ed. P. Gardiner, Free Press, N.Y. 1959.

26. Gilbert Ryle's phrase in his *Collected Papers,* vol II, Oxford 1972.

CHAPTER 5: RESISTANCE AND SOCIAL DECLINE: F. R. LEAVIS

1. See Michael Green's history of Bloomsbury and its cultural camp-followers, *Children of the Sun,* Constable 1977.

2. I introduce these terms from an unpublished paper by Charles Taylor. We shall return to them as centrepieces of the argument at the end of chapter 10.

3. *The Great Tradition,* Chatto & Windus 1958, p. 9.

4. It is where Francis Mulhern begins, in *The Moment of 'Scrutiny',* New Left Books 1979, but although I admire his book, I come to different conclusions, later in this chapter.

5. For example Terry Eagleton in *Criticism and Ideology,* New Left Books 1976, and John Goode in *New Left Review* 122, 1980, pp. 90 – 96.

6. As documented by John Ziman, in *Public Knowledge,* Cambridge, rev. edn. 1972 and *The Force of Knowledge,* Cambridge 1976.

7. B. and L. Hammond, *The Village Labourer 1760 – 1832,* Longmans Green 1911.

8. *The Town Labourer 1760 – 1832,* Longmans Green 1917. See, for Tawney's history, especially *Religion and the Rise of Capitalism,* John Murray 1926, Penguin 1965.

9. Letter to *Hudson Review,* XX, 4, 1967 – 8, p. 538.

10. The state of mind is finely recorded by Vera Brittain, in *The Testament of Youth,* Gollancz 1942, Pan 1980.

11. A point I take from an excellent preliminary paper by Nicholas Garnham 'Towards a Political Economy of Culture', *New Universities Quarterly,* 31. 3, 1977.

12. Edwin Muir, *An Autobiography,* Hogarth Press 1954, Methuen 1968, p. 48.

13. George Steiner, 'Leavis', in *Language and Silence,* Faber & Faber 1967, Penguin 1969.

14. One of whom of course was Robert Graves, whose description of the physical consequences of gassing and shellshock is unrivalled; see *Good-Bye to All That,* Jonathan Cape 1929, Penguin rev. edn. 1960.

15. He evidently thought so himself. In a letter written to a former pupil in 1969 as he launched himself into the last four books of his amazingly productive seventies, he wrote of himself as 'faced with so much still to do' and as being 'like the distance runner bracing himself for the long run-in'. I am most grateful to Andor Gomme for showing me this letter.

16. For a richly brewed narrative of this history, see James Morris's third volume of his history of imperialism, *Sound the Trumpets,* Penguin, rev. edn. 1978. For a history of the disturbances in Germany, see F. L. Carsten, *Revolution in Central Europe 1918 – 1919,* Oxford 1972.

17. A powerfully argued version of half this history appears in Keith Middlemass, *Politics in Industrial Society,* Deutsch 1979. Middlemass however talks only of corporatism; he removes the ideological content from things.

18. Q. D. Leavis, 'Caterpillars of the Commonwealth Unite! A Review of *Three Guineas*', *Scrutiny*, VII.2, 1938.

19. In, classically, T. S. Eliot, *The Sacred Wood*, Methuen 1920; I. A. Richards, *Practical Criticism*, Routledge & Kegan Paul 1923 and *The Principles of Literary Criticism*, rev. edn. Routledge & Kegan Paul 1926; William Empson, *Seven Types of Ambiguity*, Chatto & Windus 1930 and *The Structure of Complex Words*, Chatto & Windus 1936.

20. In 'Two Cultures? The Significance of C. P. Snow', *Nor Shall My Sword: Discourses on Pluralism, Compassion, and Social Hope*, Chatto & Windus 1972, p. 62.

21. 'Life' is a Necessary Word' in *Nor Shall My Sword*, pp. 12 – 14.

22. A point polemically made by Mulhern, see section 5 of *Moment of 'Scrutiny'*. His objection is in support of a partisan sociology; I agree with his description, but propose above that there are conceptual gains from such a dissolution, precisely because it is impossible to bring it off.

23. F. R. Leavis and Denys Thompson, *Culture and Environment: the Training of Critical Awareness*, Chatto & Windus 1933, p. 91.

24. *Nor Shall My Sword*, p. 59.

25. Particularly of Sturt's *The Wheelwright's Shop*, Cambridge 1923, reprinted 1970 and *Change in the Village*, Duckworth 1912, reprinted and reset 1955. It is important not to undervalue Sturt as chronicler and theorist of the change from early to late capitalism, and from rural, agrarian production to industrial, urban production. His elegiac moments are well-chosen and his eye and mouth are dry. See also the 2 vols of his *Journals*, ed. E. D. Mackerness, Cambridge 1966.

26. These three examples — Bedford, Conway, and Dawson's Landing are all discussed in Leavis's *'Anna Karenina' and Other Essays*, Chatto & Windus 1967.

27. In essays scattered throughout his work; but centrally in *D. H. Lawrence: Novelist*, Chatto & Windus 1955.

28. Especially in the essay of that name collected in *Phoenix*, Heinemann 1936, 1961.

29. Raymond Williams's phrase in *The Country and the City*, Chatto & Windus 1973, pp. 165ff.

30. *Purity and Danger* is the title of Mary Douglas's well-known study of the social boundaries which keep moral and other kinds of pollution out. She argues that people's sense of the social order demands some certainty in marking those boundaries. My argument — not against hers, of course, but simply taking up her concepts — is that moments of cultural energy depend upon a moving tension within her antimony. See *Purity and Danger: An Analysis of Concepts of Pollution and Taboo*, Routledge & Kegan Paul 1966.

31. See in order: Perry Anderson *New Left Review* 50, 1968 as cited; John Goode 'William Morris and the Dream of Revolution' as cited; and Terry Eagleton 'Raymond Williams: an Appraisal', *New Left Review*, 95, 1976; for a rather sharply discrepant example in terms of a drop in intellectual quality, see *Working Papers in Cultural Studies*, 6, University of Birmingham 1974, p. 2.

32. His deliberately unphilosophical case is philosophically supported by Roy Bhaskar in *The Possibility of Naturalism: A philosophical critique of the contemporary human sciences*, Harvester Press 1979.

33. I take a lead here in the definition of hermeneutics from H-G. Gadamer, *Truth and Method*, Sheen & Ward 1975, pp. v–xiii.

CHAPTER 6: PRACTICE AGAINST THEORY: GEORGE ORWELL
AND ADRIAN STOKES

1. F. R. Leavis 'Thought, Language and Objectivity' in *The Living Principle, 'English' as a Discipline of Thought*, Chatto & Windus 1975, pp. 43–4.

2. This counterposing of epistemology to hermeneutics I take from Richard Rorty's fine book *Philosophy and the Mirror of Nature,* Princeton University Press and Basil Blackwell 1980. There will be much more occasion to refer to Rorty later. For the broader exposition of the relation between literary criticism and social understanding, see Clifford Geertz, *The Interpretation of Cultures,* Basic Books 1973, Hutchinson 1975.

3. 'Deconstruction' these days as we note in the last two chapters has a peculiarly Parisian provenance. Here I intend it more broadly, as I later recommend, as a happier synonym for 'analysis'.

4. Most of the references here are to the useful edition of *Collected Essays,* Heinemann 2nd edn 1961. See also the admirably complete edition, *Collected Essays, Journalism and Letters of George Orwell, 1920–1950* edited by Sonia Orwell and Ian Angus, 4 vols., Secker & Warburg with Penguin 1970.

5. Recently and straightforwardly recounted by Bernard Crick, *George Orwell: A Life*, Secker & Warburg 1980.

6. Wallace Stevens, 'Credences of Summer', *Collected Poems,* Faber & Faber 1955.

7. *The Road to Wigan Pier,* Left Book Club, Gollancz 1937, Secker & Warburg 1959. It is worth explaining the joke: Wigan Pier is a non-existent seaside feature in what was, until the 1950s, quite the dreariest inland town in South Lancashire.

8. See Crick, p. 70.

9. 'Down the Mine', first printed in *The Road to Wigan Pier*, as chapter II.

10. *Road to Wigan Pier*, pp. 117–18.

11. Secker & Warburg 1938, Penguin 1962.
12. *Collected Essays*, p. 168.
13. Walter Benjamin, *Charles Baudelaire: A Lyric Poet in the Era of High Capitalism,* trans. H. Zohn, New Left Books 1973, p. 159.
14. *Collected Essays*, p. 177.
15. Rorty, pp. 357 – 94.
16. Richard Wollheim, Professor of Logic at the University of London, has been one of Stokes's best advocates. He edited and introduced the anthology, *The Image in Form: Selected Writings of Adrian Stokes,* Penguin 1972. Lawrence Gowing has edited *The Critical Writings of Adrian Stokes,* in three volumes, Thames and Hudson 1978.
17. 'Adrian Stokes 1902 – 1972: A Supplement' edited by Stephen Bann for *Poetry Nation Review* 15, 1980. Wollheim's memoir is quoted from pp. 31 – 7.
18. I take the pregnancy of the phrase from Stokes's great, though courteous and undeclared antagonist Ernest Gombrich, in 'Art, History and the Social Sciences', *Ideals and Idols: Essays on Values in History and in Art,* Phaidon Press 1979. Gombrich, famously, calls for a canonical and historical aesthetics, but his history has rather less life in earnest in it than the artists themselves would think fit. Stokes provides both pre-history and phenomenology.
19. H-G. Gadamer, *Truth and Method,* Sheen & Ward 1975, quoted in Rorty, p. 358.
20. I take several phrases here from a magnificent essay by Roger Poole, 'The Bond of Human Embodiment', reviewing Maurice Merleau-Ponty's *The Prose of the World,* translated by John O'Neill, Heinemann Educational, in *Universities Quarterly,* Autumn 1974.
21. Stokes himself refers us particularly to Melanie Klein's *Contributions to Psycho-Analysis,* Tavistock 1948.
22. *Stones of Rimini,* 1934, the second volume (after *The Quattro Cento*) of a study of Italian renaissance art and architecture in Florence, Verona and Rimini. This edition by Schocken Books, New York 1969.
23. *Stones of Rimini,* p. 24.
24. In *The Aesthetics of Architecture,* Methuen 1979, pp. 144 – 51.
25. From *Colour and Form,* vol. II of *The Critical Writings,* p. 13.
26. 1945, *Critical Writings* vol. II, pp. 85 – 138.

CHAPTER 7: FABIANS IN ARMS: TONY CROSLAND AND RICHARD TITMUSS

1. A process diagrammatically and convincingly historicized by Ralph Miliband, *The State in Capitalist Society,* Weidenfeld & Nicolson 1969.
2. Published as *Social Insurance and Allied Services, A Report* by Sir William Beveridge, Cmnd 6404, 1942.

3. Walter Benjamin, *Illuminations,* Cape 1970, p. 259.

4. E. P. Thompson, *Writing by Candlelight,* Merlin Press 1980, p. 131.

5. C. A. R. Crosland, *The Future of Socialism,* Cape 1956, abridged and rev 1964.

6. *The Conservative Enemy,* Cape 1962, rev. edn 1967.

7. E. P. Thompson, *The Poverty of Theory and other Essays,* Merlin Press 1978, p. 67.

8. A point made about Tawney by Alasdair MacIntyre, in *Against the Self-Images of the Day,* Duckworth 1971, p 00.

9. For a discussion of this distinctly sectarian concept see Tom Nairn, 'The Anatomy of the Labour Party', *New Left Review* 1964, 27 – 8, and Michael Barratt Brown, *From Labourism to Socialism,* Spokesman Books 1970.

10. *Future of Socialism,* p. 79.

11. *The Conservative Enemy,* p. 127.

12. Cf. David Lipsey, 'Crosland's Socialism' in *The Socialist Agenda: Crosland's Legacy,* ed. David Lipsey and Dick Leonard, Jonathan Cape 1981, p. 42.

13. Quoted in *The Future of Socialism* p. 221 from Michael Fogarty, *Economic Control,* Routledge 1955.

14. Fred Hirsch, *Social Limits to Growth,* Routledge & Kegan Paul 1977, p. 17, see also p. 72.

15. Edited by Dick Leonard, Cape 1975.

16. As noted above by Bernard Williams in Smart and Williams, *Utilitarianism,* also and more briefly by Williams in the last chapter of *Morality; An Introduction to Ethics,* Cambridge 1976, as well as by Stuart Hampshire, *Morality and Pessimism,* Leslie Stephen Lecture 1972, Cambridge 1973.

17. Alasdair MacIntyre, *Self-Images,* p. 8.

18. Commented on by his former pupil, now a professor at the London School of Economics, Robert Pinker, in *The Idea of Welfare,* Heinemann 1979, p. 33.

19. In *Essays on the 'Welfare State',* Allen & Unwin 1958; with an introduction by Brian Abel-Smith to a new edition, 1976, pp. 215 – 43.

20. *Essays on the 'Welfare State',* p. 238.

21. Penguin 1980. See also David Donnison (*The Politics of Poverty,* Martin Robertson 1981) on his experience as Chairman of the Supplementary Benefits Commission.

22. *The Gift Relationship: From Human Blood to Social Policy,* Allen & Unwin 1970.

23. Thomas Nagel, *The Possibility of Altruism,* Oxford 1970, especially pp. 143 – 6, and chapter IX.

24. See the title essay in Peter Strawson, *Freedom and Resentment,* Oxford 1979, for a metaphysics of this process.

CHAPTER 8: CULTURE AND POLITICS: RICHARD HOGGART,
THE *NEW LEFT REVIEW*, AND RAYMOND WILLIAMS

1. *The Uses of Literacy: Aspects of working-class Life with special Reference to Publications and Entertainments,* Chatto & Windus 1957, Penguin 1958 (quotations from the Penguin edn).

2. As in Richard Johnson's contributions to *Working Class Culture: Studies in History and Theory,* ed. John Clarke *et al.,* Hutchinson 1979. See also the section, 'Culturalism', in *People's History and Socialist Theory,* ed. Raphael Samuel, Routledge & Kegan Paul 1981.

3. See J-C. Passeron, introduction to the French edition of *The Uses of Literacy,* published by *Bibliotheque des Sciences Humaines,* Paris 1971.

4. *Uses of Literacy,* pp. 37 – 8.

5. *Uses of Literacy,* pp. 154 – 5.

6. Classically analysed by Elias Canetti, *Crowds and Power,* 1932, reissued Penguin 1981. Canetti, however, moves his crowds largely through the streets, never into the bar of a working people's club.

7. In *Contemporary Cultural Studies,* University of Birmingham Occasional Paper 6, 1969.

8. Clifford Geertz, 'Notes on the Balinese Cockfight', in *The Interpretation of Cultures,* New York: Basic Books, London: Hutchinson 1975, p. 448.

9. For a general review of their treatment of this subject, see Martin Jay, *The Dialectical Imagination,* Heinemann Educational 1973, especially chapter 6. More particularly, see Leo Lowenthal, *Literature, Popular Culture, and Society,* Doubleday 1961.

10. A choice instance is provided by Nell Keddie, *Tinker Taylor,* Penguin Educational Books 1974.

11. *Border Country,* Chatto & Windus 1960, Penguin 1962.

12. In the striking and strikingly frank and formal series of interviews conducted with three of the present editors of *New Left Review,* published as Raymond Williams, *Politics and Letters,* New Left Books 1979.

13. Although it must be remembered that *Border Country* is a novel, not an autobiography. See *Politics and Letters* on 'The Welsh Trilogy'.

14. *Modern Tragedy,* Chatto & Windus 1966, p. 13.

15. *Border Country; Second Generation,* Chatto & Windus 1964; *The Fight for Manod,* Chatto & Windus 1979, which follows characters from the earlier two; and *The Volunteers,* MacGibbon & Kee 1978.

16. Oxford University Press 1977.

17. *Culture and Society 1780–1950,* Chatto & Windus 1959, Penguin 1960, pp. 205 – 6 (quotation from the Chatto edn).

18. e.g. Stuart Hall in a review of *Politics and Letters* called 'The Williams Interviews', *Screen Education* 34, Spring 1980.

19. *Politics and Letters* was edited by Williams himself, Clifford Collins and Wolf Mankowitz between 1947 and 1948. The *New Reasoner*, as noted below was forerunner to *New Left Review* and appeared between 1955 and 1957.

20. Most obviously the work of the Institute of Economic Affairs in general and of F. A. Hayek, in *The Road to Serfdom* and *The Constitution of Liberty,* in particular.

21. Michael Oakeshott, *Experience and Its Modes,* Cambridge University Press 1933; *Rationalism in Politics,* Methuen 1962.

22. The phrase, famously, is Rudolf Bahro's in *The Alternative in Eastern Europe,* translated by David Fernbach, New Left Books 1978, in which the author does try to think socialism into a practicable future.

23. See *Politics and Letters,* 'The Russian Revolution', where his determination to show allegiance leads him into downright murky argument.

24. See, variously, Bob Rowthorn, *Capitalism, Crisis and Inflation,* Lawrence & Wishart 1980; Tom Nairn: *The Break-Up of Britain,* New Left Books 1977; Fred Halliday, *Arabia Without Sultans,* Penguin 1978. The classics (it is not too much to say) are two historical volumes by Perry Anderson, *Lineages of the Absolutist State,* New Left Books 1974.

25. In a review of *Politics and Letters;* see John Dunn, 'The quest for solidarity', *London Review of Books,* 24 January 1980.

26. See his *Problems in Materialism and Culture,* New Left Books, Verso editions 1980, especially sections 2 and 5.

27. A case made in my paper, 'Nation and Community', *Sociological Review,* 25. 3, 1977.

28. See Williams's inaugural lecture, 'Drama in a dramatised society', Cambridge 1974.

CHAPTER 9: HISTORY AND BIOGRAPHY: JOHN BERGER AND E. P. THOMPSON

1. John Berger, *A Seventh Man: Migrant Workers in Europe,* Penguin 1975 (with Jean Mohr, photographer), p. 33.

2. 'On the edge of a foreign city' in *The Look of Things,* Penguin 1972, p. 22.

3. *The Look of Things,* p. 26.

4. *G: a Novel,* Weidenfeld & Nicolson 1972, p. 93.

5. *G,* p. 145.

6. *'The Moment of Cubism' and Other Essays,* Weidenfeld & Nicolson 1969, pp. 24 – 5.

7. 'Anglais Mort à Florence', *Collected Poems,* Faber & Faber 1955.

8. *Art and Revolution: Ernst Neizvestny and the Role of the Artist in the USSR,* Penguin 1969, p. 313.

9. *G: A Novel,* pp. 150 – 1.

10. *A Fortunate Man: the story of a country doctor.* Allen Lane, the Penguin Press, 1967; Writers and Readers Cooperative, reissued 1978.

11. See *A Painter of Our Time,* Penguin 1958 (reissued by Writers and Readers Cooperative).

12. *Corker's Freedom,* Methuen 1964 (reissued by Writers and Readers Cooperative).

13. *Pig Earth,* Writers and Readers Cooperative 1979.

14. See Perry Anderson, *Arguments Within British Marxism,* New Left Books 1980.

15. This association is retold by Thompson in 'The Nehru Tradition', in *Writing by Candlelight,* Merlin Press 1980.

16. He collaborated with his father in a pamphlet about his brother, *A Memoir of Frank Thompson,* London 1947. It is now, alas, unobtainable.

17. Christopher Hill, *The Century of Revolution,* Nelson 1961; *Puritanism and Revolution,* Secker & Warburg 1958.

18. E. J. Hobsbawm, *Labouring Men: Studies in Labour History,* Weidenfeld & Nicolson 1964.

19. Leszek Kolakowski 'Historical Understanding and the Intelligibility of History', in *Triquarterly* 22 (USA), Fall 1971.

20. First published by Gollancz 1963, revised edition, Penguin 1968 (a tribute: it was chosen to be the 1000th Pelican since the series began).

21. *'The Poverty of Theory' and Other Essays* Merlin Press 1978.

22. As Quentin Skinner convincingly recommends in the treatment of normal texts (i.e. books). See Chapter 10.

23. I have been summarizing Stefan Korner here, in his *Categorial Frameworks,* Basil Blackwell 1970.

24. First published respectively Merlin Press 1955; Gollancz 1963; and Allen Lane, the Penguin Press 1975.

25. *Making of the English Working Class,* Penguin edn 1968, p. 664.

26. *Writing by Candlelight,* pp. 75 – 6.

27. Published by Spokesman Books, Nottingham, in 1980.

CHAPTER 10: LIFE AND DEATH IN ENGLISH ACADEMIC THEORY:
ISAIAH BERLIN, THE NEW PROVISIONALS, AND THE LEFT

1. There would be no point in listing the many French books which have lead this movement in recent intellectual history. One very useful review of the main authors is edited (and contributed to) by John Sturrock, *Structuralism and Since: from Levi-Strauss to Derrida,* Oxford 1979. But see as well an excellent English acculturation of the argument in Bernard Sharratt, *Reading Relations: A Dialectical Text/Book,* Harvester Press 1982.

2. W. B. Yeats 'The Municipal Gallery Revisited', *Collected Poems*, Macmillan 1961, p. 370.

3. In his obituary to Leavis, *Times Higher Education Supplement*, 5 May 1978.

4. A point more gracefully made by David Collard *Altruism and Economics*, Martin Robertson 1980.

5. *Vico and Herder: Two Studies in the History of Ideas*, Hogarth Press 1976.

6. Anderson 'Components of the National Culture', *New Left Review* 50, 1968, p. 19.

7. *Karl Marx: His Life and Environment*, Butterworth 1939.

8. Published together as *Four Essays on Liberty*, Oxford University Press 1969.

9. *Vico and Herder*, pp. 88 – 9.

10. Bernard Williams's 'Introduction' to Isaiah Berlin, *Concepts and Categories: Philosophical Essays*, Hogarth Press 1978, p. xviii.

11. G. A. Cohen, *Karl Marx's Theory of History: A Defence*, Oxford 1978.

12. Anthony Giddens, 'Notes on the theory of structuration' in his *Studies in Social and Political Theory*, Hutchinson 1977, p. 130.

13. See Anthony Giddens, *New Rules of Sociological Method*, Hutchinson 1976. Gadamer himself acknowledges in *Truth and Method*, Sheen & Ward 1975, that he developed his account of reflexivity only to find Collingwood there before him.

14. Richard Rorty, *Philosophy and the Mirror of Nature*, Princeton University Press and Basil Blackwell 1980, especially pp. 357 – 94.

15. Anthony Giddens, *A Contemporary Critique of Historical Materialism*, Macmillan 1981. It is worth repeating the point made earlier that Leavis is the creator of a Heideggerian philosophy in English.

16. Beginning with 'Meaning and Understanding in the History of Ideas', *History and Theory*, VIII.1, 1969. See also 'Motives, Intentions and the Interpretation of Texts', *New Literary History*, III, 1971 – 2.

17. *The Foundations of Modern Political Thought*, 2 vols. Cambridge 1978.

18. He summarizes his own ideas in a special symposium on his work in *Political Theory*, II.3, August 1974.

19. Sustained in the five-volume series of essays, *Philosophy, Politics, and Society*, which Laslett has edited with various collaborators (including Skinner) for Basil Blackwell.

20. Alisdair MacIntyre, *After Virtue: a Study in Moral Theory*, Duckworth 1981.

21. The political economist who meets him most straightly on that ground is Fred Hirsch in *Social Limits to Growth*, Routledge & Kegan Paul 1977.

22. The relevant writings of Charles Taylor include *The Explanation of Behaviour*, Routledge 1964; *Hegel*, Cambridge University Press 1975, and *Hegel and Modern Society*, Cambridge University Press 1979. See especially 'Interpretation and the Sciences of Man', *Review of Metaphysics,* January 1971 and 'The Politics of the Steady State', *New Universities Quarterly,* April 1978, a specially edited edition 'Morality and the Left', by Colin Crouch and Fred Inglis.
23. Memorably by John Dunn in *Western Political Theory in the Face of the Future,* Cambridge University Press 1979.

Bibliography

Adorno, T. W. *Minima Moralia*. New Left Books, 1974

____. (and Horkheimer, Max). *The Dialectic of the Enlightenment*. New Left Books, 1974

Anderson, Perry. 'Components of the National Culture' *New Left Review* 50, 1968

____. *Lineages of the Absolutist State*. New Left Books, 1974

____. *Arguments Within English Marxism*. New Left Books, 1980

Annan, Noel. 'The Intellectual Aristocracy' in *Studies in Social History, A Tribute to G. M. Trevelyan,* ed. J. H. Plumb, London 1955

Bahro, Rudolf. *The Alternative in Eastern Europe*. trans. D. Fernbach, New Left Books, 1978

Bann, Stephen, ed. 'Adrian Stokes 1902 – 1972', Special Supplement to *Poetry Nation Review,* 15, 1980

Barraclough, G. 'The End of an Era', *New York Review of Books,* 27 June 1974

____. 'The Great World Crisis', *New York Review of Books,* 23 January 1975

____. 'Wealth and Power: the Politics of Food and Oil', *New York Review of Books,* 7 August 1975

Barratt Brown, Michael. *From Labourism to Socialism*. Spokesman Books, 1970

Benjamin, Walter. *Illuminations*. Jonathan Cape, 1970

____. *Charles Baudelaire: A Lyric Poet in the Era of High Capitalism*. New Left Books, 1973

Berger, John. *A Painter of our Time*. Penguin, 1958

____. *Corker's Freedom*. Methuen, 1964

____. *A Fortunate Man: the Story of a Country Doctor*. Allen Lane The Penguin Press, 1967, Writers and Readers Cooperative, 1978

____. 'The Moment of Cubism' and Other Essays. Weidenfeld and Nicolson, 1969

____. *Art and Revolution: Ernst Neizvestny and the Role of the Artist in the*

USSR. Penguin 1969

——. *The Look of Things*. Penguin, 1972

——. *G: a Novel*. Weidenfeld and Nicolson, 1972, Penguin, 1975

——. *A Seventh Man: Migrant Workers in Europe*, Penguin, 1975

——. *Pig Earth*. Writers and Readers Cooperative, 1979

Berger, Peter, & Luckmann, Thomas. *The Social Construction of Reality*. Penguin, 1971

Berlin, Isaiah. *Karl Marx: His Life and Environment*. Butterworth, 1939, Oxford University Press, 1967

——. *Four Essays on Liberty*. Oxford, 1969

——. *Vico and Herder: Two Studies in the History of Ideas*. Hogarth Press, 1976

——. *Concepts and Categories: Philosophical Essays*. Hogarth Press, 1978

Bhaskar, Roy. *The Possibility of Naturalism: a Philosophical Critique of the Contemporary Human Sciences*. Harvester Press, 1979

Blackburn, Robin, ed. *Ideology in Social Science*. Fontana, 1974

Brittain, Vera. *The Testament of Youth*. Gollancz 1942, Pan 1980

Burrow, J. W. *Evolution and Society*. Cambridge University Press, 1966

Canetti, Elias. *Crowds and Power* (1932), Penguin 1981

Carsten, F. L. *Revolution in Central Europe 1918–1919*. Oxford University Press, 1972

Clarke, Peter. *Liberals and Social Democrats*. Cambridge University Press, 1978

Cohen, G. A. *Karl Marx's Theory of History: a Defence*. Oxford University Press, 1978

Cole, Margaret. *The Story of Fabian Socialism*. Heinemann 1961

Collard, David. *Altruism and Economics*. Martin Robertson, 1980

Collingwood, R. G. 'The Devil' in *Concerning Prayer*, ed. L. Dougall, London 1916

——. 'Ruskin's Philosophy', privately printed, Kendal, 1922

——. *Speculum Mentis or the Map of Knowledge*. Oxford: Clarendon Press, 1924

——. *Roman Britain and the English Settlements* Vol. I of *The Oxford History of England*, with J. N. L. Myers, Oxford: Clarendon Press 1936

——. *The Principles of Art*. Oxford: Clarendon Press, 1938

——. *An Autobiography*. Oxford University Press, 1939

——. *The First Mate's Log of the 'Fleur de Lys'*, privately printed, 1940

——. *The New Leviathan*. Oxford: Clarendon Press, 1942

——. *The Idea of History*. Ed. T. M. Knox, Oxford: Clarendon Press, 1946

Collini, Stefan. *Liberalism and Sociology: L. T. Hobhouse and Political Argument in England 1880–1914*. Cambridge University Press, 1979

Creese, W. L. *The Search for Environment*. Yale University Press, 1966

Crick, Bernard. *George Orwell: A Life*. Secker and Warburg, 1980

Crosland, C. A. R. *The Future of Socialism.* Jonathan Cape 1956, abridged and revised 1964

——. *The Conservative Enemy,* Jonathan Cape 1962, revised edition 1967

——. *Socialism Now.* Ed. Dick Leonard, Jonathan Cape, 1975

Dangerfield, George. *The Strange Death of Liberal England.* MacGibbon and Kee 1935, Paladin 1970

Daunton, Robert. *The Business of Enlightenment: 'A Publishing History of the Encyclopédie' 1775– 1800.* Harvard University Press, 1980

Davies, Ioan. 'The Management of Knowledge', *Sociology* January, 1970

Derrida, Jacques. *Of Grammatology.* trans. G. C. Spirak, Johns Hopkins University Press, 1976

Dewey, John. *Art as Experience.* Milton, Balch, NY, 1934

Donnison, David. *The Politics of Poverty.* Martin Robertson, 1981

Douglas, Mary. *Purity and Danger: an Analysis of Concepts of Pollution and Taboo.* Routledge and Kegan Paul, 1966

Dunn, John. *Western Political Theory in the Face of the Future.* Cambridge University Press, 1979

——. 'The Quest for Solidarity', *London Review of Books,* January 24, 1980

Eagleton, Terry. *Criticism and Ideology.* New Left Books, 1976

——. 'Raymond Williams: an Appraisal', *New Left Review* 95, 1976

Eliot, T. S. *Complete Poems and Plays.* Faber & Faber, 1969

——. *The Sacred Wood.* Methuen, 1920

Empson, William. *Seven Types of Ambiguity.* Chatto and Windus, 1930

——. *The Structure of Complex Words.* Chatto and Windus, 1936

——. Letter to *Hudson Review,* XX.4, 1967 – 8

Fetjo, Francois. *A History of the People's Democracies.* Penguin, revised edition 1974

Gadamer, Hans-Georg. *Truth and Method.* Sheen and Ward, 1975

Gardiner, P., ed., *Theories of History.* New York: Free Press, 1959

Garnham, N. 'Toward a Political Economy of Culture'. *New Universities Quarterly* 31.3, 1977

——. 'Revolution and Reform', 'Morality and the Left', special issue of *New Universities Quarterly,* ed. C. Crouch and F. Inglis, Spring 1978

Geertz, Clifford. *The Interpretation of Cultures.* Basic Books 1973, Hutchinson 1975

Gellner, Ernest. *The Devil in Modern Philosophy.* Routledge, 1974

Giddens, Anthony. *Capitalism and Modern Social Theory.* Hutchinson, 1974

——. *New Rules of Sociological Method.* Hutchinson, 1976

——. *Studies in Social and Political Theory.* Hutchinson, 1977

——. *A Contemporary Critique of Historical Materialism.* Macmillan, 1981

Gombrich, Ernest. *Ideals and Idols: Essays on Value in History and in Art.* Phaidon Press, 1979

Goode, John. 'William Morris and the Dream of Revolution' in *Literature and Politics in the 19th Century*. Ed. John Lucas, Methuen, 1971

———. 'The Moment of Scrutiny': review-article, *New Left Review* 122, 1980

Graves, Robert. *Goodbye to All That*. Jonathan Cape 1929, Penguin revised edition 1960

Green, Michael. *Children of the Sun*. Constable, 1977

Green, T. H. *Works*. Ed. R. L. Nettleship, 3 vols. Longmans Green, 1911

———. *Prolegomena to Ethics*. Ed. A. C. Bradley, reissued with an introduction by R. M. Lemos, Thomas Crowell, New York, 1969

H. M. Government. *Social Insurance and Allied Services, A Report by Sir William Beveridge*. Command 6404, HMSO 1942

Hall, Stuart. 'The Williams Interviews', *Screen Education* 34, Spring 1980

Halliday, Fred. *Arabia Without Sultans*. Penguin, 1978

Hammond, B. and L. *The Village Labourer 1760– 1832*. Longmans Green, 1911

———. *The Town Labourer 1760– 1832*. Longmans Green, 1917

Hampshire, Stuart. *Morality and Pessimism*. Cambridge University Press, 1973

Harrison, Andrew. *Making and Thinking*. Harvester Press, 1978

Harrod, Roy. *The Life of John Maynard Keynes*. Macmillan, 1951

Hawthorn, Geoffrey. *Enlightenment and Despair: A History of Sociology*. Cambridge University Press, 1976

Hayek, F. A. *The Road to Serfdom*. Routledge, 1974

———. *The Constitution of Liberty*. Routledge and Kegan Paul, 1960

Hill, Christopher. *Puritanism and Revolution*. Secker and Warburg, 1958

———. *The Century of Revolution*. Nelson, 1961

Hirsch, Fred. *Social Limits to Growth*. Routledge and Kegan Paul, 1977

Hirschman, Albert. *Essays in Trespassing: Economics to Politics and Beyond*. Cambridge University Press, 1981

Hobhouse, L. T. *The Labour Movement* (1897). Edited with an introduction by Philip Poirier, Harvester Press, 1974

———. *Democracy and Reaction*. Unwin, 1904, edited with an introduction by Peter Clarke, Harvester Press, 1974

———. *Liberalism* (1911). Edited with an introduction by Alan Grimes, Thomas Crowell, New York 1964

———. 'Workmen's Insurance', *Nation* IX, 1911

Hobsbawm, Eric. *Labouring Men: Studies in Labour History*. Weidenfeld and Nicolson, 1964

Hobson, J. A. *The Psychology of Jingoism*. Grant Richards, 1901

———. *Elements of Social Justice*. Allen and Unwin, 1927

———. *Imperialism: A Study*. 3rd revised edition, Allen and Unwin, 1938

Hoggart, Richard. *The Uses of Literacy: Aspects of Working-class Life with special reference to Publications and Entertainments*. Chatto and Windus 1957, Penguin 1958

_____. *Contemporary Cultural Studies.* University of Birmingham, 1969

Hollis, Martin. *Models of Man.* Cambridge University Press, 1977

Inglis, Fred. *Ideology and the Imagination.* Cambridge, 1975

_____. 'Nation and Community: A Landscape and its Morality', *Sociological Review* 25.3, 1977

James, Henry. *The Letters.* Ed. Leon Edel, 4 volumes, Scribner, New York, 1962

Jay, Martin. *The Dialectical Imagination: a History of the Frankfurt School 1923–50.* Heinemann Educational, 1973

Johnson, Harry G. *On Economics and Society.* University of Chicago Press, 1975

Johnson, Richard. 'Culture and the Historians' in *Working Class Culture: Studies in History and Theory.* Ed. John Clarke *et al.,* Hutchinson 1979

Johnson, W. M. *The Formative Years of R. G. Collingwood.* Martinus Nijhoff, The Hague, 1967

Keddie, Nell. *Tinker, Tailor: the Myth of Educational Deprivation.* Penguin, 1974

Keynes, John Maynard. 'The Economic Consequences of the Peace' (1919), vol. II of *The Collected Writings of John Maynard Keynes,* ed. Elizabeth Johnson and Donald Moggridge, Macmillan, 22 volumes (1956–   ) (*JMK*)

_____. *A Treatise on Probability* (1921) *JMK* Vol. VIII

_____. *Essays in Persuasion* (1931) *JMK* Vol. IX

_____. *Essays in Biography* (1933) *JMK* Vol. X

_____. *The General Theory of Employment, Interest, and Money* (1936) *JMK* Vol. VII

Klein, Melanie. *Contributions to Psycho-Analysis.* Tavistock Press, 1948

Kolakowski, Leszek. 'Historical Understanding and the Intelligibility of History', *Triquarterly* 22, Fall 1971

Korner, Stefan. *Categorial Frameworks.* Basil Blackwell, 1970

Laslett, P. *et al.,* eds. *Philosophy, Politics and Society,* 5 series, 1956–79, Basil Blackwell

Lawrence, D. H. *Phoenix.* Heinemann, 1936, 1961

Leavis, Frank Raymond. *The Great Tradition.* Chatto and Windus, 1933

_____. *The Common Pursuit.* Chatto and Windus, 1952

_____. *D. H. Lawrence: Novelist.* Chatto and Windus, 1955

_____. *'Anna Karenina' and Other Essays.* Chatto and Windus, 1967

_____. *Nor Shall My Sword: Discourses on Pluralism, Compassion, and Social Hope.* Chatto and Windus, 1972

_____. *The Living Principle: 'English' as a Discipline of Thought.* Chatto and Windus, 1975

_____. with Denys Thompson. *Culture and Environment: the Training of Critical Awareness.* Chatto and Windus, 1933

Leavis, Q. D. 'Caterpillars of the Commonwealth, Unite!' *Scrutiny,* VII, 2, 1938

Lenin, V. I. 'On Imperialism', 'What is to be Done', in *Selected Writings,* 2 vols. Foreign Languages Publishing House, Moscow 1970

Leonard, D. and Lipsey, D. eds. *The Socialist Agenda.* Jonathan Cape, 1981

Lowenthal, Leo. *Literature, Popular Culture and Society.* Doubleday, 1961

MacFarlane, Alan. *The Origins of English Individualism.* Basil Blackwell, 1979

Macintyre, Alasdair. 'A Mistake about Causality in Social Science' in *Philosophy, Politics, and Society* (2nd series), ed. Peter Laslett & W. G. Runciman, Basil Blackwell, 1962

———. *A Short History of Ethics.* Routledge and Kegan Paul, 1967

———. *Against the Self-Images of the Age.* Duckworth, 1971

———. *After Virtue: A Study in Moral Theory.* Duckworth, 1981

MacKenzie, Norman and Jeanne. *The First Fabians.* Weidenfeld and Nicolson, 1977

MacLure, J. S. *Educational Documents: England and Wales 1816 – 1968.* Methuen, 1965

Macpherson, C. B. 'Post – Liberal Democracy' in *Democratic Theory.* Oxford University Press, 1973

McLellan, David. *Marxism After Marx.* Macmillan, 1979

Mandelstam, Nadezhda. *Hope Against Hope.* M. Hayward transl. Collins, 1971

Marcuse, H. *One-Dimensional Man.* Beacon Books, 1964

Marx, Karl (with Friedrich Engels). *The German Ideology.* Ed. T. J. Arthur, Lawrence and Wishart, 1970

Merleau-Ponty, M. *The Prose of the World.* Heinemann Educational Books, 1974

Middlemass, Keith. *Politics in Industrial Society.* André Deutsch, 1979

Miliband, Ralph. *The State in Capitalist Society.* Weidenfeld and Nicolson, 1969

Mink, Louis. *Mind, History and Dialectic: the Philosophy of R. G. Collingwood.* Indiana University Press, 1969

Moggridge, Donald. *Keynes.* Fontana, 1976

Morris, James. *Sound the Trumpets.* Penguin revised edition, 1978

Morris, May. *William Morris, Artist, Writer, Socialist.* 2 vols. Basil Blackwell, 1936

Morris, William. *Three Works by William Morris.* Ed. A. L. Morton, Lawrence and Wishart, 1968

———. *The Political Writings of William Morris.* Ed. A. L. Morton, Lawrence and Wishart, 1973

Muir, Edwin. *An Autobiography.* Hogarth Press, 1954, Methuen, 1968

Mulhern, Francis. *The Moment of 'Scrutiny'.* New Left Books, 1979

Nagel, Thomas. *The Possibility of Altruism.* Oxford University Press, 1970

Naipaul, V. S. *Guerrillas.* Penguin, 1977

_____. *A Bend in the River.* André Deutsch, 1979

Nairn, Tom. 'The Anatomy of the Labour Party'. *New Left Review,* 27 – 28, 1964

_____. *The Break-up of Britain.* New Left Books, 1977, rev. edn 1982

Nettleship, R. L. *Memoir of Thomas Hill Green.* Longmans Green, 1906

Oakeshott, Michael. *Experience and Its Modes.* Cambridge University Press, 1933

_____. *Rationalism in Politics.* Methuen, 1962

Orwell, George. *The Road to Wigan Pier.* Gollancz, 1937, Secker and Warburg, 1959

_____. *Homage to Catalonia.* Secker and Warburg 1938, Penguin 1962

_____. *Collected Essays.* 2nd edition, Heinemann, 1961

_____. *Collected Essays, Journalism and Letters of George Orwell 1920 – 1950.* Ed. Sonia Orwell and Ian Angus, Secker and Warburg with Penguin, 1970

Passeron, J-C. Introduction to *The Uses of Literacy.* French translation, 1971

Pevsner, N. *Pioneers of Modern Design: from William Morris to Walter Gropius,* revised edition, Penguin 1960

Pinker, Robert. *The Idea of Welfare.* Heinemann, 1979

Poole, Roger. 'The Bond of Human Embodiment'. *Universities Quarterly,* Autumn, 1974

Ransome, Arthur. *The Autobiography of Arthur Ransome.* Ed. with epilogue Rupert Hart-Davis, Jonathan Cape, 1976

Rawls, John. *A Theory of Justice.* Oxford: Clarendon Press, 1971

Richards, I. A. *Practical Criticism.* Routledge and Kegan Paul, 1923

_____. *The Principles of Literary Criticism.* Routledge and Kegan Paul, 1926

Richter, Melvin. *The Politics of Conscience: T. H. Green and his Age.* Weidenfeld and Nicolson, 1964

Robinson, Joan. *Economic Philosophy.* Penguin, 1964

Rorty, Richard. *Philosophy and the Mirror of Nature.* Princeton University Press and Basil Blackwell, 1980

Rowthorn, Bob. *Capitalism, Crisis and Inflation.* Lawrence and Wishart, 1980

Runciman, W. G. *Relative Deprivation and Social Justice.* Routledge and Kegan Paul, 1966

Ryle, Gilbert. *Collected Papers.* 2 vols., Oxford University Press, 1972

Samuel, Raphael, ed. *People's History and Socialist Theory.* Routledge and Kegan Paul, 1981

Scruton, Roger. *The Aesthetics of Architecture.* Methuen, 1979

Searle, John. *Speech-Acts.* Cambridge, 1969

Shackle, G. L. S. *Epistemics and Economics.* Cambridge University Press, 1972

_____. 'Time and Choice' Keynes Lecture, *Proceedings of the British Academy,* LXII, 1976

Sharratt, Bernard. *Reading Relations: a Dialectical Text/Book.* Harvester Press, 1982

Skinner, Quentin. 'Meaning and Understanding in the History of Ideas', *History and Theory,* VIII.1, 1969

_____. 'Motives, Intentions, and the Interpretation of Texts', *New Literary History,* III, 1971—2

_____. 'Some Problems in the Analysis of Political Thought and Action', *Political Theory,* II.3, 1974

_____. 'Hermeneutics and the Role of History', *New Literary History*, VII, 1975—6

_____. *The Foundations of Modern Political Thought.* Cambridge University Press, 2 vols., 1978

Smart, J. J. C. and Williams, Bernard. *Utilitarianism: For and Against.* Cambridge University Press, 1973

Strawson, Peter. *Freedom and Resentment.* Oxford University Press, 1979

Steiner, George. *Language and Silence.* Faber and Faber 1967, Penguin 1969

Stevens, Wallace. *Collected Poems,* Faber and Faber, 1955

Stokes, Adrian. *The Critical Writings of Adrian Stokes.* ed. Lawrence Gowing, 3 vols., Thames and Hudson, 1978

_____. *The Image in Form: Selected Writings of Adrian Stokes,* ed. Richard Wollheim, Penguin 1972

_____. *Stones of Rimini.* London 1934, Schocken Books 1969

Sturrock, John. *Structuralism and Since: from Levi-Strauss to Derrida.* Oxford University Press, 1979

Sturt, George. *Change in the Village.* Duckworth 1912, reset 1955

_____. *The Wheelwright's Shop.* Cambridge University Press 1923, 1970

_____. *Journals of George Sturt,* E. D. Mackerness *ed.,* Cambridge University Press, 1966

Tawney, R. H. *Religion and the Rise of Capitalism.* John Murray 1926, Penguin 1965

Taylor, Charles. *The Explanation of Behaviour.* Routledge and Kegan Paul, 1964

_____. 'Interpretation and the Sciences of Man' *Review of Metaphysics* 25; January 1971

_____. *Hegel* Cambridge University Press, 1975

_____. 'The Politics of the Steady State', 'Morality and the 'Left', Special issue of *New Universities Quarterly,* ed. C. Crouch and F. Inglis, Spring 1978

_____. *Hegel and Modern Society.* Cambridge University Press, 1979

Thompson, Edward Palmer. *There is a Spirit in Europe: a Memoir of Frank Thompson*. London, 1947

———. *William Morris: Romantic to Revolutionary*. Merlin Press 1955, reprinted with a postscript, 1977

———. *The Making of the English Working Class*, Gollancz 1963, revised edition, Penguin 1968

———. *Whigs and Hunters: the Origins of the Black Act*. Allen Lane, the Penguin Press 1975

———. *'The Poverty of Theory' and other Essays*. Merlin Press, 1978

———. *Writing by Candlelight*. Merlin Press, 1980

———. *Protest and Survive*. Spokesman Books, 1980

———. *Zero Option*. Merlin Press, 1982

Titmuss, Richard. *Problems of Social Policy*. Allen and Unwin, 1950

———. *Essays on the 'Welfare State'*. Allen and Unwin, 1958, new edition 1976

———. *The Gift Relationship: from Human Blood to Social Policy*. Allen and Unwin, 1970

Tomlinson, Charles. *The Way of a World*. Oxford, 1969

Townsend, Peter. *Poverty in the United Kingdom*. Penguin, 1980

Wallace, John. *Destiny His Choice: the Loyalism of Andrew Marvell*. Cambridge University Press, 1968

Wallas, Graham. *Human Nature in Politics*. Macmillan, 1908

———. *The Great Society*. Macmillan, 1911

Waltzer, Michael. *The Revolution of the Saints: a Study in the Origins of Radical Politics*. Weidenfeld and Nicolson, 1966

Wiggins, David. 'Myth, Invention, and the Meaning of Life', *Proceedings of the British Academy* LXII, 1976

Williams, Bernard. *Utilitarianism: For and Against* (with J. J. C. Smart) Cambridge University Press, 1973

———. *Morality: an Introduction to Ethics*. Cambridge University Press, 1976

———. 'Introduction' to Berlin (1978)

Williams, Raymond. *Culture and Society 1780–1950*. Chatto and Windus 1959, Penguin 1960

———. *Border Country*, Chatto and Windus, 1960, Penguin 1962

———. *Second Generation*. Chatto and Windus, 1964

———. *Modern Tragedy*. Chatto and Windus, 1966 verso: New Left Books, rev. edn, 1979

———. *The Country and the City*. Chatto and Windus, 1973

———. *Drama in a Dramatised Society*. Cambridge University Press, 1974

———. *The Volunteers*. MacGibbon and Kee, 1978

———. 'A Man Confronting a Very Particular Mystery' (obituary of F. R.

Leavis) *Times Higher Education Supplement,* 5th May 1978
_____. *Politics and Letters.* New Left Books, 1979
_____. *The Fight for Manod.* Chatto and Windus, 1979
_____. *Problems in Materialism and Culture.* New Left Books, 1980
Yeats, W. B. *Collected Poems.* Macmillan, 1961
Ziman, John. *Public Knowledge.* Cambridge University Press, revised edition 1972
_____. *The Force of Knowledge.* Cambridge University Press, 1976

Index